The Washington Post

Washington ALBUM

A PICTORIAL HISTORY OF THE NATION'S CAPITAL

Bob Levey and Jane Freundel Levey

TO TERESA —
ENJOY!
Bob Levey
MAY 7, 2001

Your city!
Jane Freundel Levey

The Washington Post

Washington ALBUM

A PICTORIAL HISTORY OF THE NATION'S CAPITAL

Bob Levey and Jane Freundel Levey

Washington Post Books
1150 15th Street, N.W.
Washington, D.C. 20071

First Edition

The main text of this book is composed in Galliard, with other types in Hoefler Champion and Poynter Condensed.

Manufactured by Chroma Graphics, Largo, Md., in association with Alan Abrams

ISBN: [1-930691-00-9]

Editor and Publisher: Noel Epstein
Graphic Designer: Robert Barkin
Project Coordinator: Susan Breitkopf

Front Cover: Detail from "The Planning of Washington" by Garnet W. Jex, © The George Washington University 2000, The George Washington University Permanent Collection, Courtesy of The Dimock Gallery.

Back Cover (Clockwise from top right): Larry Morris for The Washington Post; Library of Congress; Lucian Perkins for The Washington Post; The Washington Post; Library of Congress; Margaret Thomas for The Washington Post.

To our native Washingtonians, Emily and Allie

CONTENTS

INTRODUCTION

They arrived on a few small boats in 1800—some boxes, some crates, some chairs. The boats tried to dock at Georgetown, but they couldn't obtain slip space at that busy port. So the captains chose Lear's Wharf, a much smaller dock that used to sit near the site of the current Lincoln Memorial. There, many of the national government's modest belongings, sent a few days earlier from Philadelphia, were first unloaded at the new capital, a primitive piece of low-lying land where two rivers met. No one cheered. No one complained. No one much cared.

Today the entire world cares about what happens in Washington, D.C. Some applaud it, some mock it, and politicians routinely run against it in order to secure a place in it. Few, however, seem to be familiar with Washington's history beyond dry schoolbook accounts or fragments of information they have come upon, including some myths. Many, for example, think that the 13-floor limit on the height of Washington buildings was enacted to protect views of the Capitol or the Washington Monument. It wasn't. Others believe that Benjamin Banneker, the self-taught free black astronomer and mathematician who was instrumental in defining Washington's boundaries, also reconstructed Pierre L'Enfant's original city plan from memory. He didn't.

Even fewer appear to be familiar with the world of those who have worked, played, raised families and left their mark on Washington and its environs. How many can tell you about the baseball field in the "Swampoodle" district, site of the current Union Station, where Washington's National League team once played? How many know of the gambling barges and floating brothels that served the capital between the Civil War and World War I? How many remember that Prohibition came three years earlier to Washington than to the rest of the nation, or that as late as 1940 the Agriculture Department still had chicken pens at Constitution Avenue and 14th Street?

Washington Album, commissioned to commemorate the 200th anniversary of the government's arrival at the new capital, takes you on a tour of all of this and much more.

Its texts and more than 350 illustrations trace the growth of Picture Postcard Washington, the city of government temples and monuments. That government had only four Cabinet departments when the boats unloaded at Lear's Wharf: State, War, Navy and Treasury. A postmaster general and an attorney general had been appointed in 1789, but they did not exactly have large retinues. According to a Justice Department history, the early attorneys general did everything, including typing their own correspondence and emptying their own spittoons.

Washington grew chiefly as a result of national crises—the Civil War, World War I, the Great Depression, World War II—with large numbers flooding in on each occasion and overwhelming the city. But it grew for other reasons as well. It grew when the capital became a fashionable destination, particularly for nouveau riche industrialists during the Gilded Age. It grew because Americans demanded more programs to protect them against life's risks, from farm price swings to poverty in old age. It grew as the United States emerged as the world's military and economic superpower.

This book, however, is less a survey of institutional Washington than of the people of the capital—who they have been, how they have dealt with both everyday life and national crises, how they have struggled against constant obstacles, how their city has changed and is still changing today.

You will find here a capital that once was remarkably innocent. It might not surprise you that during the age of Andrew Jackson, Washingtonians walked right into the White House to eat a giant piece of cheese—weighing 1,400 pounds—that had been sent to the president. But even in the 1930s, Washingtonians still could walk unannounced into the executive mansion.

You will find real estate speculators and developers doing deals from the very beginning, auto traffic and commuting starting to create issues nearly a century ago and air traffic causing unusual problems. At the predecessor to Reagan National Airport, for example, the runways bisected Arlington's Military Road, forcing guards to drag chains across the road to halt traffic during takeoffs and landings.

You will find people scrambling for places to live during national crises. Boardinghouses put four or six in a room during the Civil War and similarly packed them in during World War I. (Tragically, that helped spread the Spanish flu, which killed 3,500 in Washington in the fall of 1918.) In the swollen city of World War II, which feared German air attacks and grumbled about rationing, you will see people who were forced to live on houseboats and lovers who could find no privacy.

Importantly, this book is also about tensions—especially the struggles between the two cities, national and local, between blacks and whites, and between city and suburbs.

The two Washingtons have had an uneasy relationship from the outset. In a capital that is a beacon of democracy, Washingtonians still lack full representation in Congress and do not control their own budget. You will thus find, among other things, images of fights for home rule across several decades. Similarly, racial tensions are a constant theme in Washington history. Often with strategic support from Howard University's great legal minds, African Americans successfully protested to gain jobs, to desegregate schools, restaurants and theaters and to overcome restrictive housing covenants. Race tensions have crested many times in the capital—during the slavery debates preceding the Civil War, during 1919 riots in which whites attacked black neighborhoods, after the assassination of the Rev. Martin Luther King, Jr. in 1968.

Washington also had to contend with government agencies, white families and retailers heading for the suburbs during World War II or the early Cold War years (most suburban builders refused to sell homes to African Americans). The trend accelerated as a result of the 1968 riots and the high District crime rates of the 1990s. Ever since, the capital has been in a competition with the suburbs, which ultimately drew middle-class African American families as well. The points of contention have included malls, sports teams, live theater, restaurants and efforts to attract other new businesses.

The District can still count each year on droves of tourists, but the suburbs have acquired a new advantage: the growing high-tech firms of the Dulles Airport corridor in Virginia and the biotech companies of the Interstate 270 corridor in Maryland. These and other companies are playing a key role in redefining the Washington metropolitan area—making it less "transient" than is generally imagined and moving it closer at last to fulfilling George Washington's dream of having a thriving commercial center on the Potomac.

It should be noted that the book's essays and captions are based on the most recent Washington-area scholarship and that a number of its illustrations have rarely or never been published before. Some photographs from *The Washington Post's* archives, for example, are appearing here in print for the first time. Similarly, so far as we are aware, this is the first time that *Pittsburgh-Courier (Washington Edition)* photos of middle-class African American life in the 1940s and 1950s are appearing in book form.

Washington is a unique city with a rich history, one that we have been privileged to explore for many years. We hope that you will enjoy exploring it with us in the pages that follow.

ACKNOWLEDGMENTS

In creating *Washington Album*, we have benefited from the work of dozens of historians whose research has sharpened and corrected our understanding of the city's history. Any errors, however, are of course our own.

While we have made every effort to credit their original work in the text and bibliography, a few friends and scholars demand special acknowledgment here: Kenneth R. Bowling, Marvin Caplan, Steven J. Diner, Emily Eig, Tom Frail, Howard F. Gillette, Jr., Don A. Hawkins, James O. Horton, Elizabeth Clark-Lewis, Kathryn Allamong Jacob, Richard W. Longstreth, David Merlin-Jones, Eugene L. Meyer, Alfred Moss, Philip W. Ogilvie, Peter Perl, Pamela Scott, Larry Van Dyne and especially Kathryn Schneider Smith and Sam Smith.

In addition, we found the pioneering work of Constance M. Green still invaluable, along with that of Letitia Woods Brown, Frederick Gutheim, W.M. Kiplinger, Leroy O. King, Jr., Margaret Leech and the Junior League of Washington.

We are greatly indebted to the energy and creativity of editor/publisher Noel Epstein and graphic designer Robert Barkin, as well as to the tireless and good-humored work of Susan Breitkopf. Special thanks also go to Gail Redmann, Jack Brewer, Barbara Franco and especially Anne W. Rollins, of the Historical Society of Washington, D.C.; Lucinda P. Janke, Kiplinger Washington Collection; Nick Natanson, National Archives; Sam Daniel, Maja Keech, Beverly Brannon, Mary Ison, Jan Grenci and Jennifer Brathovde, Library of Congress; Mary Ternes, Matthew Gilmore, Karen Bell, Fay Haskins and Roxanna Deane, D.C. Public Library; Donna Wells, Joellen El Bashir, Raul Gordon, Robin Van Fleet and Janet Sims-Wood, Moorland-Spingarn Research Center, Howard University; Leslie Taylor Davol, New-York Historical Society; Matthew Wasneiwski, Capitol Historical Society; Caroline Alderson, General Services Administration; Jay Sumner, *Washingtonian*; Kathy Myrick; and May Eng, Office of Personnel Management.

At *The Washington Post*, additional thanks to Jennifer Domenick, Carmen Chapin, Kim Klein, Aimee Sanders, Elisabeth Carlson, Virginia Rodriguez, Suzannah Gonzales and especially Lynn Ryzewicz. Finally, we are grateful to Paul Phillips Cooke, John Hechinger, Sr., Henry Whitehead, and Shirley L. and Paul S. Green for sharing their wisdom.

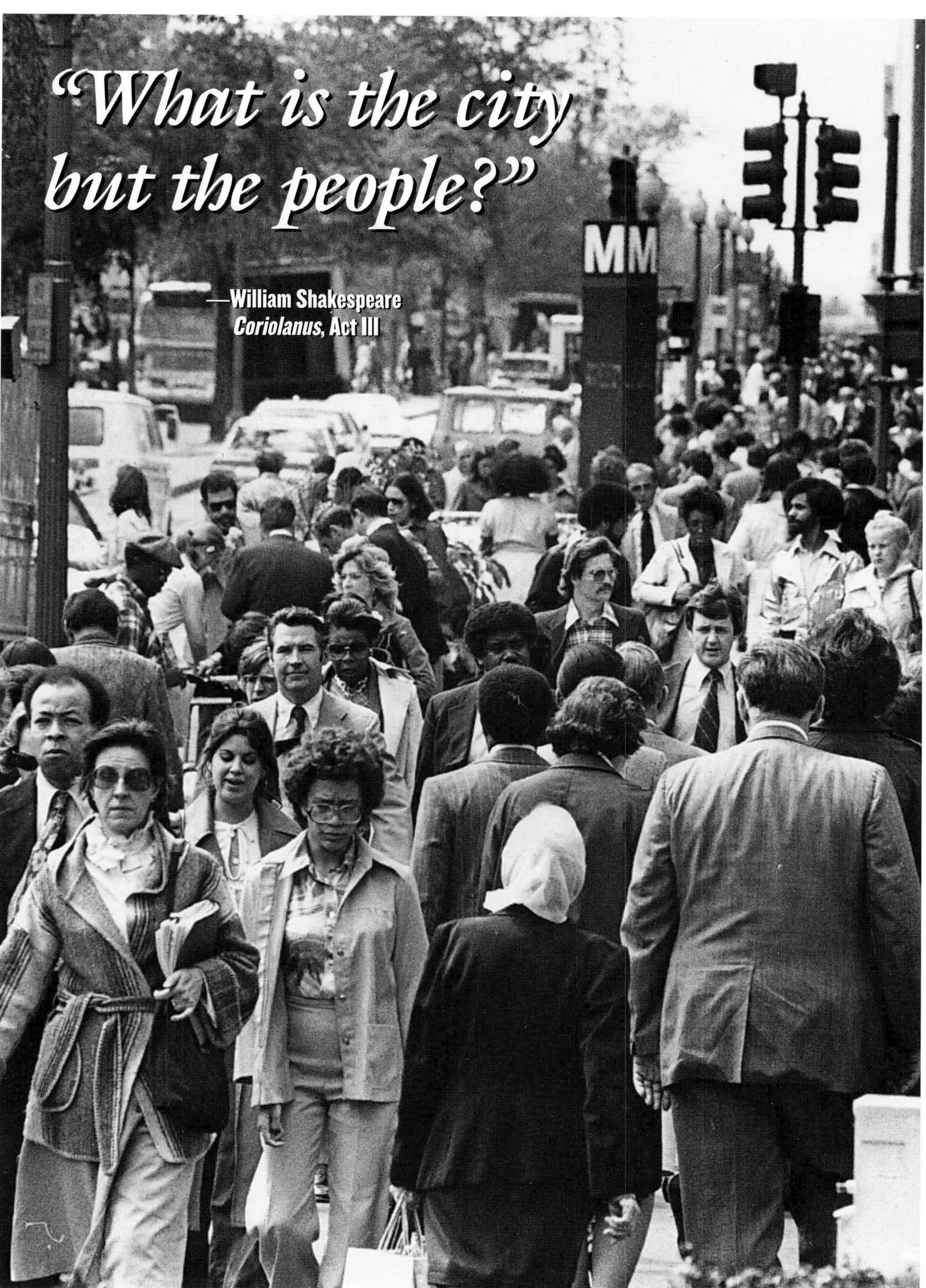
"What is the city but the people?"
—William Shakespeare
Coriolanus, Act III

CHAPTER 1

PELICANS IN THE WILDERNESS

AT a public Sale of Lots in the City of WASHINGTON, Peter Charles L'Enfant of George Town Maryland became purchaser of Lot number thirty in square number one hundred twenty seven for the confideration of ninety nine pounds current Money of Maryland on the terms and conditions publifhed at the fame fale: And he hath accordingly paid one-fourth part of the faid confideration money, and given Bond, with fecurity, for the payment of the refidue; on the payment whereof, with intereft, according to the faid Bond the faid Peter Charles L'Enfant or his affigns will be entitled to a conveyance in fee.

18th October 1791
Square No 127. Lot No 30

Th. Johnson
Dd Stuart } Commrs
Danl Carroll

199

Painter Garnet Jex imagined the above 1791 view of the new capital, seen from the heights above Georgetown and including the major actors in creating Washington. At left are the first presidentially appointed commissioners, responsible for executing the city plan: David Stuart, Thomas Johnson and Daniel Carroll. To their right is architect William Thornton, who won the competition to design the Capitol. Holding the map is city designer Pierre L'Enfant, and President Washington sits astride the horse. At his foot is surveyor Andrew Ellicott, and to Ellicott's right is Benjamin Banneker, the self-taught free black astronomer and mathematician who made the astronomical observations necessary to lay out the city's boundaries.

The first city commissioners signed a 1791 receipt (inset) for the sale of a lot to Pierre (*aka* Peter) L'Enfant. The brilliant but temperamental designer was dismissed in February 1792 for being uncooperative. Among other high-handed moves, he began demolishing Commissioner Carroll's nephew's house because it would have occupied part of the future New Jersey Avenue, S.E.

George Washington envisioned the new capital of the United States as "The Rome of the New World," according to historian James Sterling Young. The president wanted glistening, wide boulevards. He wanted a prestigious national university. He wanted a thriving commercial center, nourished by Potomac River links to the Ohio River valley.

What the nation got instead for the first two-thirds of the 19th century was mostly a rattletrap, a muddy backwater that embarrassed visiting diplomats, stumbled commercially and failed to attract significant population or investment. "There sits the president, like a pelican in the wilderness," wrote a Philadelphia editor in 1803.

As always, politics explained a great deal.

Congress had meandered to eight locations since 1774, from major cities like New York to farm villages like Lancaster, Pa. In 1790, while it was meeting in Philadelphia, former Revolutionary War soldiers laid siege to its members, demanding long-delayed back pay—and sympathetic local militias did little to protect the lawmakers. So Congress decided to create a permanent capital out of whole cloth, a federal enclave protected by forces without local responsibilities or ties. But where should it be built? Northerners wanted it in their region, while Southerners insisted that it be more central to their homes than the previous meeting places in Pennsylvania, Maryland, New Jersey and New York.

Not for the last time in American government, the solution was found in a bargain over money. Treasury Secretary Alexander Hamilton had proposed that Congress assume the states' Revolutionary War debts, a notion opposed by Southerners, who feared that it would lead to too much federal control, to an "unconstitutional seizure of state authority," as historian Kenneth R. Bowling puts it. So Secretary of State Thomas Jefferson persuaded Hamilton and James Madison, then a Virginia member of the House, to strike a deal: The capital would be placed in the South in return for Southern support of a debt-assumption bill. The bargain worked, resulting in a capital that, unlike its European counterparts, would be orphaned from the nation's financial and cultural centers.

The Congress directed George Washington to choose a government seat of up to "10 miles square" on the Potomac, between Conococheague Creek at Williamsport, Md., and the Eastern Branch (Anacostia) near Georgetown. He picked 64,000 acres, mostly farmland and dense woods, at the junction of the

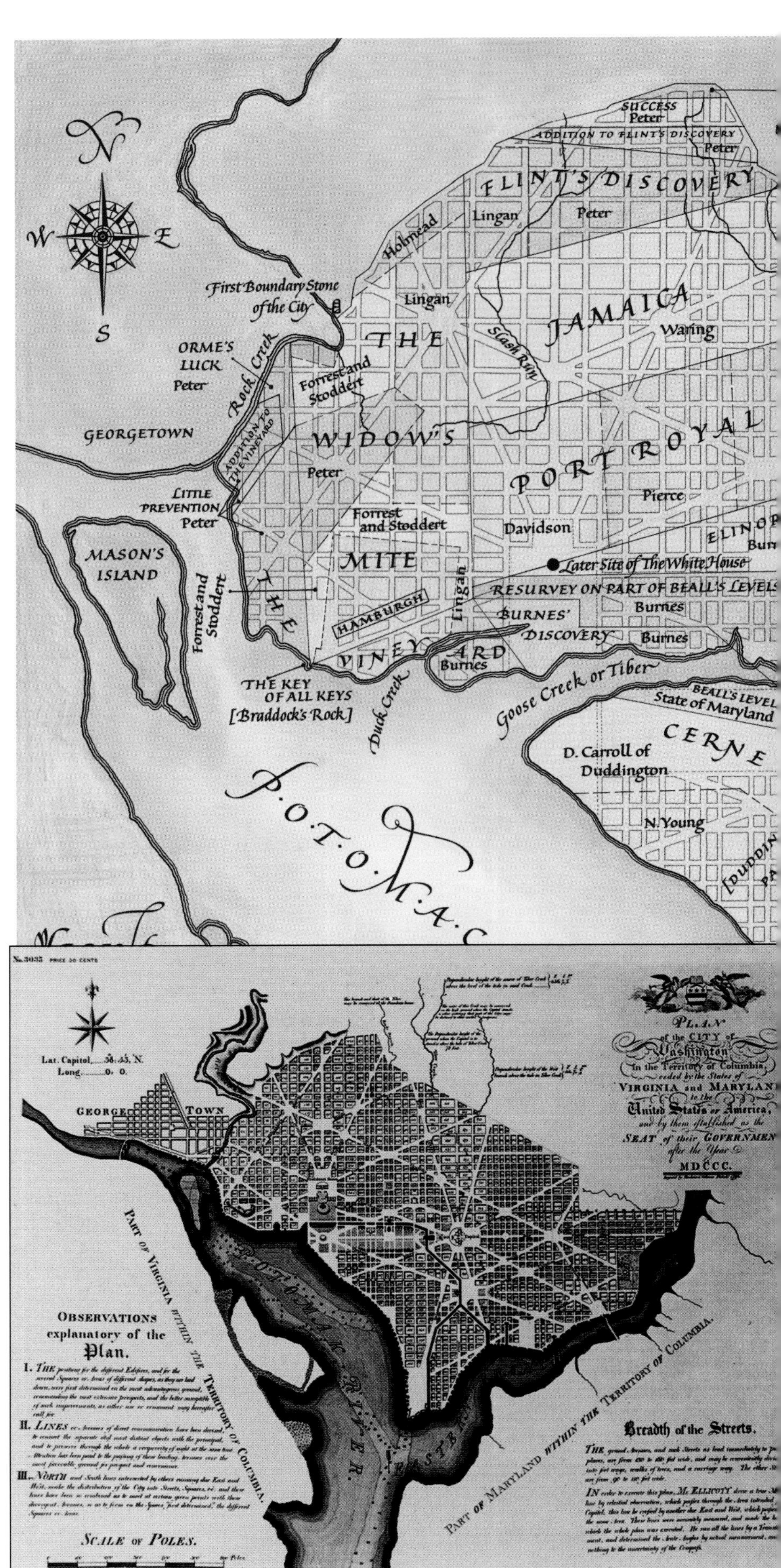

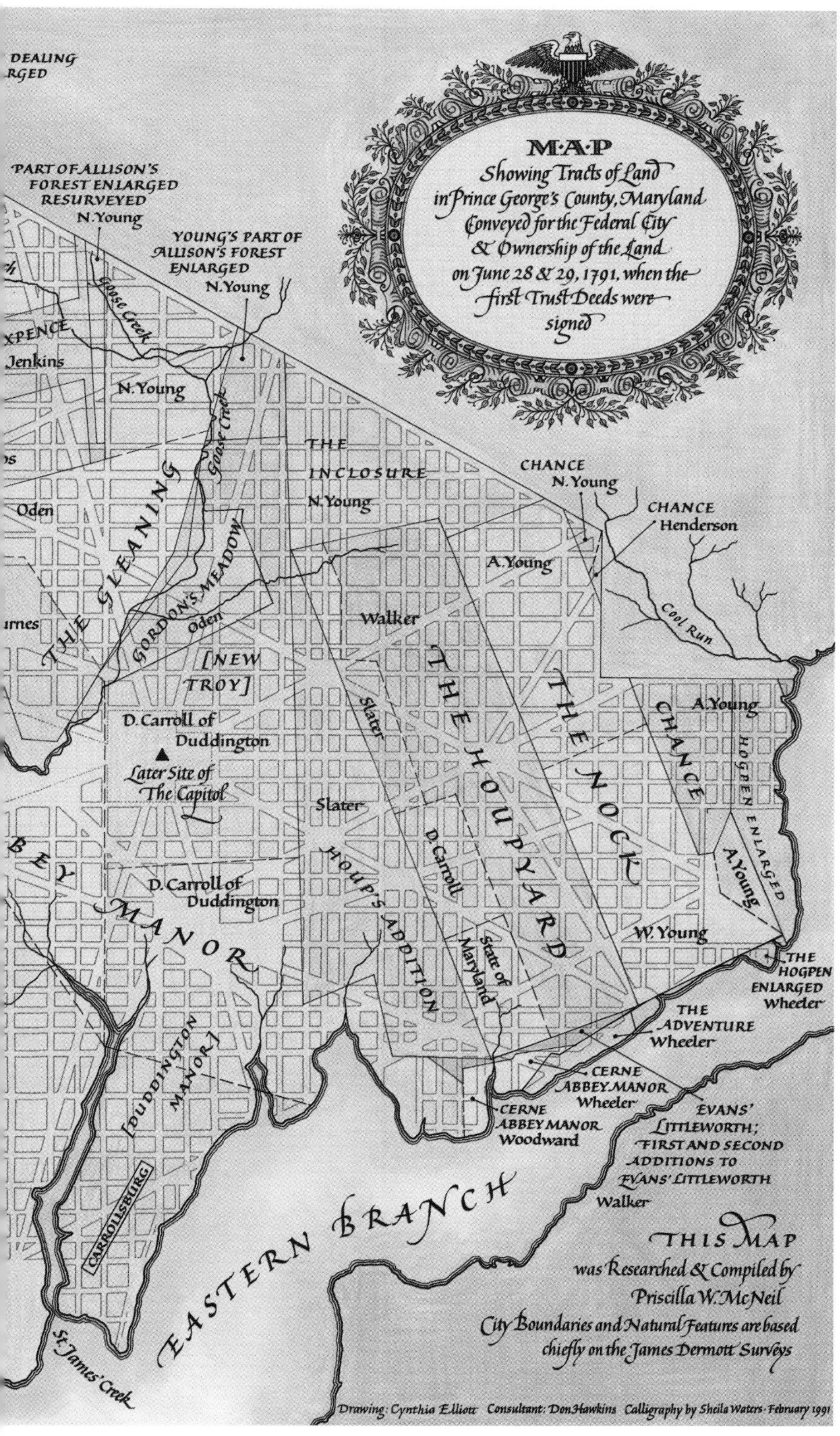

The Ellicott version of Pierre L'Enfant's city plan (left) was published in 1792, soon after L'Enfant was dismissed. Drawn from drafts left behind by L'Enfant, the map became the basis for land sales and construction as well as for future planning. (Contrary to local legend, mathematician Benjamin Banneker did not design the city or reconstruct L'Enfant's plan from memory.) The extraordinary plan combined the popular American street grid with European-style diagonal avenues, placed to take advantage of hills and natural vistas. The map (above) of the owners of land designated for the city in 1791, compiled in 1991 by Priscilla W. McNeil and drawn by Don A. Hawkins, dispels the myth that the area was a wilderness.

Potomac and Anacostia, almost exactly midway between the northernmost and southernmost points of the new republic.

Some grumbled that the president's choice was likely to enhance the value of his own large landholdings—8,500 acres (and 10 miles of river frontage) at and near Mount Vernon, and another 60,000-plus acres, two-thirds of which lay along the Potomac-Ohio river system. In picking the capital's site, however, he specified that no federal buildings be erected on the Virginia side of the District of Columbia, and admiration for the president was in any case so intense that few dwelled on the question of financial conflicts.

Maryland and Virginia, anticipating economic benefits, were happy to cede land for the capital. Maryland gave 60 square miles of territory, including Georgetown. Virginia gave 30 square miles, including Alexandria. The remaining 10 square miles lay under the Potomac and Anacostia rivers. Maryland threw in $72,000 in cash, and Virginia anted up $120,000, to get the city started. President Washington carved the city into plots and offered them for sale, but after land auctions of the early 1790s failed to raise much money, Maryland lent the city an additional $250,000.

In 1791 the president picked Pierre L'Enfant, a young French artist and soldier who had served with him during the Revolutionary War, to design the new capital. L'Enfant came up with a street system made up of a basic grid joined by oddly angled streets that eventually were named for states, and he used the existing landscape to excellent effect. As historian C.M. Harris writes, "Nature, the natural shape of the land, would organize the major sites and coordinates."

Especially notable was L'Enfant's decision to place the key government buildings, the Capitol and the White House—the "poles" of his design—atop slopes or hills. While this reflected the separation of powers embodied in the Constitution, the decision also pleased local landowners, who believed that it would result in real estate sales and development around both buildings.

For the Mall L'Enfant envisioned a huge expanse of lawn extending from the Capitol to the Potomac River, with a manmade waterfall cascading down from the Capitol's West Front. The city would be dotted by public squares containing a grand nondenominational church, a national bank, the judiciary, a theater, markets, a mercantile exchange and monuments, and within the capital would be a City Canal that extended Tiber Creek, which ran partly along today's Constitution Avenue, to the Anacostia.

In addition, the 15 existing states each would be assigned a square to fill with statues and monuments honoring their own sages and heroes. L'Enfant also set aside public areas for colleges and schools and anticipated the arrival of lobbying enterprises by reserving space for "every Society whose object is national."

Jefferson and others, however, found L'Enfant's plan too elaborate for a struggling new country. They succeeded in deleting the national bank, the theater, the waterfall and the mercantile

THE FIRST SPECULATORS

As Duke de la Rochefoucauld-Liancourt wrote after visiting Washington in 1797, "In America, where, more than in any other country in the world, a desire for wealth is the prevailing passion, there are few schemes which are not made the means of extensive speculations; and that of the erecting Federal-City presented irresistible temptations . . ."

Washington's plan for developing the city relied on the cooperation of the existing landowners, who deeded their land to the federal government. They would be paid for any lots used for public squares and buildings. They would not be paid for land used for streets. The deal was made palatable because the government would return to the landowners a portion of the lots not needed for the government's use, which meant most of the land. The landowners could then sell these lots at what were expected to be high prices. The government would do the same with its share and use its proceeds to build the new city. Washington kept the actual location of the city secret until the last minute, hoping to hold down the price it would have to pay to the landowners.

The government tried selling its lots at three public auctions between 1791 and 1793, but only a handful were purchased. Conditions were ripe for private speculators, and 28-year-old financier James Greenleaf (left) of Boston began buying up tracts. The terms of sale included a pledge to build brick houses on some lots. Greenleaf brought in two Pennsylvania partners, former Senator Robert Morris and John Nicholson, said he had the backing of Dutch financiers and purchased thousands of lots. Unfortunately, the partners could neither find buyers for the lots nor build houses fast enough. By 1797 the group had declared bankruptcy, the three men were sent to debtor's prison and real estate prices plummeted.

Wheat's Row (opposite, top), at 1313 4th Street, S.W., was built by the group in 1795. It is one of a handful of buildings that survived the razing of Southwest in the 1950s. The Six Buildings (opposite, middle), built by Isaac Pollock on the 2100 block of Pennsylvania Avenue, housed the early State Department. Two of its structures remain today. Carroll's Row (opposite, bottom), housing for members of Congress, opened in 1809 on the site of today's main Library of Congress. Even George Washington got into the act: In 1799 he built a double townhouse designed by Dr. William Thornton on North Capitol Street to be used as a boarding house, as seen in this sketch by William G. Newton (left).

exchange. The temperamental L'Enfant did not take well to such instruction from his employers, and it didn't help that he ordered the house of a nephew of Daniel Carroll, one of the capital's three commissioners appointed by Washington, to be demolished. L'Enfant was dismissed in 1792. Still, his plan was largely adopted.

His and Washington's expectations for commercial development, however, were not to be realized. The Potomac never became the commercial gateway to the Ohio River valley that they had envisioned. The construction of two canals to link the Potomac with the Ohio failed before reaching the far side of the Appalachians. Instead, New York State's Erie Canal in the 1820s and then the Baltimore & Ohio Railroad in the 1830s began to monopolize domestic commerce, helping New York City and Baltimore grow into major commercial centers.

Indeed, Baltimore had been winning the race for Middle Atlantic dominance from the outset. As historian David R. Goldfield notes, farmers in northern Maryland and central Pennsylvania had already built relationships in 1800 with Baltimore millers and shippers. Washington would not attract major regional farming business until the 1850s, when northern Virginia farmers turned to Washington as a city in which to sell and from which to ship.

Now, without key canal transportation westward, Washington failed to attract more than minor manufacturing, and neither Georgetown nor Alexandria

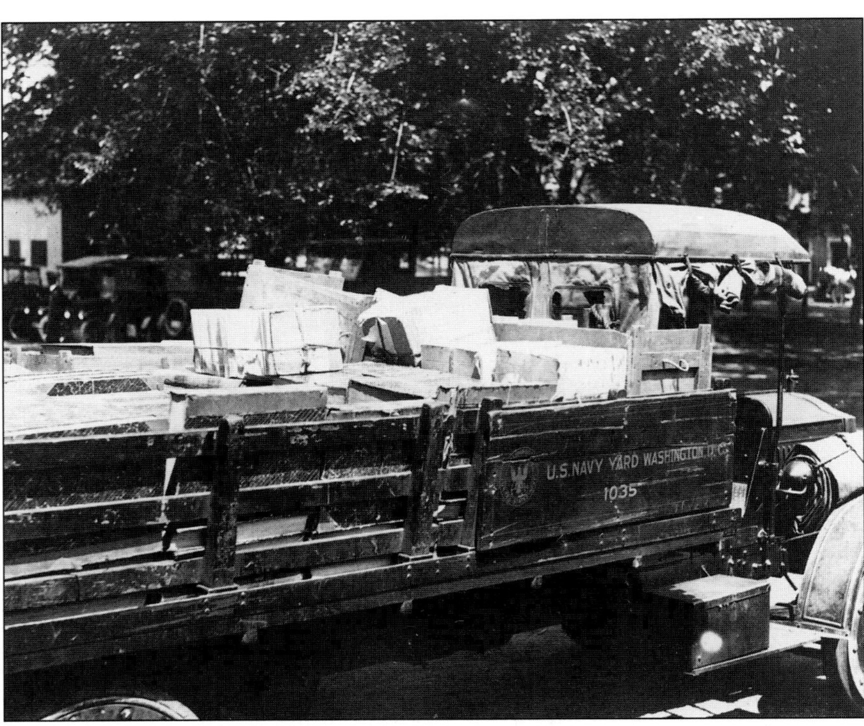

It's easy to see why visitors scoffed at L'Enfant's "city of magnificent intentions" (Charles Dickens, 1842) and why Americans didn't rush to invest in the city. The entire first census of the nation's 1790 population of less than 4 million is written on the papers in the small bundle atop the truck in this 1922 photograph. The government consisted of the president, 26 senators, 65 representatives, the secretaries of state, war, the navy and the treasury, the postmaster and a handful of clerks. Why did anyone need a 6,100-acre capital city?

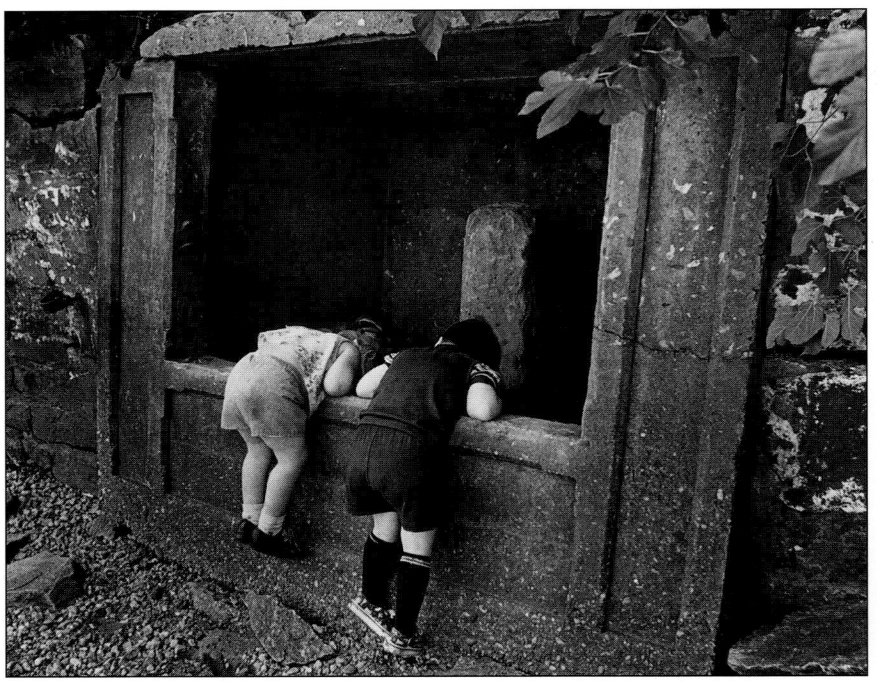

Two children strain to read the inscription on the Jones Point, Alexandria, boundary marker identifying the point from which Andrew Ellicott laid out the boundaries of the 10-mile-square Territory of Columbia. Forty stones were set at one-mile intervals along the diamond's route through parts of Virginia and Maryland (the Virginia portions, Alexandria and Arlington County, were returned to that state in 1846). Most of the stones remain in place today.

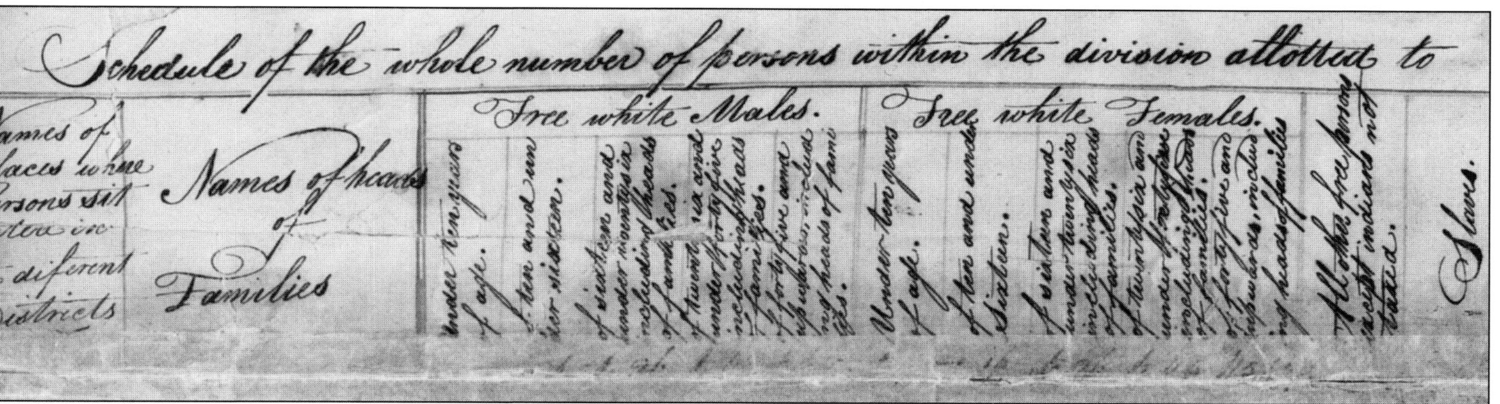

This page from the census of 1800 suggests the makeup of the Territory of Columbia's population. That year it counted 14,093 inhabitants, most in Georgetown and Alexandria. Of the total, 10,266 were white, 3,244 were slaves and 783 were free African Americans. Of the slave owners in Washington City, nearly all held fewer than 10, suggesting that most slaves worked in the household rather than in the fields.

became the major ports of Washington's dreams. In fact, Alexandria, far from the District's central city, prospered less than Georgetown, and the Virginia port balked at the heavy debt required to build the canal system. For these and other reasons, Alexandria and Arlington were returned to Virginia in 1846.

As it turned out, L'Enfant's separation of government buildings also made it difficult to create a nucleus for community and initially slowed the city's growth. Washington's citizens, moreover, had to struggle to win the sympathies of transient, part-time legislators whose "primary allegiance," as historian Howard Gillette notes, "lay with their own states." L'Enfant's state squares, for example, depended on investments from those states, but the states never bit. Why would they? Shouldn't farmers back home devote scarce resources to their own state capitals? They did—and Washington languished.

The city long lacked a sewage system, paved streets and sufficient housing. Literature of the early 1800s is full of references to members of Congress who set out from the Capitol by carriage after dark for a hotel just a few blocks away,

A DESCRIPTION OF THE SITUATION AND PLAN

OF THE

CITY OF WASHINGTON,

NOW BUILDING FOR

THE METROPOLIS OF AMERICA,

AND ESTABLISHED AS THE PERMANENT RESIDENCE OF CONGRESS AFTER THE YEAR 1800.

THE CITY of WASHINGTON, in the diſtrict of COLUMBIA, now building for the permanent ſeat of the Government of the United States, ſtands at the junction of the rivers Potomac and the Eaſtern Branch, extending about four miles up each, including a tract of territory, exceeded in point of convenience, ſalubrity, and beauty, by none in America, if any in the world:—For, although the land is apparently level, yet, by gentle and gradual ſwellings, a variety of elegant proſpects are produced, while there is a ſufficient deſcent to convey off the water occaſioned by rain.

Within the limits of the city are twenty-five never-failing ſprings of excellent water; and, by digging wells, water of the beſt quality is readily had; beſides, the never-failing ſtreams that now run through that territory, are alſo to be collected for the uſe of the city.

The EASTERN BRANCH is one of the ſafeſt and moſt commodious harbours in America, being ſufficiently deep for the largeſt ſhips, for about four miles above its mouth; while the channel lies cloſe along the edge of the city, and is abundantly capacious.

The City, being ſituated upon the great poſt road, exactly equidiſtant from the northern and ſouthern extremities of the union, and nearly ſo from the Atlantic Ocean to the Ohio river, upon the beſt navigation, and in the midſt of the richeſt commercial territory in America, commanding the moſt extenſive internal reſources, is by far the moſt eligible ſituation for the reſidence of Congreſs; and as it is now preſſing forward, by the public ſpirited enterpriſe of the people of the United States, and by foreigners, it will grow up with a degree of rapidity, hitherto unparalleled in the annals of cities, and will ſoon become the admiration and delight of the world.

The inland navigation of the Potomac is ſo far advanced, that craft loaded with produce now come down that river and its ſeveral branches, from upwards of one hundred and eighty miles to the great falls, which are within fourteen miles of the New City. The canals at the great and little falls are nearly completed, and the locks in ſuch forwardneſs, that, in the courſe of the enſuing ſummer, the navigation will be entirely opened between tide water and the head branches of the Potomac, which will produce a communication by water between the City of Waſhington, and the interior parts of Virginia and Maryland, by means of the Potomac, the Shannandoah, the South Branch, Opecan, Cape Capon, Patterſon's Creek, Conoochegue, and Monocaſy, for upwards of two hundred miles, through one of the moſt healthy, pleaſant, and fertile regions in America, producing, in vaſt abundance, tobacco of ſuperior quality, hemp, Indian corn, wheat and other ſmall grain, with fruit and vegetables peculiar to America, in vaſt abundance, and equal in quality to any in the United States.

The lands upon the Potomac above the City of Waſhington, all around it, and for ſixty miles below, are high and dry, abounding with innumerable ſprings of excellent water, and are well covered with large timber of various kinds. A few miles below the City, upon the banks of the Potomac, are inexhauſtible mountains of excellent freeſtone, of the white and red Portland kinds, of which the public edifices in the city are now building. Above the City, alſo upon the banks of the river, are immenſe quantities of excellent coal, limeſtone, and marble, with blue ſlate of the beſt quality.

The founding of this City, in ſuch an eligible ſituation, upon ſuch a liberal and elegant plan, will by future generations be conſidered as a high proof of the judgement and wiſdom of the preſent Preſident of the United States, while its name will keep freſh in mind, to the end of time, the many virtues and amiable qualities of that great man.

The plan of this City, agreeably to the directions of the Preſident of the United States, was deſigned and drawn by the celebrated Major L'ENFANT, and is an inconceivable improvement upon all other cities, combining not only convenience, regularity, elegance of proſpect, and a free circulation of air, but every thing grand and beautiful that can poſſibly be introduced into a city.

Two haſty impreſſions of this plan were uſhered to the public laſt ſpring, one done at Philadelphia upon a ſmall ſcale, and another done at Boſton upon a larger;—theſe did not exhibit the ſoundings of the harbours, and were defective with regard to the limits of the City upon the Eaſtern Branch.

The laſt and beſt impreſſion of the plan is that lately publiſhed at Philadelphia upon the large ſcale, although it contains ſeveral miſtakes in the ſoundings of the Eaſtern Branch; for, where there is thirty-five feet water, it only ſhews twelve and eighteen. This river has, however, been ſounded by authority, and is found to contain thirty and thirty-five feet to near the upper end of the city, where it is eighteen and twenty feet deep.

The City is divided into ſquares or grand diviſions, by the ſtreets running due North and South, and Eaſt and Weſt, which form the ground-work of the plan. However, from the Capitol, the Preſident's Houſe, and ſome of the important areas in the City, run tranſverſe avenues or diagonal ſtreets, from one material object to another, which not only produce a variety of charming proſpects, but remove that inſipid ſameneſs that renders ſome other great cities unpleaſing. Theſe great leading ſtreets are all one hundred and ſixty feet wide, including a pavement of ten feet, and a gravel walk of thirty feet planted with trees on each ſide, which will leave eighty feet of paved ſtreet for carriages. The reſt of the ſtreets are in general one hundred and ten feet wide, with a few only ninety feet, except North, South, and Eaſt Capitol Streets, which are one hundred and ſixty feet. The diagonal ſtreets are named after the reſpective ſtates compoſing the Union, while thoſe running North and South are, from the Capitol Eaſtward, named, EAST FIRST STREET, EAST SECOND STREET, &c. and thoſe Weſt of it are in the ſame manner called WEST FIRST STREET, WEST SECOND STREET, &c. thoſe running Eaſt and Weſt are from the Capitol Northward named, NORTH A STREET, NORTH B STREET, &c. and thoſe South of it are called SOUTH A STREET, SOUH B STREET, &c.

The ſquares, or diviſions of the City, have their numbers inſerted in the plan, and amount to eleven hundred and fifty.—The rectangular ſquares generally contain from three to ſix acres, and are divided into lots of from forty to eighty feet front, and their depth, from about one hundred and ten to three hundred feet, according to the ſize of the ſquare.

The irregular diviſions produced by the diagonal ſtreets are ſome of them ſmall, but are generally in valuable ſituations.—Their acute points are all to be cut off at forty feet, ſo that no houſe in the City will have an acute corner.—The lots in theſe irregular ſquares will all turn at a right angle with the reſpective ſtreets, although the backs of the houſes upon them will not ſtand parallel to one another, which is a matter of no conſequence.

By the rules declared and publiſhed by the Preſident of the United States, for regulating the buildings within the City, all houſes muſt be of ſtone or brick—their walls muſt be parallel to the ſtreets, and either placed immediately upon them, or withdrawn therefrom at pleaſure. The walls of all houſes upon ſtreets one hundred and ſixty feet wide muſt be at leaſt thirty feet high; but there is no obligation impoſed to build or improve in any limited time.

The area for the CAPITOL (or houſe for the Legiſlative Bodies) is ſituated upon the moſt beautiful eminence in the City, about a mile from the Eaſtern Branch, and not much more from the Potomac, commanding a full and complete view of every part of the City, as well as a conſiderable extent of the country around.—The PRESIDENT'S HOUSE will ſtand upon a riſing ground, not far from the Banks of the Potomac, poſſeſſing a delightful water proſpect, together with a commanding view of the CAPITOL, and ſome other mat- parts of the City.

Due ſouth from the Preſident's houſe, and due weſt from the Capitol, run two great pleaſure parks or malls, which interſect and terminate upon the Banks of the Potomac, and are to be ornamented at the ſides by a variety of elegant buildings, and houſes for foreign Miniſters, &c.

Interſperſed through the City, where the moſt material ſtreets croſs one another, are a variety of open Areas, formed in various regular figures, which in great cities are extremely uſeful and ornamental.

Fifteen of the beſt of theſe Areas are to be appropriated to the different States compoſing the Union; not only to bear their reſpective names, but as proper places for them to erect ſtatues, obeliſks, or columns, to the memory of their favourite eminent men.—Upon the ſmall eminence, where a line due weſt from the Capitol, and due ſouth from the Preſident's houſe would interſect, is to be erected an equeſtrian ſtatue of GENERAL WASHINGTON, now PRESIDENT of the UNITED STATES.—The building where Maſſachuſetts and Georgia ſtreets meet, is intended for a *Marine Hoſpital*, with its gardens.

The AREA at the ſouth end of Eaſt Eight Street is for the GENERAL EXCHANGE, and its public walks, &c.—The broad black line, which runs along part of NORTH B STREET, and, ſeparating, joins the Eaſtern Branch at two places, is a CANAL, which is to be eighty feet wide, and eight feet deep.—The AREA, where SOUTH G STREET croſſes the canal, is intended to contain a CITY HALL, and a baſon of water; there being now a very large ſpring in the middle of it.

The AREA, at the junction of the rivers, is for a FORT, MAGAZINES, and ARSENALS.

At the eaſt end of EAST CAPITOL STREET is to be a BRIDGE, and the preſent Ferry is at the lower end of KENTUCKY STREET, where the great road now croſſes the Eaſtern Branch.—The Tyber, which is the principal ſtream that paſſes through the City, is to be collected in a grand Reſervoir beſide the Capitol, from whence it will be carried in pipes to different parts of the City; while its ſurplus will fall down in beautiful caſcades, through the public gardens weſt of the Capitol, into the canal.—In various parts of the City places are allotted for MARKET HOUSES, CHURCHES, COLLEGES, THEATRES, &c.

The PRESIDENT of the UNITED STATES, in locating the ſeat of the City, prevailed upon the proprietors of the ſoil to cede a certain portion of the lots in every ſituation, to be ſold by his direction, and the proceeds to be ſolely applied to the public buildings, and other works of public utility within the City. This grant will produce about fifteen thouſand lots, and will be ſufficient, not only to erect the public buildings, but to dig the canal, conduct water through the City, and to pave and light the ſtreets, which will ſave a heavy tax that ariſes in other cities, and conſequently render the lots conſiderably more valuable.

The grants of money made by *Virginia* and *Maryland*, being hitherto ſufficient, few of the public lots have yet been ſold; but a ſale is advertiſed to commence on the 17th day of September next, when it is expected the demand will be conſiderable, as the monied men in America have now turned their attention to that great national object.

When the writer of this left Waſhington, on the end of January laſt, moſt of the ſtreets were run, and the ſquares divided into lots.—The canal was partly dug, and the greateſt part of the materials provided for the public buildings, which are to be entirely of freeſtone poliſhed, and are now carrying on with all poſſible expedition.—Laſt ſummer ſeveral private houſes were erected, and a great many proprietors of lots were preparing to build this enſuing ſummer.

In conſequence of the eſtabliſhment of NATIONAL FAITH, ORDER, and GOOD GOVERNMENT, by the NEW CONSTITUTION, immenſe fortunes have been amaſſed in America within theſe three years paſt, by the National Debt and Bank Stock appreciating to their full value, as well as by the rapid riſe in the value of back lands.—The public lots in the City of Waſhington open the next field for ſpeculation in America, and there is every probability of their being run up to an enormous price, as ſoon as the public buildings are conſiderably advanced; for although lands in America, from their quantity, are leſs valuable than thoſe in Britain, yet lots in cities generally ſell as high.

Having every opportunity to be thoroughly acquainted with the ſubject, the preceding conciſe account of the progreſs of that grand and novel undertaking is reſpectfully offered to the public, by

Their obedient Servant,

GEORGE WALKER.

LONDON, *York Hotel, Bridge-ſtreet, Black-friars,*
March 11, 1793.

The job of selling the new city to investors abroad fell to real estate speculators like George Walker, whose pitch (above) was published in European papers in 1793. Walker traveled to London and Amsterdam, where either his hyperbole — "an inconceivable improvement upon all other cities" — or his charm resulted in sales of a few lots. Walker is credited with first suggesting the city's site, but he failed as a land speculator, declaring bankruptcy in 1804.

only to run afoul of ruts, bogs and thieves. As late as 1820, when the first municipal trash collection began, pigs were allowed to run wild in the streets, the better to assure that rotting food scraps were cleaned up. There were no signs, no gas lights, no street markers. In a celebrated incident, First Lady Abigail Adams became hopelessly lost en route from Baltimore to Washington, wandering in woods near Bladensburg, Md., for hours, and had to hire a vagabond to guide her to safety.

Washington was also from the start a financially dependent city, although Congress was careful to provide a taste of local government. In 1802 it enacted a charter for the City of Washington, providing for a presidentially appointed mayor and an elected city council, and two years later the first publicly funded schools opened. Starting in 1820, Congress let the city elect its own mayor as well. The lawmakers were extremely reluctant, however, to appropriate money for roads or other improvements or to give the city any edge in the competition for trade with the Western territories.

On May 15, 1800, according to a local survey, only 372 residences stood in the city—109 brick, the rest wood. In 1802, only 233 people in a population approaching 4,000 owned property. Poor relief, a rudimentary form of welfare, accounted for 42 percent of the city's spending. In that year, other than soldiers, the federal government employed only 291 people. The civilian federal workforce grew to only 625 by 1829.

That clearly wasn't much of a nucleus for a capital city. Most

The Frederick Road—today's Wisconsin Avenue—began life as a Native American trail. This circa 1800 view, painted by Rebecca Wister Morris Nourse, captures the lightly populated landscape from the vicinity of today's R Street. In the distance is Mason's Island (now Roosevelt Island).

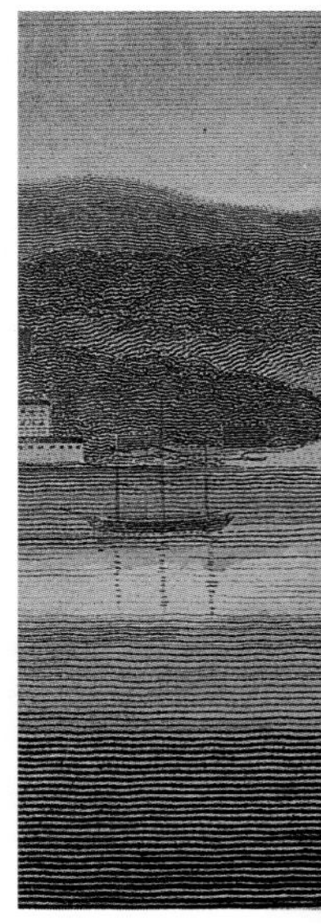

Artists often created city vistas that combined actual details with future plans. This view, the best that exists of how Washington looked when government belongings arrived in 1800 at Lear's Wharf (at center), is no exception. While accurately portraying most city land as vacant, it exaggerates the number of buildings lining the waterfront. It also shows the Capitol, to the left of the tall masts, with two wings connected by a dome. In reality, only the north (Senate) wing was completed in 1800, as seen (inset) in William Birch's watercolor.

Americans, residents and not, thought of Washington as more of a village, and one that, despite some notable buildings, was not exactly elegant or well maintained. In 1803, for example, part of the Senate ceiling fell, narrowly missing Vice President Aaron Burr, who was presiding. In the same year, visitors to the Senate gallery were warned not to place their feet on a restraining board at the gallery's edge, because dirt and debris were falling from their shoes onto the heads of the senators below.

In 1810, the city had only two places of public amusement: a racetrack, where drunkenness and

fights were frequent, and a theater, where scruffy boys gained admission by lifting floorboards and sneaking in. By 1814, the first of many motions to move the capital somewhere else—anywhere else—had been introduced in the House.

During the city's first half century, population consisted chiefly of three groups—farmers, skilled craftsmen and laborers (often Irish, but also African-American, both slave and free) and government officeholders, with sprinklings of others, from shopkeepers and silversmiths to ministers and millwrights. Subsistence farming flourished, and the "sin industries" of gambling and drinking found regular clienteles.

Since legislative sessions lasted only three months a year, elected representatives always had a sense of transience. Nearly all lived and ate in hotels and boardinghouses. Few set up permanent housekeeping in Washington or stayed after their terms ended. Similarly, because Congress was not in session all year, work for laborers ebbed and flowed. Many workers swung between full employment and the almshouse, the first of which opened in Washington in 1809 on the site of what is now D.C. General Hospital.

The capital's early development may have been hindered most of all, however, by its Southern character. Having been forged from two slave-holding states, Washington, too, permitted slavery from the outset. That meant that the city was unattractive to most skilled immigrants, who could not hope to compete with slave labor, as well as to early

Surveyor Nicholas King rendered the city's rustic conditions in his circa 1803 watercolor. The building at right is Blodget's Hotel, at 8th and E streets, N.W., built as the prize in a lottery for a city where investors waited—in vain—for the federal government to fund improvements. The hotel, never awarded to anyone, eventually housed a variety of local and federal offices. The small building at left was probably a laborer's shanty.

CITY OF WASHINGTON, ss.

I CERTIFY, That the bearer hereof, Eliza Washington a bright Mulatto Woman 31 years old living in the first Ward of said City

hath produced to me, satisfactory evidence of the legality of her title to freedom, pursuant to an act of the Corporation of the city of Washington, entitled "An act concerning free negroes, mulattoes and slaves," passed on the thirty-first day of May in the year eighteen hundred and twenty-seven, she is therefore permitted to reside in the said city of Washington, she complying with the provisions contained in the above recited act.

In testimony whereof, I have hereunto set my hand and affixed the seal of the Corporation of the said city of Washington, this 30th day of October Anno Domini one thousand eight hundred and twenty-seven

Register of the City of Washington.

From 1808 to 1862, Washington City's Black Code governed the lives of free blacks and slaves. After 1806, Virginia barred freed slaves from that state, but the capital had no such prohibition. In 1812, though, the City Council ordered free blacks to register and to carry proof of their free status at all times. Eliza Washington's registration certificate theoretically protected her from being abducted by slave traders.

Top: Robert Brent was the City of Washington's first mayor, serving by presidential appointment from 1802 to 1812. (The city charter granted by Congress in 1802 let Alexandria and Georgetown continue autonomous operations.) In 1812, the City Council was allowed to elect the mayor, and in 1821 the people were given that right, which they exercised until 1871. Under Brent, the city improved streets that were marked out but as yet uncleared, granted business licenses, started a police force and provided funds for the poor, victims of the inconsistencies of construction work.

Above right: Yarrow Mamout was one of 894 free blacks living in Georgetown in 1820. When portrait painter Charles Willson Peale captured his likeness a year earlier, Mamout was more than 100 years old. Born in Africa and raised a Muslim, he was brought as a slave to the Maryland colony and eventually was freed by his Georgetown owner as a reward for hard work. Mamout bought a cart and earned his living hauling goods, one of the few occupations approved for free blacks at the time. He eventually bought a house and other property, despite having made bad investments with white merchants.

manufacturers, who considered slave labor unreliable.

Slave trading was not abolished in Washington until 1850, far too late to mend the economic damage it had done. And while anti-slavery leaders badgered Congress to end slavery outright in the capital, Congress refused to take that step until 1862, well after the outbreak of the Civil War.

As the 1850s ended, the capital surely was not the new Rome of Washington's dream. The City Canal was forever polluted. The beginnings of the Washington Monument stuck strangely out of the ground, while the Treasury Department, Post Office and Patent Office buildings, all begun in the 1830s, were similarly incomplete. Americans' allegiance to the city, moreover, was anything but universal. Predominantly Southern but including many people from elsewhere, the capital throbbed with the sectional antagonism that would lead to the Civil War. Indeed, in December of 1860, when South Carolina became the first state to secede from the union and its representatives made a great show of resigning from Congress, George Washington's capital was in danger of passing into oblivion.

Farmers worked the land within the city and out in Washington County, that part of the Territory beyond Boundary Street (Florida Avenue) and across the Eastern Branch (Anacostia River), raising food for city residents. The first city market was a gathering of traders on the President's Square nearly opposite the White House. In 1801 it was moved to Market Square, where the National Archives stands today. The Center Market operated on that location until 1931.

BY DESIGN

When Jefferson, Washington and the city's first commissioners decided to hold competitions for the designs of key buildings, they appealed to the few existing professional architects as well as to architect-builders with some design training, builders, and gentlemen-architects for whom design was an avocation.

James Hoban (below), an Irish-born architect, was responsible for the White House's design and construction and contributed to the Capitol. Benjamin Henry Latrobe (right) had received training as an architect in Europe. After engineering Philadelphia's water supply, he came to Washington in 1803 as Jefferson's surveyor of public buildings. He designed the Navy Yard and numerous private estates in the city. Latrobe also contributed to the design of the Capitol and oversaw much of its rebuilding after the British burned it in 1814.

Dr. William Thornton (below right) was an English-educated physician and a gentleman-architect who won the competition for the design of the Capitol. Today's Capitol, however, is significantly different from his winning plan because of the impact of the War of 1812, the amount of time needed to build such a massive project, flaws in the amateur's original plan and the rapid growth of the national legislature, which soon demanded more space.

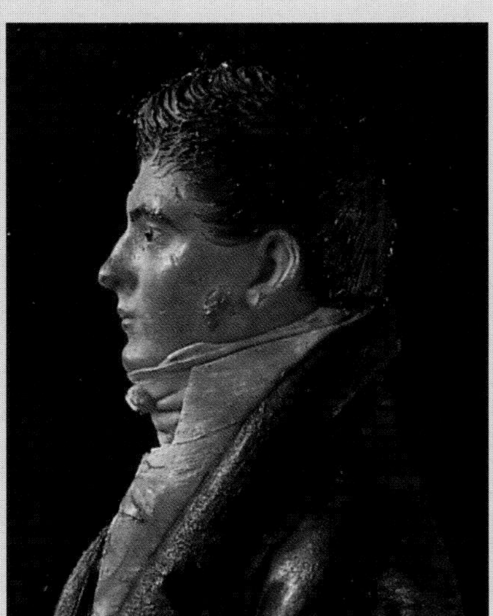

In this watercolor of "An Overseer Doing His Duty," painted in 1798 by architect Benjamin Henry Latrobe, slaves clear a field in the Chesapeake region. Of the land chosen for the capital, bounded by today's Florida Avenue and the Anacostia and Potomac rivers, some was still wooded, but much was under cultivation by slave labor.

Edward Savage's portrait of George Washington and his family in 1796 illustrates the first president's unfulfilled ambitions for the capital. Washington wrote of a city that would serve as "the channel of commerce" for "the trade of a rising empire." Savage's backdrop is the Potomac, which Washington dreamed of linking commercially to the Ohio River by means of a series of canals. The first president's left hand rests on a map of the city, his right hand on the shoulder of his step-grandson, representing future generations.

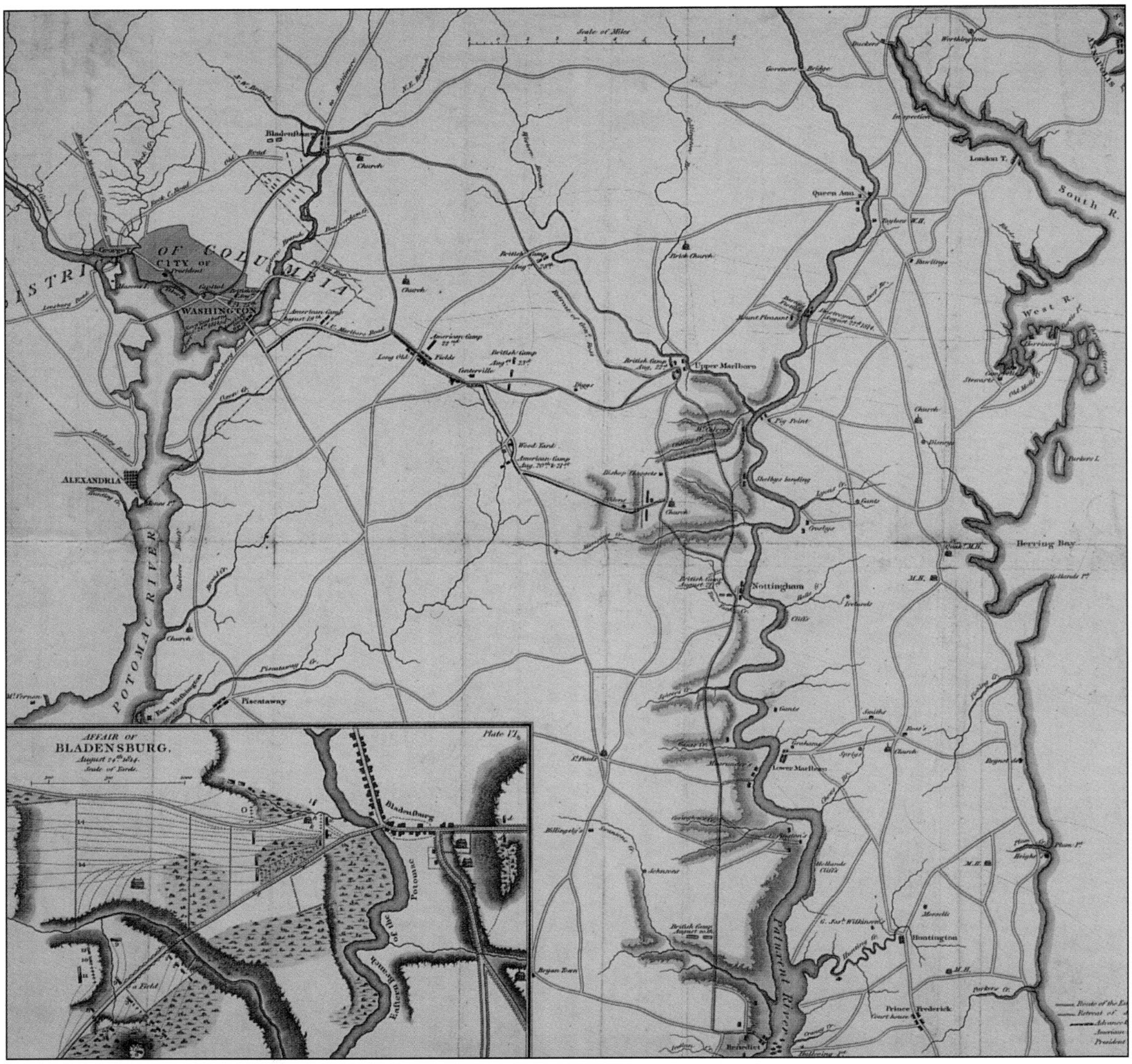

During the War of 1812, the British nearly destroyed the fledgling capital. In August 1814, British troops landed on the Patuxent River at Benedict, Md., and advanced via the shortest overland route through Bladensburg (left). The government fled, leaving public buildings practically empty. British soldiers burned the arsenal, State, War and Treasury buildings (lower left), the White House (below) and the Capitol (bottom). The Navy Yard's commandant torched the yard to prevent it from falling into enemy hands. Even before the British were defeated in 1815, Congress considered relocating the government, but a loan from local bankers helped persuade it to stay and rebuild.

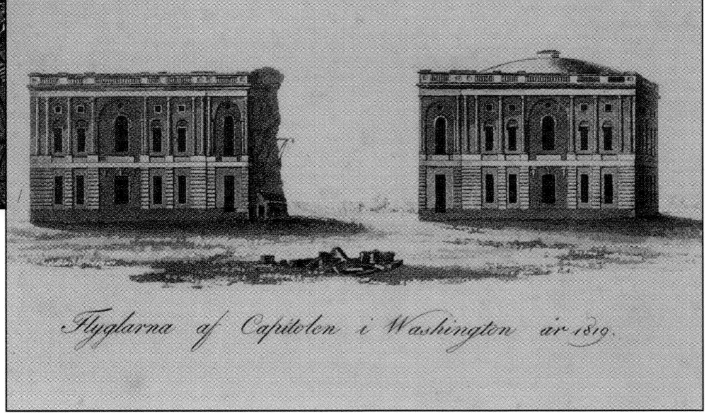
Flyglarna af Capitolen i Washington år 1819.

President John Quincy Adams officiated at the groundbreaking (above) for the Chesapeake and Ohio Canal on July 4, 1828. The success of the Erie Canal, completed in 1825 and linking New York to the Great Lakes, had triggered a wave of canal building. The C&O was intended to connect the Atlantic seaboard to the Ohio River. On the same day, however, ground was broken for the Baltimore & Ohio Railroad. By 1839, when the drawing at left was made by August Kollner of a train passing near the capital, the B&O had beaten the canal to the Ohio Valley and, in 1835, had opened a spur to Washington's depot at Pennsylvania Avenue and Second Street, N.W.

Fortunately for the new capital, it included the ports of Georgetown and Alexandria. Georgetown served as the main supply depot and shelter for those who built the city. The title of this aquatint by George Isham Parkyns, "View of the Suburbs of the City of Washington," is a bit of hyperbole, since Washington was hardly populated enough then to be urban, let alone to have a suburb. Georgetown, on the other hand, was an important port, with the Potomac there deep enough for ocean-going vessels.

A secretary of the British Legation created a sensation by riding his "velocipede" on Pennsylvania Avenue in 1827. By 1830, Washington City was finally starting to fill in. The population totaled 18,826, six times the number when Congress first arrived. Street life had begun to resemble that of other small cities, and odd attractions easily drew crowds. However, the city was still small enough for President Adams to bathe undisturbed and in privacy in the Potomac on summer mornings.

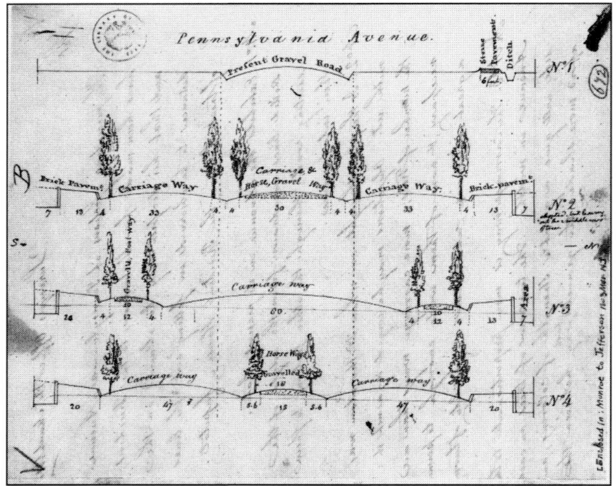

Thomas Jefferson influenced the city's plan and, in 1803, struck by the enormity of L'Enfant's 160-foot-wide avenues, suggested designs (left) to make the streets more pleasant and more to human scale. L'Enfant also had suggested dividing the avenues with trees to create a central carriageway bordered by gravel walks. By 1824, fast-growing poplars had created a grand approach to the Capitol's West Front, as seen in this oil painting (above) by Charles Burton. The original Capitol dome by Bulfinch, seen here, was actually under construction at the time.

Baroness Hyde de Neuville, wife of the French minister, painted this watercolor of F Street, possibly the 1400 block, in 1821. Historian Bernard Herman identified the brick house on the right as typical of the "urban plantations" that developed in Washington and other Southern cities. It includes a number of household workspaces, screened from the street by fences, that theoretically also contained domestic slaves.

"The City of Washington From Beyond the Navy Yard," 1834, by William James Bennett, shows the growing capital from across the Anacostia River. On the opposite shore, to the right, is the Navy Yard's shipbuilding facility. Above it is the rebuilt Capitol, with the Bulfinch dome. The regularity and size of the buildings stretching between the Capitol and the White House probably are exaggerated, but the gently rolling landscape that attracted Washington and L'Enfant is still visible despite nearly 50 years of development.

As the city developed, social life changed from male-dominated gatherings in inns and taverns to mixed-company events at private homes. In 1827, journalist John Agg and his wife, Elizabeth Blackford, received a standing invitation (below left) to the bimonthly Wednesday evening receptions at Kentucky statesmen Henry Clay's Decatur House on Lafayette Square. In 1840, the Peter family, descendants of Martha Washington, held regular soirees such as the one (below right) at their Georgetown home, Tudor Place.

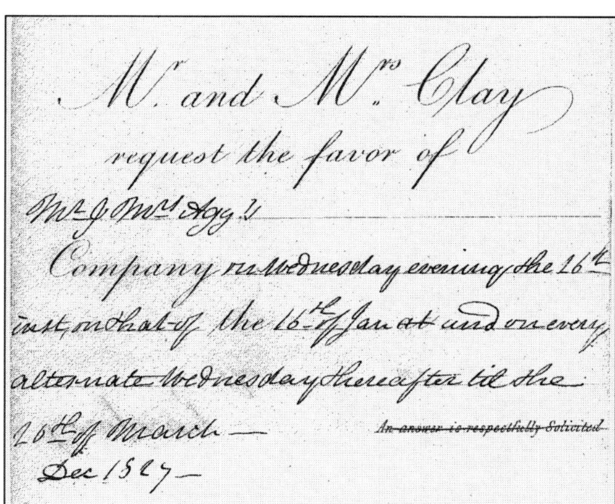

Mr. and Mrs. Clay
request the favor of
Mr & Mrs Agg's
Company on Wednesday evening the 26th
inst, on that of the 16th of Jan ~~at~~ and on every
alternate Wednesday thereafter til the
26th of March —
~~An answer is respectfully Solicited~~
Dec 1827 —

In addition to housing the Navy Yard, the city's waterfront areas were used for manufacturing. This 1839 wash drawing by August Kollner shows Washington's steamboat wharf and its glass factory, which produced windowpanes for local and distant clients, along with the bluffs that once lined the Potomac's edge.

Washington's legislators, lobbyists and journalists put aside their antagonisms during long evenings at such gambling houses as Pendleton's "Palace of Fortune" on Pennsylvania Avenue. The Palace's inner room, seen above, was for serious gamblers, who won and lost fortunes at the faro table. The outer parlors were devoted to drinking, smoking and dissecting the day's political events.

Until the 1930s, citizens and visitors alike had virtually unlimited access to the president. In 1837, the aging Andrew Jackson received a 1,400-pound cheese from admirers in upstate New York. The cheese, put on display in the White House vestibule, finally was tasted at an afternoon reception. For hours citizens hacked away at it, leaving a carpet slippery with shavings and only a small piece for the president.

William McLeod painted this view of the Capitol in 1844 from near the site of today's Union Station. L'Enfant expected the city to develop commercial and residential areas east of the Capitol, but the city first grew west of the Capitol toward the White House. The small buildings in the foreground may have been farmer's outbuildings or frame dwellings of the city's poor, whose ranks grew when the erratic progress of city construction led to long spells of unemployment for laborers and craftsmen.

This plan by architect Robert Mills won the 1836 competition for a monument to George Washington. It included a colonnaded pantheon as well as a 500-foot obelisk. While L'Enfant's 1791 plan called for a monument to the first president, Congress failed to act, so in 1833 private citizens raised the funds. Ground was broken in 1848, by which time so many had objected to Mills' fussy design that the monument was limited to a grand obelisk.

The farms of nearby Maryland and Virginia changed from labor-intensive tobacco cultivation to other crops as the 18th century ended, so the region's need for slaves diminished. At the same time, however, demand for slaves in the Deep South had grown, so Washington City became a center of slave trading. An American Anti-Slavery Society poster from 1836 shows the "Slave House of J.W. Neal & Co." of 7th Street south of Center Market, which offered "cash for young Negroes."

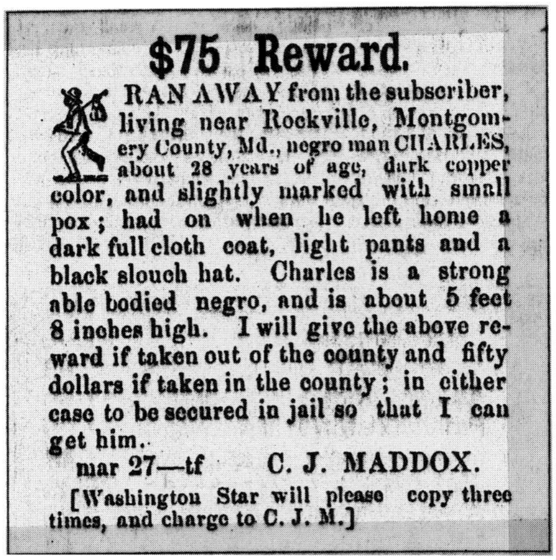

$75 Reward.

RANAWAY from the subscriber, living near Rockville, Montgomery County, Md., negro man CHARLES, about 28 years of age, dark copper color, and slightly marked with small pox; had on when he left home a dark full cloth coat, light pants and a black slouch hat. Charles is a strong able bodied negro, and is about 5 feet 8 inches high. I will give the above reward if taken out of the county and fifty dollars if taken in the county; in either case to be secured in jail so that I can get him.

mar 27—tf C. J. MADDOX.

[Washington Star will please copy three times, and charge to C. J. M.]

This ad appeared in the *Montgomery Sentinel* in 1857. Local slaves who escaped frequently fled to Washington, blending in with the large free black population. By 1830, free blacks already outnumbered slaves. Most had gained their freedom by hiring out their labor and paying off their masters.

©Collection of the New-York Historical Society, accession number s-225

GOOD WORKS

In 1791 David Burnes agreed to deed to the federal government more than 450 acres near the site of the White House. Overnight (especially on paper), he went from being a comfortable farmer to a relatively wealthy man.

Marcia Burnes, his daughter and heiress (left), grew into an accomplished young woman, a major catch for one of the eligible young men drawn to government service. When Marcia married Rep. John Peter Van Ness of New York in 1802, the union bridged the two elements of Washington society: landed gentry and national leaders.

Combining their wealth, the Van Nesses became Washington's earliest philanthropists. Their contributions during the capital's first 30 years included its first theater, the Washington Dancing Assembly, the Columbian Institute (designed to attract scientists, intellectuals and artists to Washington), St. John's Episcopal Church, the Freeman's Vigilant Total Abstinence Society and the Washington Female Orphan Asylum, the city's first children's welfare organization.

Facing page: Eastman Johnson's famous 1859 painting, "Negro Life at the South," is often given an alternate title: "Old Kentucky Home." But, according to art historian John Davis, the painting captures the particulars of urban slavery in the interior of a city block on F Street. L'Enfant's oversized blocks created long, narrow lots that backed onto alleys. Over time the rear of the lots housed slaves and poorer Washingtonians. The painting's dilapidated frame structure, according to Davis, was the back of a sometime tavern. The painting's figures are linked by a network of glances; the white woman at right is presented as an intruder on a rare moment of rest and repose.

©Collection of the New-York Historical Society, negative number 1574

In the 1850s, animosities between North and South were mirrored in Washington City, where most white residents sympathized with the South. The entire city was shaken in 1856, when South Carolina rep. Preston Brooks found abolitionist Charles Sumner's rhetoric so offensive that he blindsided the Massachusetts senator at his desk. Sumner was so severely caned that he did not return to the Senate for two years.

CHAPTER 2

EXPLOSIONS OF WAR

Overwhelmed Union soldiers and panicked picnickers flee Confederate forces at the First Battle of Bull Run in Manassas, Va., on July 21, 1861. Many Washingtonians had tagged along to see the battle, but the entertaining spectacle turned terrifying as the ill-prepared Union troops fled the 25 miles back to Washington City.

Washingtonians did not believe at first that either they or their city were in much danger from the ragtag Confederate Army. So in 1861, when word spread that a big battle was brewing in nearby Manassas, Va., several wagonloads of Washingtonians treated it as a chance for an entertaining day trip. According to historian Margaret Leech, an "army of sightseers" with picnic lunches rode to the battlefield, expecting to see the rebels "run for Richmond."

But in that First Battle of Bull Run and throughout the Civil War's early stages, it was Union forces that shed most of the blood. And when Confederate troops under General Jubal Early invaded the District of Columbia from the north in 1864, the capital was shaken by how close the fighting had come.

The war not only exploded Washington's comfortable assumptions. The capital itself exploded with people as a result of the con-

On July 12, 1864, the war crossed into Washington City. General Jubal Early's Confederate troops marched down Seventh Street Road (Georgia Avenue) from Silver Spring and attempted to take Fort Stevens before being repulsed. In this artist's rendering, President Lincoln is at left observing the action. Newspapers reported that after a sharpshooter killed the medical officer standing with the president, Lincoln was taken to a safer spot.

flict. More than 200,000 soldiers would move through the city between 1861 and 1865, far more than Washington was prepared to handle. With the troops came supplies of food, weapons and horses, prostitutes, pickpockets and undertakers, prizefighters, actors and other goods and services. At the same time, about 40,000 freed and escaped slaves flooded into the city, taxing scarce resources in the free black community.

The overwhelmed capital had to deal with much else as well. What should it do, for example, about its own slaves and slave owners? Even though he knew freeing the slaves would cripple the Southern economy and the South's ability to wage war, President Lincoln had avoided taking that step early in the war, because some slave-holding border states were loyal to the Union. Had these states seceded—Maryland, Delaware, Kentucky and Missouri, plus the western counties of Virginia that would soon become West Virginia—the capital would have been surrounded by hostile forces. As an experiment in freeing slaves while keeping their owners loyal, Lincoln did free the slaves of the District of Columbia in April 1862—and Congress provided up to $1 million to compensate their owners. Washington was, in fact, the only place with stop-slavery bounties. More than 900 slave owners received payments for nearly 3,000 slaves before the program ended in

The City Canal, photographed circa 1861, was a persistent symbol of the capital's failure to thrive. The artery carried construction materials to various buildings, but it was never wide enough to permit much traffic. Because the city lacked sewers, the canal became a repository of waste and garbage. The rest of the city was equally unattractive. The great influx of people forced Washington to modernize some city services, but without much of a commercial base, no booster constituency was promoting more improvements.

Members of the 12th New York Regiment stand in formation beside their flimsy accommodations on Franklin Square, at 14th and K streets, N.W., in June 1861. The troops that poured into the city commandeered almost every open space and large public building. Quiet residential neighborhoods like Franklin Square became boisterous scenes of drilling soldiers, complete with buglers and drummers.

January 1863, when the Emancipation Proclamation was issued, freeing slaves in "rebellious" states. Loyal slave-holding states were permitted to keep their property for the duration of the war.

Washington also worried about spies and saboteurs. Many in the capital with deep Southern roots, including hundreds of military officers, congressmen and other officials, had followed the example of Robert E. Lee and joined the Confederate cause, while others had left for Canada or elsewhere. In 1862, for example, banker William Corcoran left for Paris, where his son-in-law was the secretary of the Confederate legation, and remained there until the war ended (his art gallery became a military clothing depot). But the government feared sabotage by many Southerners who remained or had since slipped in, and it jailed hundreds of real or suspected traitors. Some journalists and officials even doubted the loyalty of First Lady Mary Todd Lincoln, who had two brothers in the rebel army. Rumors raged that even she was passing presidential secrets to Confederate leaders.

But the city's basic problem was coping with its population explosion. With sewers nonexistent, the foul-smelling City Canal—barely used by watercraft—nearly filled up with garbage. Troops commandeered all kinds of public spaces, from the Capitol Rotunda to the Mall to neighborhood squares. Churches, dance halls, schools and other buildings, including Corcoran's country estate, served as hospitals for the wounded and dying. Boarding houses regularly packed four or six to a bed. The constant battering of unpaved streets by heavy wagons, troops and horses left deep ruts and puddles everywhere, creating a "metropolis of mud and dust," as one observer wrote.

While freed or "contraband" slaves who had escaped from the Confederacy had expected Washington to be a haven, social supports other than the almshouse were scarce. Churches and clubs of the city's free black community rushed to assist them, initiating fund-raising efforts in Washington and in Northern cities. The Contraband Relief Association was founded in 1862 by more than 40 blacks, including Elizabeth Keckley, an educated woman who had purchased her own freedom in the 1850s and had become a seamstress and companion to Mary Todd Lincoln. The National Freedmen's Relief Association of the District of Columbia, one of a series of such regional groups, was organized by sympathetic white Washingtonians in 1862. In addition, Northern abolitionists arrived to provide humanitarian, educational and vocational aid.

Because Union soldiers would hire and protect them, many former slaves clustered around the military encampments that dotted the city, or in nearby Arlington, Va., on the grounds of Robert E. Lee's

Because Washington was near so many campsites and battlegrounds, it quickly became a center for military hospitals. The government built Lincoln Hospital at East Capitol Street and Massachusetts Avenue, seen above, as a model facility. Others were rigged up in existing buildings. According to historian Martin Murray, the sick and wounded were housed in 56 facilities, including churches, hotels, schools and dance halls. Among the hundreds of volunteer aides were (briefly) children's author Louisa May Alcott and (for much longer) poet Walt Whitman.

Troops of the Sixth Massachusetts Regiment, en route to Washington, battle hostile Sout sympathizers in Baltimore in April 1861. Maryland was divided over whether the slave-ho state should stay in the Union. After Baltimore secessionists bloodied the Massachus forces and broke the vital rail link to the North, Lincoln sent troops to occupy Baltimore arrest secessionist state lawmakers. With those legislators behind bars, Maryland's gove kept the state in the Union.

former estate (today's Arlington National Cemetery). Freedmen's shanties also littered the alleys of the notorious Murder Bay (now the western half of the Federal Triangle) and elsewhere. The Freedmen's Bureau, a federal agency created in 1865, made only a small dent in the former slaves' problems when it offered lots in Barry's Farm in rural Anacostia. Most freedmen preferred the crowded city to the Bureau's unimproved and inaccessible plots.

The Civil War disruptions left indelible marks on the capital. By 1870, long after most troops had left, Washington's permanent population had nearly doubled, from 60,000 in 1859 to almost 110,000. Civilian federal employment had nearly quintupled, from 1,268 to 6,000. The city itself was scarred by partially felled trees, which troops had used for firewood, piled-up mule carcasses, deeply rutted streets and makeshift housing.

Moralists and promoters, meantime, grew concerned about crime and prostitution. In an 1869 history of the city, Dr. John B. Ellis wrote that the chief clientele of the numerous bordellos that remained was "the floating population" that appeared when Congress was in session. He quoted one madam as saying that "it would be impossible to carry on the Government" without her aid.

The more sensitive post-war issue, however, was the question of voting rights for the burgeoning black population. After President Lincoln's 1865 assassination, the Radical Republican leaders who briefly gained control of Capitol Hill were frustrated by President Andrew Johnson's unwillingness to punish the South or to assist the freedmen. To prevent the return to power of former Confederate leaders and to secure civil rights for freedmen, the radicals pushed for black voting rights. But first they wanted to test black suffrage in the District.

Hoping to defeat the Radicals' plan, the city council in December 1865 asked white male voters if black men should be permitted to vote. The tally: 35 for, 7,056 against. But the Radicals were undaunted. A year later Congress passed a bill allowing all men in the District to vote, and black men cast ballots for the first time anywhere in the South in March 1867, helping to elect a Republican mayor of Georgetown.

Ratification of the 14th Amendment in 1868 gave all freedmen the right to vote. That year, black Republicans helped sweep white Republican Sayles Bowen into office as Washington City's mayor and elected two African American council members, John F. Cook and Stewart Carter.

But political support was one thing, economic support another. Whenever local politicians tried to boost the city's image and revenue, Congress shot down their proposals. In 1869, for example, local business leaders proposed holding a world's fair in Washington. They raised $2 million. But

Office seekers and contractors throng the White House corridors in 1861 shortly after Lincoln's inaugural. A new administration always attracted those seeking postmaster, consular and other posts. When the Civil War erupted, lucrative war contracts made Washington opportunities even more tantalizing.

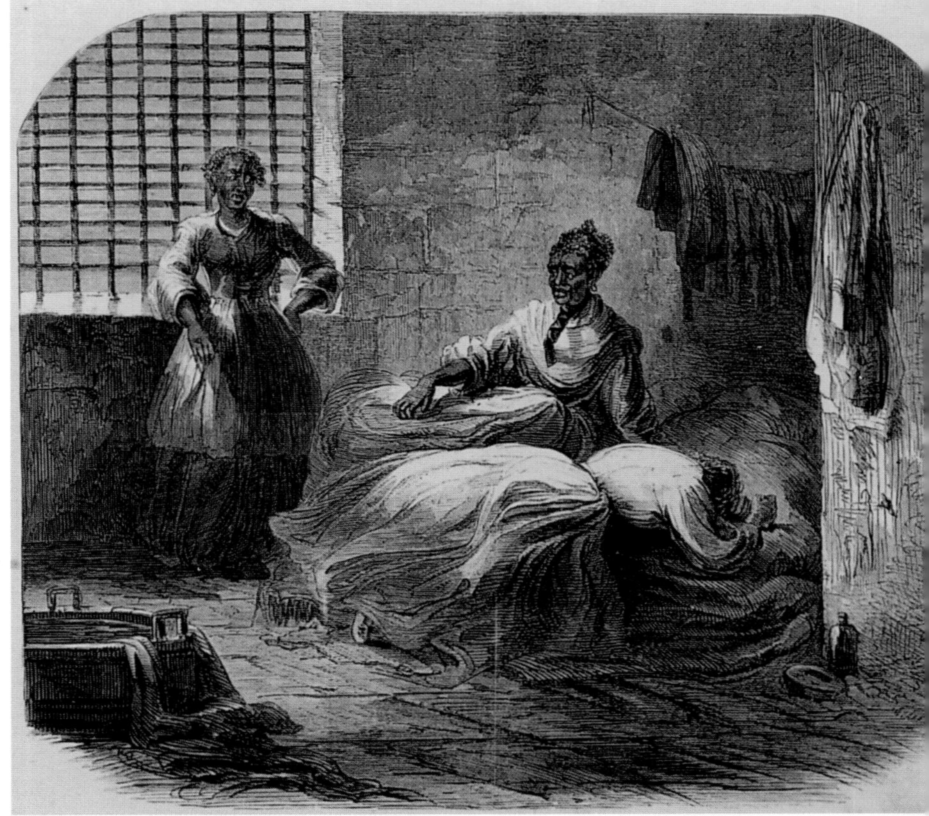

After slave trading was outlawed in the District, it flourished in Alexandria. The Price, Birch Company operated out of this building until 1861, when it was commandeered by Union forces for use as a military prison and later as a barracks for slaves who had escaped from the Confederacy and were thus deemed "contraband of war."

Facing page: Fugitive slave women held in a Washington jail in 1861 await return to their owners. While contraband slaves were not returned, many escaped slaves had fled from District or Maryland owners who were loyal to the Union. Technically, they remained property that the city had to return. The District marshal, believing most runaways did not have rebel owners, ordered mass arrests, and jails were swiftly overcrowded. Lincoln finally ordered the marshal not to arrest any such slaves unless they had committed crimes.

Congress refused to appropriate the required matching sum. The idea of inviting the world to see a ramshackle, ill-lit, polluted backwater "seems to me altogether out of the question," said Nevada Senator William Stewart. He declared Washington "the ugliest city in the whole country" and a terrible advertisement for a United States that hoped to impress the world as a nation on the rise.

Some politicians urged again that the capital be moved elsewhere, to a city closer to the geographic center of a nation that now stretched farther from east to west than it did from north to south. In part to prevent the loss of the capital, and in part to prevent the black population from taking over the political life of the city, local leaders hammered out a compromise with Congress in 1871. Banker W.W. Corcoran and Alexander H. "Boss" Shepherd, an ambitious plumbing contractor and real estate salesman who was a crony of President Ulysses Grant's, were the chief advocates.

The compromise ended 51 years of locally elected city leadership. It combined the separate governments of Washington City, Georgetown and Washington County into a single territorial government, which consisted of an appointed governor and upper legislature, plus an elected lower legislature and a non-voting delegate to Congress.

To no one's surprise, Shepherd was asked by

President Grant to head the Board of Public Works under the new government, and he leapt at the chance. Under his leadership, hills were leveled and streets were graded, paved and lit. Thousands of trees were planted, and much of the city received its first sewer and gas lines. In 1871 the squalid cluster of market stalls along the canal was leveled, and construction began on a grand new Center Market building on what is now the site of the National Archives. It was described at the time as the largest building of its kind in the United States, a point of civic pride for a city then known more for what it lacked. Shepherd's crews also filled in the City Canal to create B Street (now Constitution Avenue).

However, Shepherd, named governor in 1873, greatly exceeded his budget, which infuriated Capitol Hill. He also indulged in the questionable habit of making the earliest improvements to property that he and his friends owned. Congress pulled the plug on local self-government in 1874 and re-established itself as the sole authority over the city (via three presidentially appointed commissioners), an arrangement that would last for 94 years.

Conservative white Washingtonians were willing to give up their voting rights so long as those of the black population were also canceled. To sweeten the deal, Congress guaranteed an annual federal payment of 50 percent of the

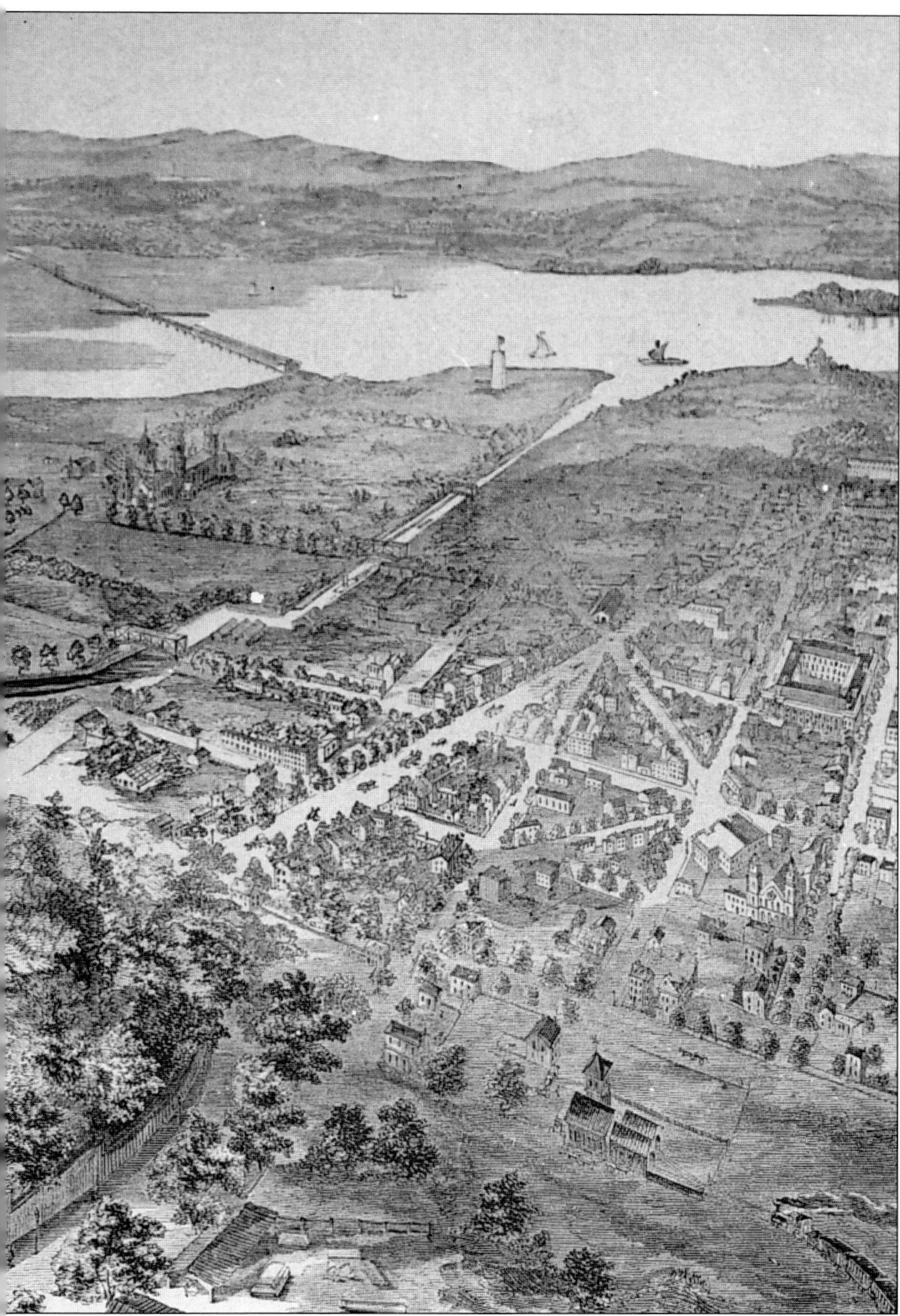

This 1861 engraving of Washington was based on a *Harper's Weekly* sketch made from one of a small fleet of gas-filled reconnaissance balloons developed by Smithsonian scientists. The balloons rose beyond the reach of Confederate fire, letting officers observe enemy positions with impunity. In the lower left is the Capitol, still being enlarged according to Thomas U. Walter's 1851 design. President Lincoln ordered construction to continue despite the war. "If people see the Capitol going on," he reportedly said, "it is a sign we intend the Union shall go on."

Members of the Washington militia are inducted into the federal army in 1861. For weeks such ceremonies took place in front of the War Department next to the White House. As news of the attack on Fort Sumter spread, loyalists rushed to enlist while Southern sympathizers, including most officers commanding the Navy Yard, left for more hospitable locales.

city's budget. (Congress kept its part of the bargain only until after World War I, when it was no longer clear how much money it would provide, creating an unending annual struggle to fund the city.)

Religious congregations of all faiths at this time built churches and synagogues, many of which survive to this day. At the same time, African Americans entered schools in record numbers and showed "dramatic gains in levels of literacy," according to historian Howard Gillette. Of course, the schools they attended were segregated and would remain so for 80 years. With the schools and the city's Southern style as examples, segregation spread to other institutions, even though Congress never succeeded in passing "Jim Crow" legislation to cover other aspects of city life.

Post-war Washington, capital of the Union victory, drew even more newcomers eager to participate in the remaking of a nation. African Americans of national reputations, such as ex-slave and abolitionist Frederick Douglass, came to lobby for black rights and stayed. Ohio lawyer John Mercer Langston came to head the new Howard University Law School and was appointed legal counsel of the city's Board of Health by President Grant. They were absorbed into the city's old elite black community, whose wealth was built primarily on catering and the operation of restaurants and hotels. By the late 1870s, Washington, with its superior opportunities for education and culture, thanks to the opening of Howard University in 1867 and to occupational opportunities in the Republican-controlled bureaucracy, drew black aristocrats from around the nation. The succeeding generations of local elites occupied key positions in the city government, schools and the professions.

Another class of elites flocked to Washington at this time as well: intellectuals and scientists. The Smithsonian Institution, founded as a national research institution, the Coast Survey, Patent Office, and Naval Observatory had all drawn scientists to the city before the war. In the unsettled post-war era, Americans worried about how to bring order to a chaotic world. Many found comfort in taking the scientific approach. Soon the Smithsonian broadened its activities to include the Bureau of Ethnology (studying Native Americans), and during or after the war the U.S. government created the Geological Survey, the Army Medical Museum, the Fish Commission and the Department of Agriculture.

Intellectuals, activists, an expanded labor force—and the arrival of a new class of millionaires—all helped the newly spiffed up city settle in for its next phase: a golden era for Washington.

Washington became a research and manufacturing center for war materials. The arsenal on Greenleaf's Point produced weapons and ammunition and served as a military prison. The Navy Yard led the transition from sailing ships to steamships and produced improved cannons.

RD, WITH SHAD FISHERS IN THE FOREGROUND.—[See Page 246.]

This 1939 photograph (right) shows a view of the Virginia hills from the ramparts at Fort Washington on the Potomac. Despite the capital's disastrous experience in the War of 1812, when the Civil War began Fort Washington was the only installation that existed to defend the city. In August 1861, troops began building 48 more forts, batteries and other defense works, as seen in red in the War Department map on the facing page. Battery Rodgers (above) was created at Jones Point in Alexandria.

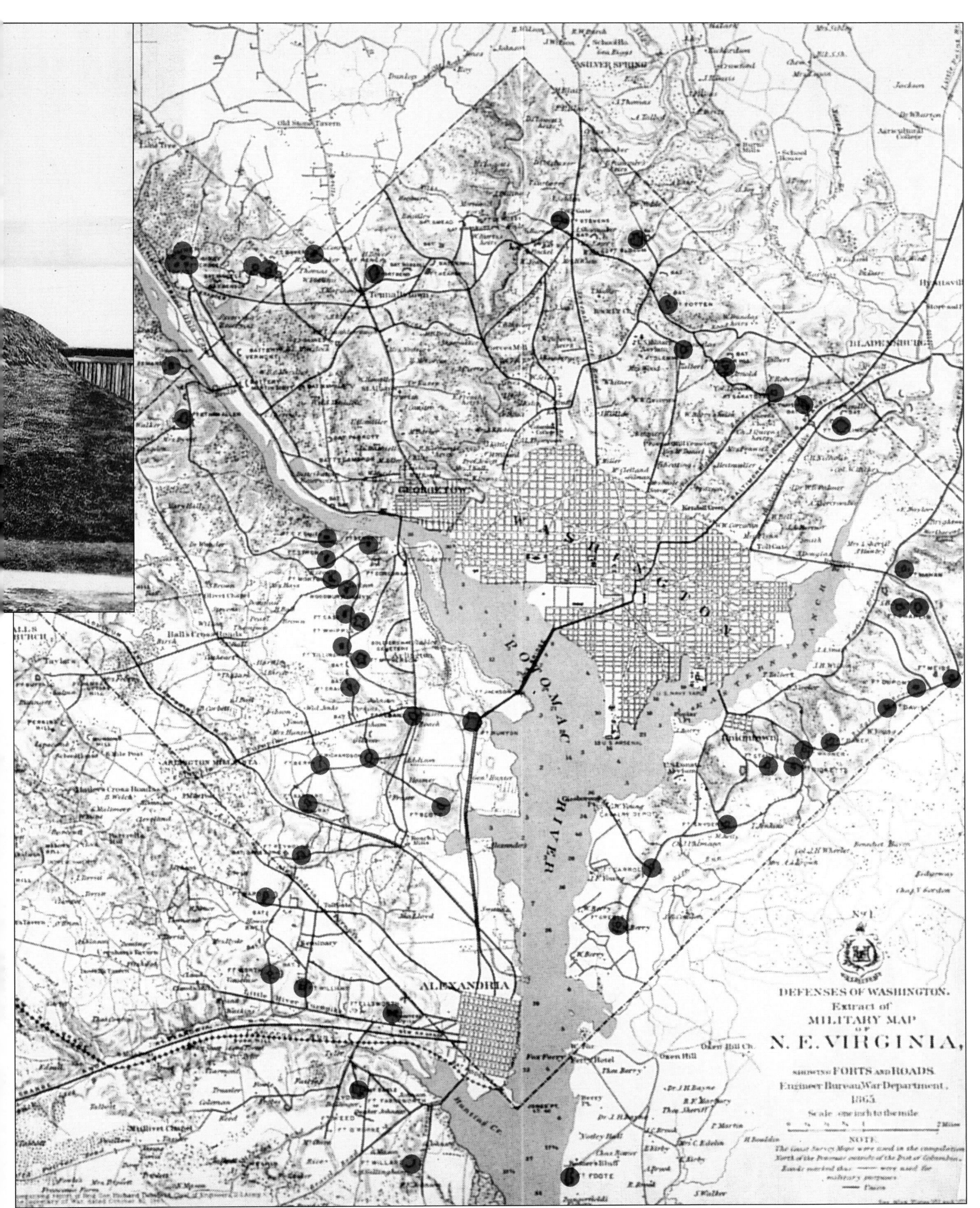
No. 1
DEFENSES OF WASHINGTON.
Extract of
MILITARY MAP
OF
N. E. VIRGINIA,
SHOWING FORTS AND ROADS
Engineer Bureau War Department,
1865
Scale one inch to the mile
NOTE
GEORGETOWN
WASHINGTON
POTOMAC RIVER
ALEXANDRIA
SILVER SPRING
BLADENSBURG
Old Stone Tavern
Tennallytown
Uniontown
Hunting Cr.

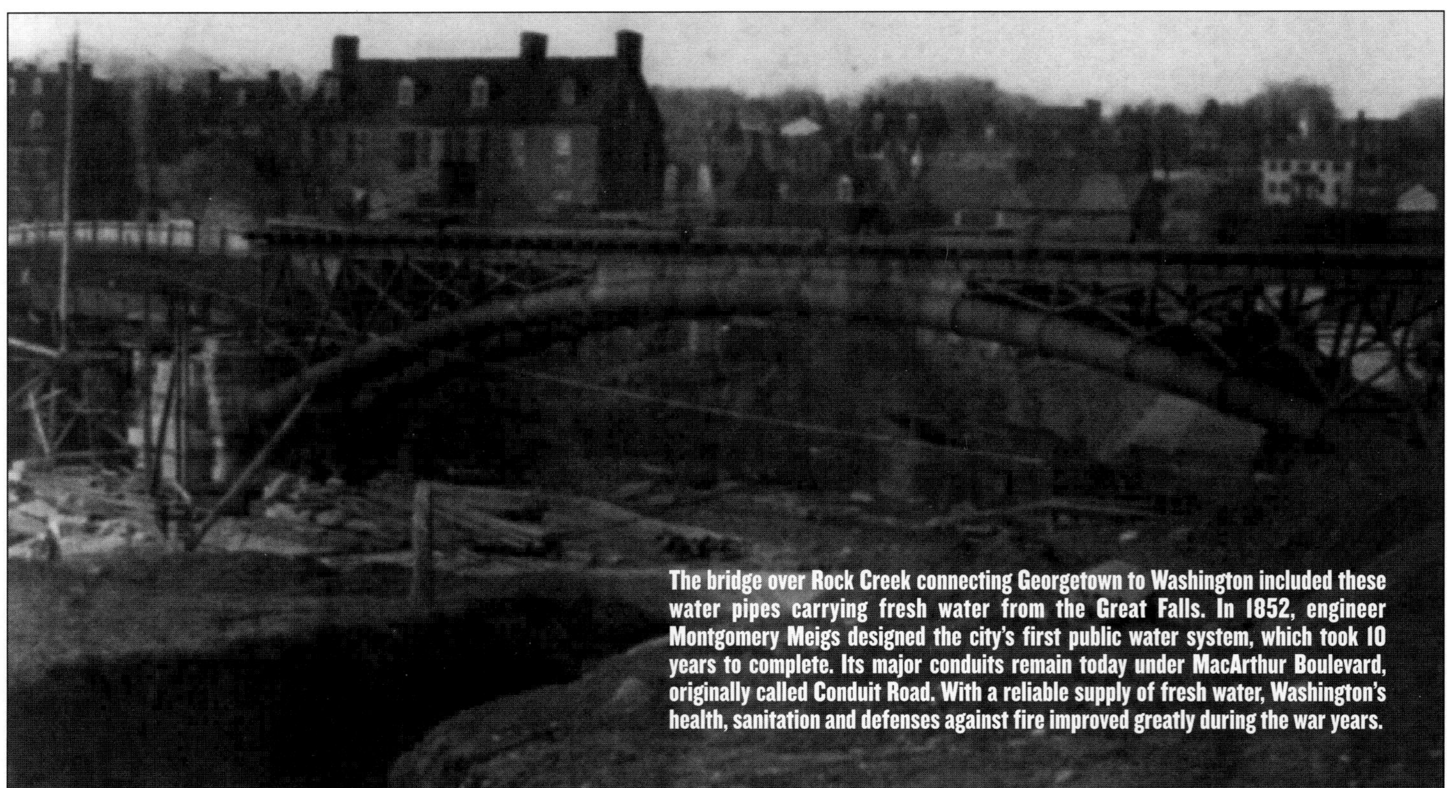

The bridge over Rock Creek connecting Georgetown to Washington included these water pipes carrying fresh water from the Great Falls. In 1852, engineer Montgomery Meigs designed the city's first public water system, which took 10 years to complete. Its major conduits remain today under MacArthur Boulevard, originally called Conduit Road. With a reliable supply of fresh water, Washington's health, sanitation and defenses against fire improved greatly during the war years.

On August 6, 1862, businesses closed early so Washingtonians could gather at the Capitol to hear Lincoln and national and local leaders speak at the "Great War Meeting."

Three former slaves pose with officers of the Second Rhode Island Volunteer Infantry regiment in their camp in the Brightwood section of Washington, circa 1862. At first the thousands of escaped slaves were restricted to labor, support and guard duties, but by the middle of 1863 they were serving in combat as well.

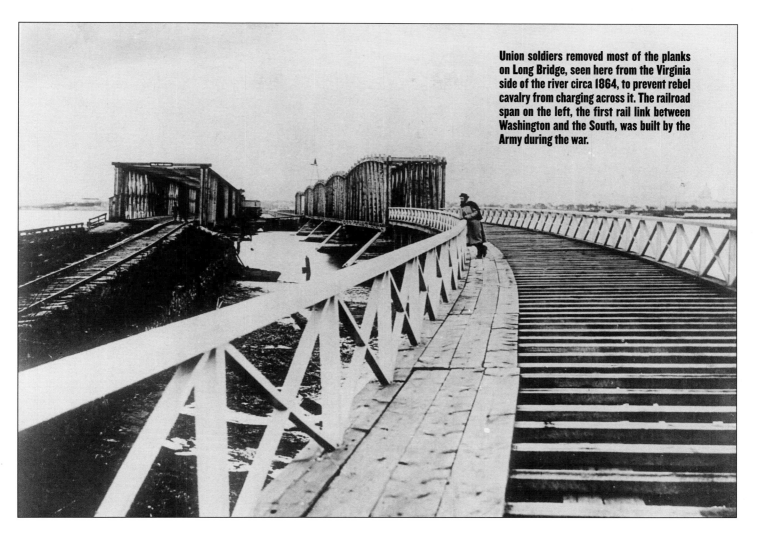

Union soldiers removed most of the planks on Long Bridge, seen here from the Virginia side of the river circa 1864, to prevent rebel cavalry from charging across it. The railroad span on the left, the first rail link between Washington and the South, was built by the Army during the war.

This engraving from the *New-York Illustrated News,* "A Stormy Day at the Aqueduct Bridge, Georgetown, D.C.," shows military supplies and troops moving across the Potomac to Union-held Alexandria County in 1861 or 1862. The bridge's trough, originally built to carry the water of the Alexandria Canal across the river to link to the C&O Canal, was drained and converted to wagon use in August 1861.

Workers pose in front of the Government Horse Shoeing Shop. Washingtonians easily found war-related work.

Washington schoolchildren gather on the Capitol steps on May 23, 1865, to serenade Union troops lining up for the grand review of the victorious Army of the Republic. A little more than six weeks earlier, Lee had surrendered at Appomattox Courthouse, Va. The parade was the city's first joyous occasion since the shock of President Lincoln's death at the hand of rebel actor John Wilkes Booth on April 15. The Capitol's columns are still draped in black crepe.

Female clerks leave the Treasury Department in February 1865. In the early 1850s, the Patent Office "outsourced" copying work to women at home, but the work was sent in male relatives' names to prevent females from appearing on official rosters. In 1853 a few women clerks, including Clara Barton, were allowed to work at the Treasury. Some 10 years later, the U.S. Treasurer began openly hiring about 600 "Treasury girls," mostly to cut up sheets of currency. As more departments began hiring females, men tried to discredit the women, whispering about the morals of those who lived unchaperoned, accusing them of seducing members of Congress for jobs and attacking them as too frivolous for office work.

This 1866 engraving shows more than 15,000 African Amercians celebrating the fourth anniversary of emancipation in the District. Congress had abolished slavery in Washington on April 16, 1862, nine months before the Emancipation Proclamation. Washington's African American community celebrated its freedom each April until 1901, when dissension in the community about the events' style led to their demise. The celebration was revived by Loretta Carter Haynes in 1991 and continues today.

DOUGLASS' DISDAIN

Frederick Douglass, seen here with his grandson Joseph, came to Washington in 1872 to promote civil rights for African Americans. During his stay, the former slave, memoirist, abolitionist, pro-feminist and journalist embraced the light-skinned, educated elites of Washington and disdained the less-educated classes. His pronouncements were typical of leaders who did not want powerful whites to associate them with their less fortunate brethren.

In 1886, he said that the rowdy annual Emancipation Day parade consisted of "gaudy display and straggling processions, which empty the alleys and dark places of our city into the broad daylight of our thronged streets and avenues, thus thrusting upon the public view a vastly undue proportion of the most unfortunate, unimproved, and unprogressive class of the colored people, and thereby inviting public disgust and contempt, and repelling the more thrifty and self-respecting among us. . ."

This ticket admitted its owner to President Andrew Johnson's 1868 impeachment hearings. The charges against Johnson turned on a technicality about his right to fire a government appointee, but the real cause was his constant vetoes of Reconstruction legislation. In addition to the District black suffrage bill, he vetoed (and was overturned on) the 1866 Civil Rights Act, which declared African Americans to be citizens.

In Thomas Nast's "The Georgetown Election," a black Washingtonian votes for the first time in March 1867 as President Andrew Johnson, holding his overridden veto of black voting rights for Washington, scowls. With the overwhelming support of black voters (one third of the total voting population), George Welch, a white equal-rights candidate, won the Georgetown mayor's race.

Members of "The Oldest Inhabitants Association of the District of Columbia" pose on the steps of City Hall in 1879. According to historian Kathryn Allamong Jacob, the association was founded in 1865 by a group of "disgruntled old residents" to distance themselves from the upstart Republicans and the nouveau riche who dominated the capital during and after the Civil War. Membership was confined to white males over age 50 who had been residents for 45 years. The group today is integrated by race and gender and admits individuals aged 40 or older who have lived or worked in Washington for 20 years.

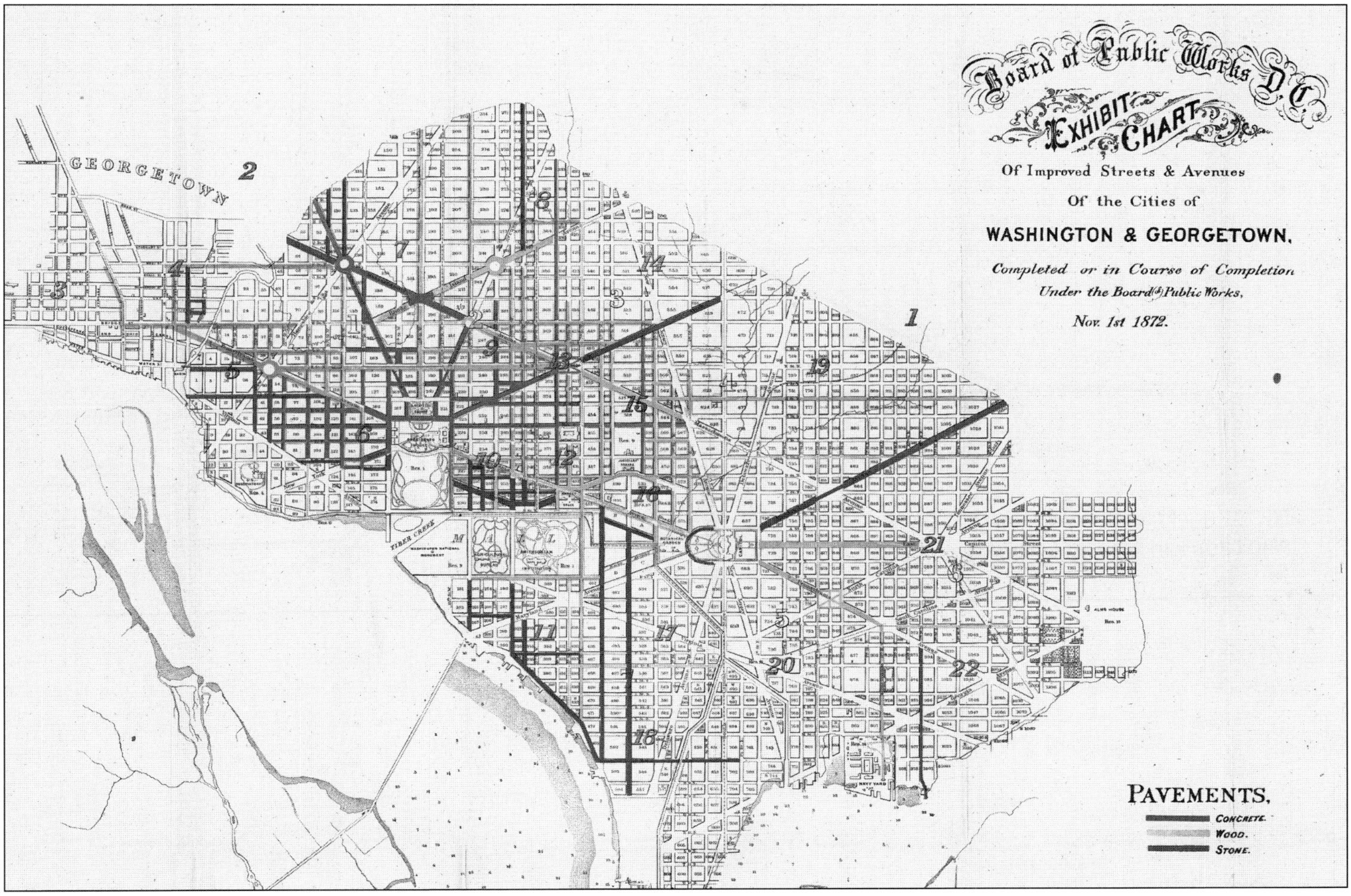

Board of Public Works D.C.
Exhibit Chart
Of Improved Streets & Avenues
Of the Cities of
WASHINGTON & GEORGETOWN.
Completed or in Course of Completion
Under the Board of Public Works,
Nov. 1st 1872.

PAVEMENTS.
Concrete.
Wood.
Stone.

This map shows the streets paved and graded by Boss Shepherd's contractors, who also installed water and sewer pipes, planted 50,000 shade trees and filled in the City Canal to create B Street (now Constitution Avenue). In addition to widespread opposition to black voting, Shepherd's overspending helped bring about the end of the territorial government and the imposition of a presidentially appointed commission form of rule, which lasted from 1878 until 1973.

This statue of Boss Shepherd, the last governor of the District's territorial government, once stood in front of the District Building on Pennsylvania Avenue. While his improvements bankrupted the city, they also put an end to calls for moving the capital elsewhere.

Patent examiners search the files in the U.S. Patent Office in 1869. One of the government's first functions, the right to grant patents turned the capital into a collector of models. Housed in a number of central buildings, including today's National Portrait Gallery, the models were a major 19th century tourist attraction.

The Department of Agriculture, circa 1870. The department was established in 1862, but agricultural research and related functions had been carried on by the Patent Office virtually since the nation's founding. As the war ended, the department was assigned a plot on the Mall that had been used as a Union cattle yard. Its grand building, among the first major post-Civil War projects, symbolized the nation's desire to return to business as usual.

A "veteran caller," or expert party crasher, shares in the generous refreshments at a private gathering following the official White House New Year's reception in January 1873. Washingtonians of means regularly joined diplomats and politicians at grand-scale White House events. Society was still small enough that known crashers were politely tolerated, though the artist couldn't resist a few raised eyebrows.

One of the penalties of the popularity of public officials, as shown above, was the easy accessibility of even the humblest of citizens. Even Cabinet-level officials such as Treasury Secretary Francis E. Spinner (right), who served from 1861 until 1875, kept an open office. According to journalist Ben: Perley Poore, it was unclear whether the visitors thought Spinner could "distribute greenbacks at pleasure to all who came" or whether his "remarkable signature" made him seem a remarkable man.

This composite Currier & Ives portrait of "The First Colored Senator and Representatives" was widely distributed in 1872. These legislators were the most visible members of the educated African American elite who flocked to Washington after the war. The capital's African American community included a small, equally educated group who had lived as free men before the war, native-born free black laborers, former urban slaves (many of whom were skilled artisans) and ill-educated former plantation slaves. The legislators' arrival marked the beginning of a wave of immigration by elite African Americans, attracted by opportunities with the federal government and Howard University, which opened in 1867.

Wormley's Hotel, at 15th and H streets, N.W., opened in 1871. The free-born James Wormley was perhaps the city's most successful African American entrepreneur of his era. He began as a chef and moved into catering, a business in which many local blacks made fortunes before the war when other opportunities were closed to them. By 1863 he was operating lodging houses, a confectionery and a restaurant in addition to cooking for private parties. His hotel and lodging houses had a white clientele, including Radical Republican Charles Sumner. Ironically, the hotel was the site for the "Wormley Agreement," resulting in the Compromise of 1877 that removed Union troops from the South. Wormley's portrait (left) was the work of noted society painter Henry Ulke.

THE TOURISM TRADE

Tourists are the bread and butter of Washington, and meeting their needs is the metropolitan area's largest service industry. The earliest visitors came specifically to attend congressional debates in the days of the great orators. They also came to view the few grand federal buildings and, until the Civil War, wandered freely in the White House and departments. Union victory in the Civil War brought new prestige to the capital, and by the 1870s writers were extolling Washington as a national shrine to which all Americans should make at least one pilgrimage. Increasingly, the tourists who came were people of means like these visitors to the Capitol in 1871 (left). By 1900, an industry had grown up to show off the city, and visitors no longer limited their forays to congressional session. Sightseeing cars with trained guides like the one at right, photographed in 1905, led the way. By the late 1940s, trips to Washington were rites of passage for students like these (below), photographed in 1948.

Americans and visitors from other countries still make their way to the city to find inspiration in the symbols of government, education and delight in its museums, and stimulation in the city's off-the-Mall neighborhoods. They still like to be guided, as did this tired bunch in 1974 (opposite page, bottom), and they may no longer be elegant, as evidenced by this dressed-for-comfort Georgia family in 1991 (below left). But in 1998, 21.2 million of them found their idea of America here.

OBSERVATION AUTOMOBILE
"THE ONLY WAY"
FISCHER SYSTEM.
LEAVES EVERY DAY
10 A.M. 2 & 4 P.M. FARE ROUND TRIP $1.00
1333 PENNA. AVE.

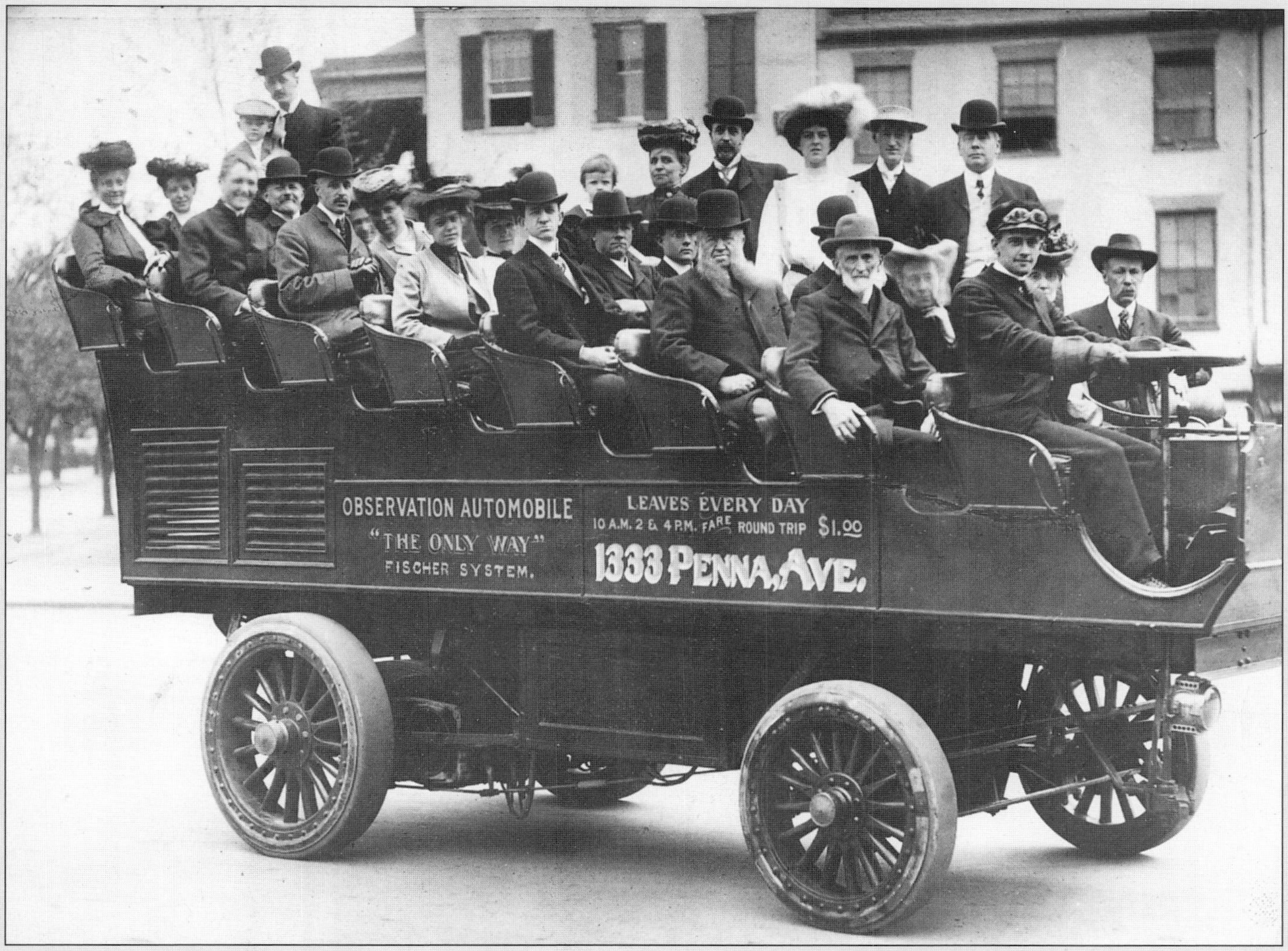

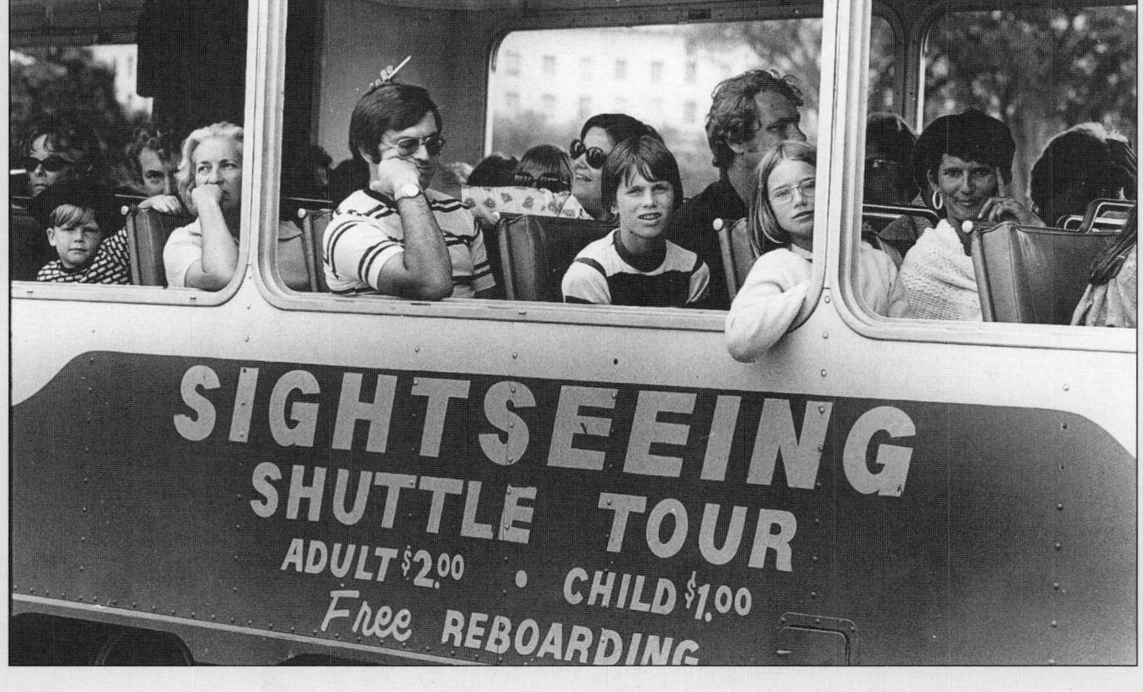

SIGHTSEEING
SHUTTLE TOUR
ADULT $2.00 • CHILD $1.00
Free REBOARDING

CHAPTER 3

A CAPITAL TRANSFORMED

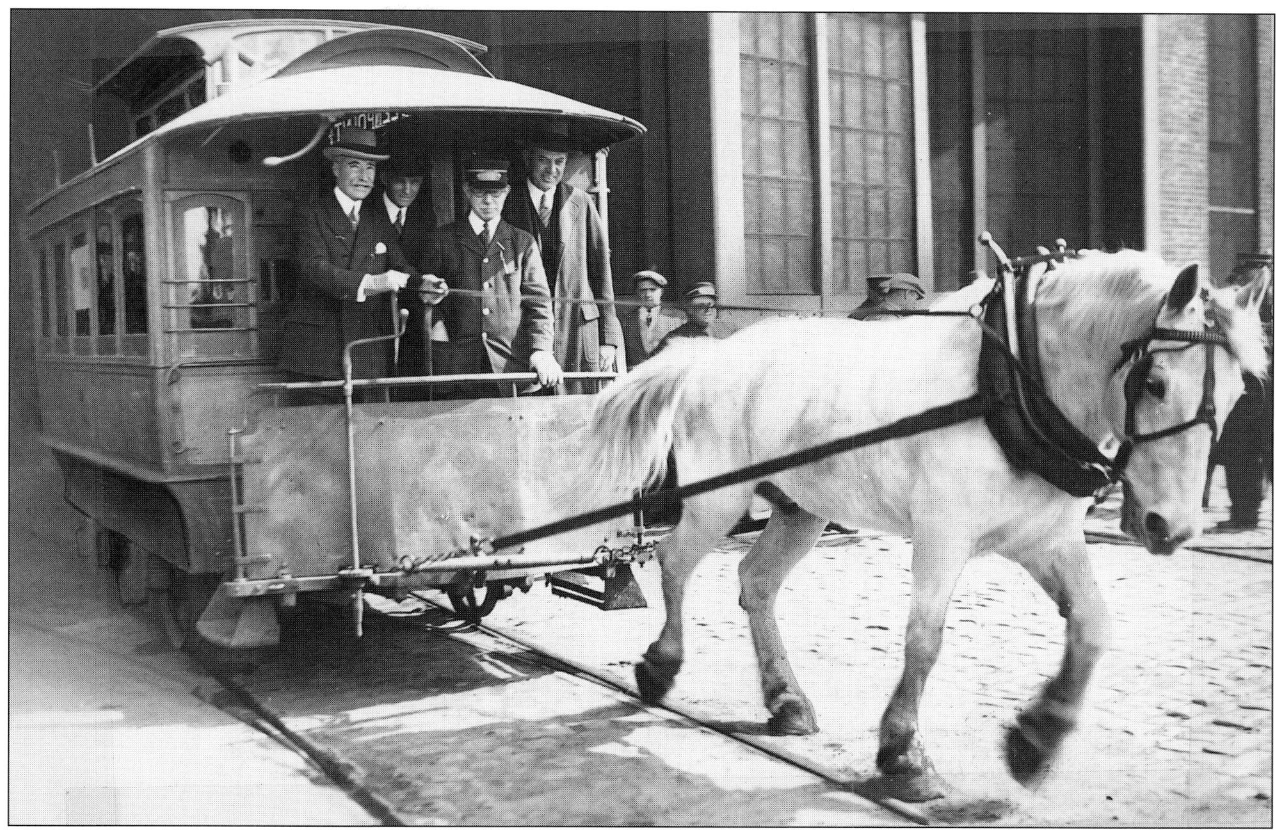

A powerful horse pulls a street railway car in a demonstration of the type introduced in 1862. Horsecars with steel wheels riding on steel rails dominated public transportation until 1888, when electrified streetcars were introduced. Congress had chartered privately run street railways early in the Civil War for both war workers and freight. A network of horsecars soon dominated the relatively level portion of the city south of Florida Avenue.

Washington may have been called "the ugliest city in the whole country" in the late 1860s, but by 1884 the *Century Magazine* reported that it was "the fashion to go to Washington in winter as to Newport in summer." What was happening?

A new Washington was being born, and the transformation would continue through World War I and beyond. The remaking of the capital included many elements—a continued climb in employment, new modes of transportation and communication, construction of imposing mansions, apartment buildings and rowhouses, a redesigned Mall and downtown core graced with grand buildings and new monuments, the rise of Washington tourism and much more.

For transportation, for example, residents until 1860 had taken omnibuses, vehicles with four flimsy wheels, hard seats for about 16 and cramped standing room for four more, pulled by one tired horse. These urban stagecoaches bumped over rut-

One of the last Metropolitan Railroad horsecars prepares to cross Wisconsin Avenue in Georgetown in the 1890s. New electrified streetcars now easily carried passengers up the steep hills of Wisconsin Avenue and 16th Street all the way to the District line. Farms along the way made way for housing developments, and the middle class began commuting longer distances to work.

ted dirt roads when the weather was good and lurched through mud and slush when it wasn't.

In 1860, rails were laid in downtown Washington, and horsecars seating 20, with velvet seats and stained-glass windows, provided some comfort while riding along the tracks. It wasn't until 1888, though, that privately operated electric streetcars revolutionized local life, opening such previously remote parts of town as Cleveland Park and Anacostia to development and creating the new Washington commuter.

The first automobile reportedly arrived in Washington in 1897, but roads were still bumpy (and sometimes nonexistent), and car prices were far beyond the means of most residents. So except for the rich, the car remained essentially a curiosity. It was only in 1908, with the introduction of Ford's Model T, that other Washingtonians could afford the new vehicles, and they began snapping them up. By 1920, about 56,000 private cars were registered in the District—a number that tripled over that decade. According to historian Howard Gillette, by 1929 only a third of Washington commuters still used public transportation.

The telephone was another post-Civil War addition to the capital. In 1878, Alexander Graham Bell hired a local agent to erect the city's first telephone poles and wires, and before long many women were employed in the new job of telephone operator.

Bell himself became a Washington resident in 1882, part of a nouveau riche class that began arriving after the war, men who

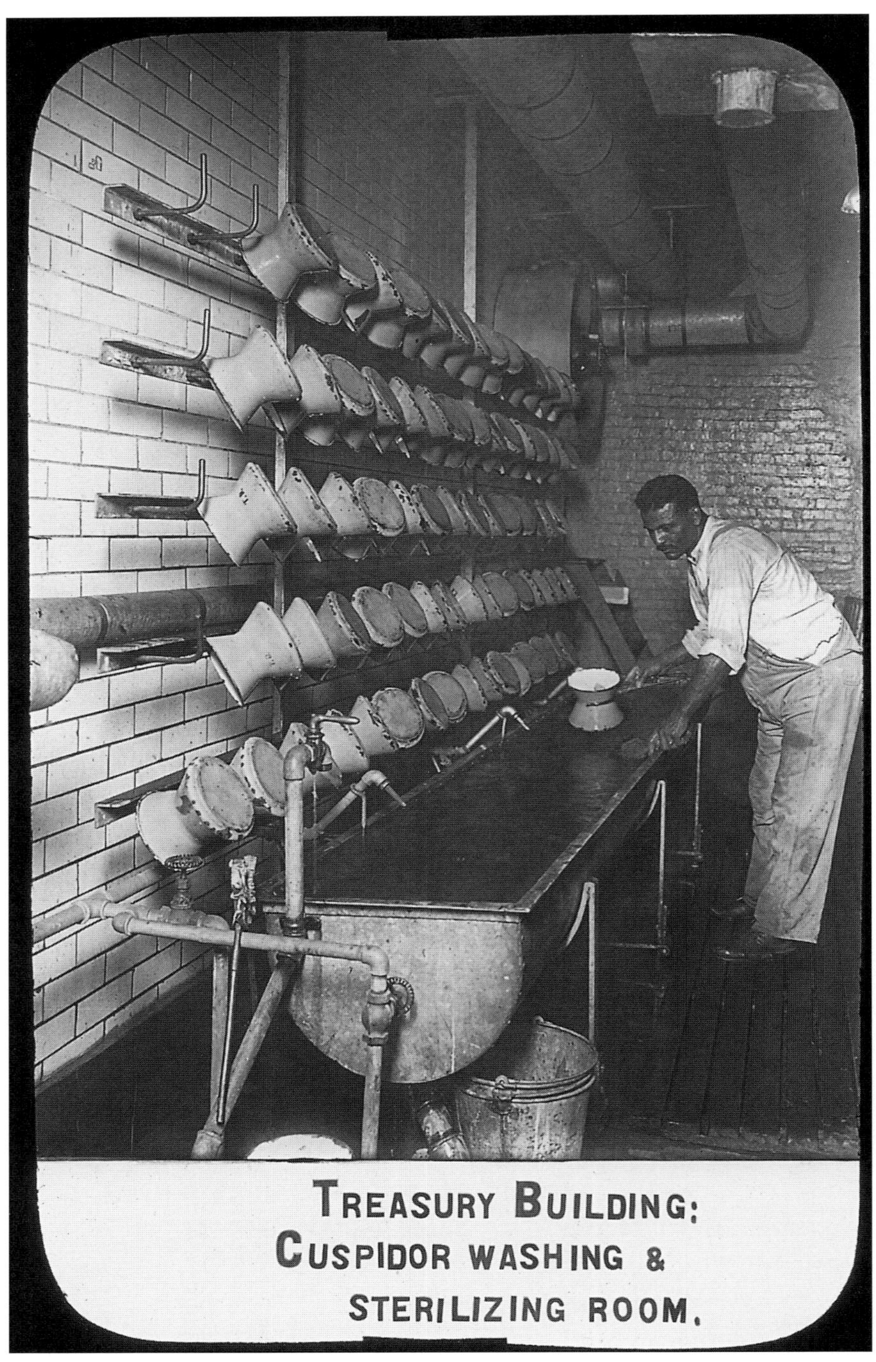

A Treasury Department employee sterilizes cuspidors circa 1915. From the city's earliest days, European visitors were horrified by the widespread acceptance of tobacco chewing and spitting. As early as 1842, Charles Dickens called Washington "the headquarters of tobacco-tinctured saliva" and described public buildings where visitors "are implored to squirt the essence of their quids, or 'plugs'... into the national spittoons, and not about the bases of the marble columns."

By 1883, Boss Shepherd's improvements to the Dupont Circle area had created a landscape of extremes. In the foreground of Delancey Gill's 1883 drawing is a shanty of one of the African American families who dominated the neighborhood. In the left background is "Stewart's Folly," a five-story mansion designed by Adolph Cluss for Nevada Senator William M. Stewart. Stewart, who made his fortune in gold and silver mining, was ridiculed when he built the house in 1873 where Riggs Bank is today. But he knew that his friend Shepherd was about to bring water mains, sewers, paved streets and electricity to the area. The utility poles carried telephone and telegraph wires as well as electrical wires for street lighting.

In 1885, when this picture was taken from the Washington Monument, Foggy Bottom was a relatively undeveloped mix of federal buildings, working-class housing and waterfront industrial companies. The dirt road at center is Virginia Avenue. To its upper left, along the waterfront, are storage tanks of the Washington Gas Light Company, current site of the Watergate complex (1). The company, founded in 1848, baked coal to produce the gas stored in the tanks until it was used to light streets and interiors. The three-masted ship is docked at the site of Lear's Wharf, where federal government belongings were unloaded in 1800.

had made fortunes in mining, steel, oil, steam engines, munitions and other industries. Some came briefly, to lobby on such issues as tariffs or patent rights, such as Andrew Carnegie's patent for the Bessemer steel-making process and Bell's for the telephone, or to secure lucrative government land grants for railroads or timber. Others stayed for the entire "social season," when Congress was in session, or longer, buying mansions on tony Dupont Circle or nearby, mingling with political and diplomatic elites as well as with intellectuals and what remained of Washington's antebellum aristocracy. Often, as historian Kathryn Allamong Jacob notes, the new millionaires did not have the pedigrees to be accepted by their hometown establishments and thus found Washington much more to their liking.

The nouveau riche and the newly opened neighborhoods helped send real estate prices skyrocketing. A local savings and trust company, for example, bought a 40-acre parcel in Kalorama Heights, about a mile north of Dupont Circle, in 1873 for $15,000. Fourteen years later, the same parcel, still undeveloped, sold for $300,000.

Government clerks with a few dollars to invest bought small tracts and waited for the fever to inflate their investments. Locals built houses to rent while Congress was in session, and in the 1880s apartment buildings with high-priced rental accommodations began going up. According to historian Constance Green, more than 2,450 private buildings, mostly houses, were constructed in

1887 alone. In 1894 Washington had eight apartment houses. By 1900 their number had multiplied to 72.

Yet none was permitted to be taller than 13 stories. This was not, as commonly believed, because of a desire to protect views of the Capitol or any other public buildings or monuments. The rule stemmed from concern over a building that still stands in the 1600 block of Q Street, N.W.—the Cairo. Twelve stories high, the Cairo was the city's tallest building when it went up in 1894. Neighbors complained vigorously that it blotted out the sun and posed a fire hazard, since firefighters' ladders couldn't reach its upper floors. The District's commissioners agreed and promptly limited the height of future city buildings to 13 stories, a restriction that has never been lifted. More than anything else, it accounts for Washington's low-rise feel.

As private building flourished, so too did creation of new government edifices. The Pension Building was completed in 1885, the Library of Congress in 1886, the State, War and Navy Building (now the Old Executive Office Building) in 1887, the Post Office Building in the 1890s. At the same time, Congress set aside Rock Creek Park in 1890 to provide a refuge for Washingtonians.

Nothing, however, did more to redefine the public city than the McMillan Commission, appointed by Congress in 1900 as part of the centennial of the government's arrival in Washington. Its work, which ended 100 years of uncontrolled development, led not only

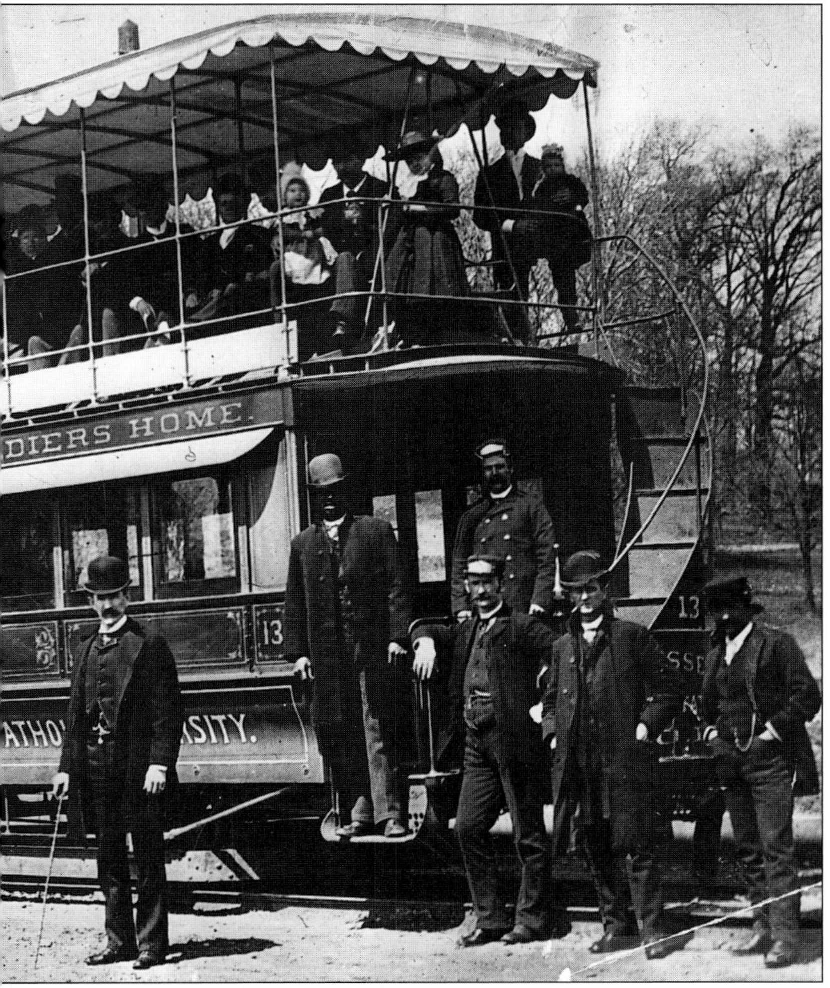

Clockwise, from upper left:

Cycling—relatively affordable, liberating and slightly frivolous—was one of the nation's first fads, and Washington proved no exception, as evidenced by these cyclists photographed by the White House in 1868. National organizations such as the League of American Wheelmen, whose members enjoyed train/cycle excursions, lobbied for better roads.

Sightseers examine water pipes awaiting connection to the reservoir south of Soldiers' Home in 1889. The water supply then originated from the Potomac via the Georgetown reservoir. It proved inadequate for the city's growing needs, especially in the eastern sections where the gravity-propelled system tended to sputter out. The McMillan reservoir, the city's second, finally opened near Howard University in 1907.

Passengers and crew of a "motor car" and its double-decker trailer pose on North Capitol Street circa 1891. The Eckington and Soldiers' Home Railway Company was chartered in 1888 to build the city's first electric railway from 7th and New York Avenue, N.W., to Fourth and T streets, N.E.

to the redesign of the Mall but to creation of the Federal Triangle, Union Station, the Jefferson and Lincoln memorials and parks and parkways.

All of the construction, private and public, both reflected and helped create growing Washington employment. New or expanded bureaucracies were taking care of pensions for war veterans, the settlement of Western lands, the collection of education information and the growing demand for patents and an accurate census. The Interstate Commerce Commission was established in 1887, as was the Bureau of Engraving, (though Washington had begun printing "greenbacks" in 1862 to finance the Civil War).

Congress didn't neglect its own needs. In 1884 it authorized a clerk for each member, requiring more office space on Capitol Hill. The lawmakers by then had lengthened their sessions, sometimes sitting for up to seven months in non-election years. It took the introduction of air conditioning in the House in 1928 and in the Senate in 1930, however, to let Congress stay longer on a more regular basis.

In all of these and other areas —at the Interior Department, the Justice Department, the later-divided Department of Commerce and Labor—employment was climbing, a trend that would continue to accelerate. Indeed, at the turn of the century, the federal workforce began expanding to levels previously unimaginable, climbing from 25,000 in 1903 to 65,000 by 1927.

In part, this was a result of World War I, which nearly doubled

The Gilded Age not only brought nouveau riche industrialists to the capital, where they built mansions near "Stewart's Folly" and Dupont Circle. It also sent them to Congress. In 1890 *Puck* published this commentary on an increasingly common method of achieving national elective office.

Washington's National League team, known as both the "Statesmen" and the "Senators," plays in the Swampoodle section, site of the current Union Station, circa 1888. Swampoodle owed its moniker to the many springs and streams that created puddles and ponds after heavy rains. A line drive through the McDowell & Sons grain elevator was a home run for sure.

Charles Glover, a founder of the second Board of Trade, created in 1889, was president of Riggs Bank. Historian Constance Green described him as "violent-tempered" but credited him with arranging for public parks and creating the foundation that would build the National Cathedral. With Washington ruled by Congress and three presidentially appointed commissioners, the powerful Board of Trade acted as an unofficial, self-appointed city council until the 1970s. Some considered this "representative aristocracy" an ideal quasi-government in a time of widespread city corruption.

In 1894, Warwick & Hiss advertised its billiard parlors, on 13th Street, N.W., near Pennsylvania Avenue, as "the most elegant in Washington." The emporium was located in Murder Bay, southeast of the Treasury, bordered by Pennsylvania and Constitution avenues. From the Civil War until the 1920s, the neighborhood was notorious as the city's red light district and as home to the destitute.

Anna J. Cooper taught Latin at M Street (later Dunbar) High School, earned a Ph.D. from the Sorbonne at age 67 and served as principal of Dunbar. She championed academic training for African Americans at a time when Booker T. Washington's emphasis on industrial education was in vogue. Teachers like Cooper were prominent in the city's separate "colored" schools, which enjoyed a national reputation and drew African Americans to Washington for their children's education. Cooper later led Frelinghuysen University, a night school for working black adults. She died at age 105 in 1964. A traffic circle in LeDroit Park is named in her honor.

the city's overall population, as the Civil War had before it, though this time the women who flocked to town came to type and file. With them came an acute housing shortage, despite the city's building boom and construction of a few dormitories for single women. A single room in a boarding house, occupied by three or four women, rented for nearly as much as an entire house had before the war.

Residents, new women workers and thousands of young men training in nearby camps for the conflict in Europe thronged the city. Citizens stood in line to read war bulletins in front of the *Washington Post* building on E Street, near the National Theatre, to eat at restaurants, mail a letter, see a movie and make a telephone call. Flags flew everywhere, and, beginning in August 1918, a siren blew at noon and workers stopped their labors to pray for victory. Soon many presumably also prayed that they would not be struck down by the Spanish influenza epidemic, which killed thousands of Washingtonians that fall.

With so many unattached young women and men in town, entertainment opportunities seemed endless. "Nearly every day I see daring exhibition aeroplane flights over the city," wrote "government girl" Josephine Lehmann in her diary in 1918, "and at night the sky is shot through with many searchlights playing on the dome of the Capitol. Some thrilling thing is going on all the time and the city is full of soldiers, sailors, aviators, etc. A dozen or more were at the dance" hosted by her landlady for 75 young people the previous evening. "There are always men and dances and places to go."

On Armistice Day in November 1918, Washington had more than 100,000 residents who had not been in the capital when the war broke out in Europe in 1914. Many, like young Josephine, who had come to Washington from rural Michigan, stayed to continue their city lives.

The expanding federal workforce prompted Congress in 1926 to approve another $50 million construction program. The money was devoted to buildings in the city's downtown core, including the Supreme Court, the Government Printing Office and the Commerce Department. More than 20,000 employees occupied the buildings when they were completed in 1938.

In the private sector, in addition to booming real estate and retail businesses, a tourism industry had begun to emerge in the 1880s, together with a growing number of luxury hotels, mainstays of today's Washington economy. Advances in railroad travel made touring attractive to a new leisure class, and its members were intrigued by images of the capital presented in such illustrated publications as *Harper's Weekly*.

Despite all the prosperity, however, in racial terms Washington was still two cities. African Americans remained a major part of the population (about one-third until after World War II), but they made little headway in their efforts to earn as much money as whites, despite post-Civil War civil rights laws guaranteeing non-discrimination. To be sure, an elite, educated African American

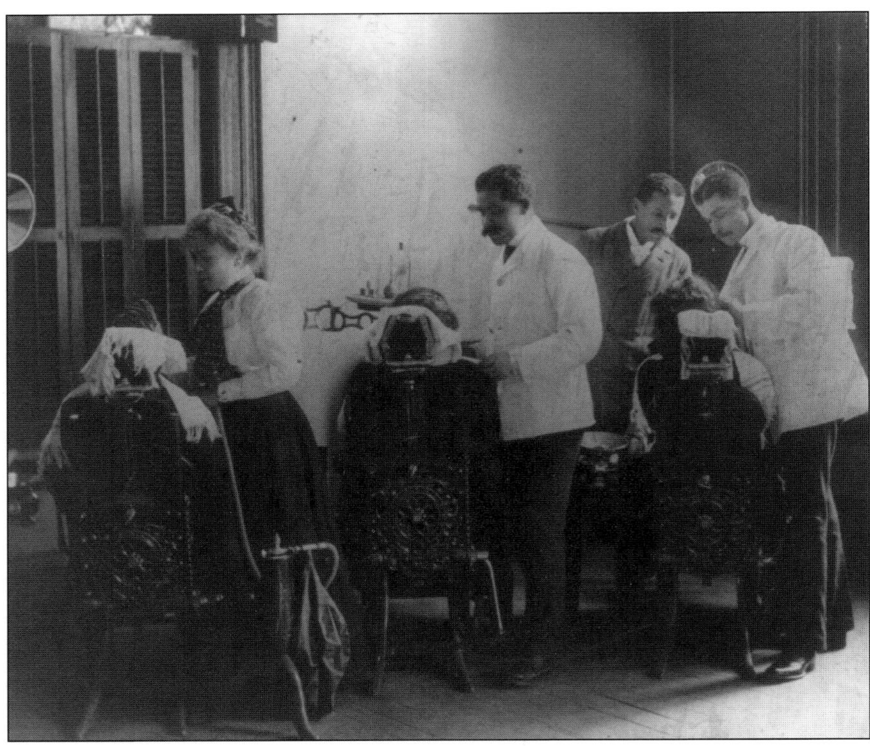

Dental students practice on brave volunteers at Howard University in 1900. Chartered by the federal government in 1867 as a non-segregated institution, Howard quickly became an important black intellectual center. It supplied a large percentage of the black professionals for Washington and other African American communities across the nation.

First graders of the Miner Normal School practice proper dental hygiene, circa 1919, outside their model elementary school. Myrtilla Miner, a white educator interested in training black elementary school teachers, founded the school in 1851. It operated until 1860 despite fierce opposition from some whites. In 1863 Congress incorporated and reopened the school to train teachers for the freed men and women who flooded the city. After a series of mergers, Miner was folded in 1977 into the University of the District of Columbia.

Students in a white elementary school pose for photographic pioneer Frances Benjamin Johnston in 1899. Johnston, a Washington cultural leader, was commissioned to photograph the city's schools for the Paris Exposition (World's Fair) of 1900.

Legend has it that this proud driver leading admiring boys on Pennsylvania Avenue in 1897 is piloting the city's first auto. With wide and straight avenues, Washington was then considered a first-rate motoring city. In 1906 the House adopted a resolution calling for a speed limit of 12 miles per hour on straightaways, 5 mph at street crossings and 4 mph around turns (only the 12-mph standard became law). Three years earlier, the city commissioners introduced the first driving exams and gave cars moving north or south the right of way over those moving east or west. They didn't specify how to negotiate diagonal streets.

community continued to play important roles in the school system, the arts and the professions. For the most part, though, black men were relegated to unskilled or menial work, forcing many black women to work outside their homes, usually as domestics or personal servants.

In a social history called *Horse and Buggy Days With Uncle Sam*, for example, civil servant John H. Paynter wrote that at the end of the Spanish-American War in 1898, "out of more than 500 clerks in the Internal Revenue Bureau, there were not 10 colored employees ..." Inevitably, such job discrimination led to inadequate living conditions and health care for most African Americans. At the same time, blacks had to contend with such insults as racist congressmen attempting to introduce Jim Crow laws and authorizing Ku Klux Klan marches down Pennsylvania Avenue.

But blacks in the federal government were still doing better than most blacks elsewhere—a point often made by whites. Paynter reports overhearing a white messenger from Kentucky who grew annoyed when a black messenger complained about his salary. The white man noted that his black fellow employee was earning $60 a month. "I know plenty of men down my way who would be glad to do this work for $30 or $40," he said.

With the arrival of Woodrow Wilson's administration in 1913, his cabinet of Southern Democrats, with his tacit approval, systematically instituted segregation in federal departments. Cabinet members spoke of the need to defer to Southern sensibilities during the era of Jim Crow. Middle-class black clerks especially resented this regressive policy, but most remained silent to keep their jobs.

Some light-skinned blacks attempted to "pass" into the white workforce. Others, such as civil rights activist Mary Church Terrell, were taken for white and assigned to work in whites-only sections. Those who were discovered to be African American were transferred to "colored" sections or hounded out of the federal service on trumped-up charges of inefficiency.

Far worse than the threat of exposure or segregation was the peril of racial violence, especially during the hard times following World War I, when some veterans were forced to become street panhandlers. In fact, in 1919, following more than a month of inflammatory newspaper articles on "posses" hunting blacks or seeking a "Negro fiend," a virtual race war erupted for four days in the city, leaving an estimated 40 dead and 150 wounded. The immediate cause of the outbreak, one of 20 race riots in U.S. cities that summer, was police questioning and release of a black suspect in an attempted sexual assault on the white wife of a military man. On a hot July night, hundreds of white soldiers and sailors randomly attacked African American residents of a largely black Southwest neighborhood.

Because police provided little protection, African Americans mobilized to defend themselves. Working-class blacks of Southwest turned mobs away from their

The Mall (right), seen circa 1863, was designed with romantic curving paths by Andrew Jackson Downing in 1851. By the turn of the century, this was considered passé and not in keeping with L'Enfant's vision. In 1900 the Senate Park (McMillan) Commission revisited the Mall design and the "monumental core of the city" and concluded that a simple linear design (below) was more functional. The commission was formed as part of the capital's celebration of the centennial of the federal government's arrival. Its members, landscape architect Frederick Law Olmsted, architects Daniel Burnham and Charles McKim and sculptor Augustus Saint-Gaudens, were determined to bring controlled planning to the city after 100 years of haphazard development. They sought to create parks and new monuments and to introduce carefully placed public buildings in the beaux-arts style: grand white marble structures based on Greek and Roman classical architecture. Their work eventually resulted in the Federal Triangle, Union Station, the Jefferson and Lincoln memorials and parks and parkways.

neighborhoods and then helped the black elite in Le Droit Park. With newspapers still fanning the flames—*The Washington Post* ran a disgraceful front-page article that included what amounted to a recruiting call for white rioters—more confrontations ensued. It took a combination of federal troops, black self-defense and heavy rain to end the violence

Despite such difficult periods, though, reliable incomes in the capital produced a vibrant downtown business community, which formed the first Washington Chamber of Commerce in 1906 and began to lobby Congress directly, as the Board of Trade (into which the chamber was later folded) still does.

In the 1920s, F Street was the locus of local shopping, principally at department stores like Kann's, Lansburgh's and Woodward & Lothrop (which limited black access to goods and services). The flourishing capital also had plenty of time for fun. Just a few blocks west, several large movie theaters (one of them seating 1,900) packed in customers all day, every day. Baseball fans cheered for their Washington Senators. Prohibition came to the capital almost three years before the rest of the nation, and speakeasies suddenly appeared all over town.

Washington, however, didn't roar during the Roaring Twenties to the extent that New York or Chicago did. In those cities, rich industrialists and their pampered offspring did most of the partying. Washington at the time had fewer socially prominent business families, and the city's style was resolutely middle-class and conservative. Washingtonians did their share of socializing and drinking of bootleg liquor, but social activities tended to center on dances and on home entertaining.

Where Washington did continue to roar during the 1920s was in real estate development. Because commuting by car was becoming more and more common, neighborhoods like Wesley Heights (1925) and Spring Valley (1929), both developed by W.C. and A.N. Miller, sprang up. The houses there were among the most expensive in the city—and they were strictly covenanted, not to be sold to "any person of the Semitic race ... [including] Armenians, Jews, Hebrews, Persians and Syrians," according to a Wesley Heights deed of the time.

The first large-scale construction of rowhouses north of Florida Avenue also took place in that decade, bringing an urban atmosphere to once-open areas and providing the growing corps of government workers a much greater range of middle-class accommodations.

By 1929, the capital was prosperous as never before. The urge for grander apartments, larger homes and larger-still backyards was turning into a flood. And before long it would be clearer than ever that Washington was a wonderful place to live and work.

This lyrical view of I Street, N.W., looking west from 10th Street, shows a typically quiet urban neighborhood circa 1901. The Yee Lee laundry washed a shirt for eight cents (the collar and cuffs, which were detachable, cost an additional 4.5 cents). The laundry occupies a typical early 19th century two-story structure, formerly a house. Small merchants, who generally lived above their shops and served their immediate neighbors, prized corner buildings. This entrepreneur probably shopped in Chinatown, located on Pennsylvania Avenue east of 4 1/2 Street, N.W., from the 1880s until 1931, when it was forced to move north to H Street to make way for a proposed municipal center.

A Potomac Electric Power Company employee changes a downtown streetlight circa 1900. PEPCO's predecessor, U.S. Electric Lighting Company of the District of Columbia, was formed in 1882. Electricity generated in its plant on 13 1/2 Street, N.W., traveled through underground conduits to supply streetlights, competing with widely used gas-powered lights.

THE FLOATING BROTHEL

This flower-bedecked houseboat, photographed in 1905, is "Madame Rose's" *Dream,* a floating brothel. Alexandria historian Frederick C. Tilp wrote that the *Dream,* a two-story, four-woman pleasure boat, usually anchored at Jones Point, site of the Woodrow Wilson Bridge. Between the Civil War and World War II, thousands of houseboats, gambling barges and floating brothels tied up along the Virginia shore. They flourished because Virginia had no jurisdiction over them and Maryland and the District, which technically control the Potomac River, ignored them. Madame Rose made the news in 1905, when her boat lost its moorings in a storm and floated a mile downriver, where fishermen rescued her and a full house of customers.

In 1904, Center Market, located where the National Archives is today, was the city's main food market. Its grand brick building, completed in 1877 according to a design by architect Adolph Cluss, was insufficient to contain all of the farmers and their wares, so the surrounding streets served as outdoor additions to the selling space.

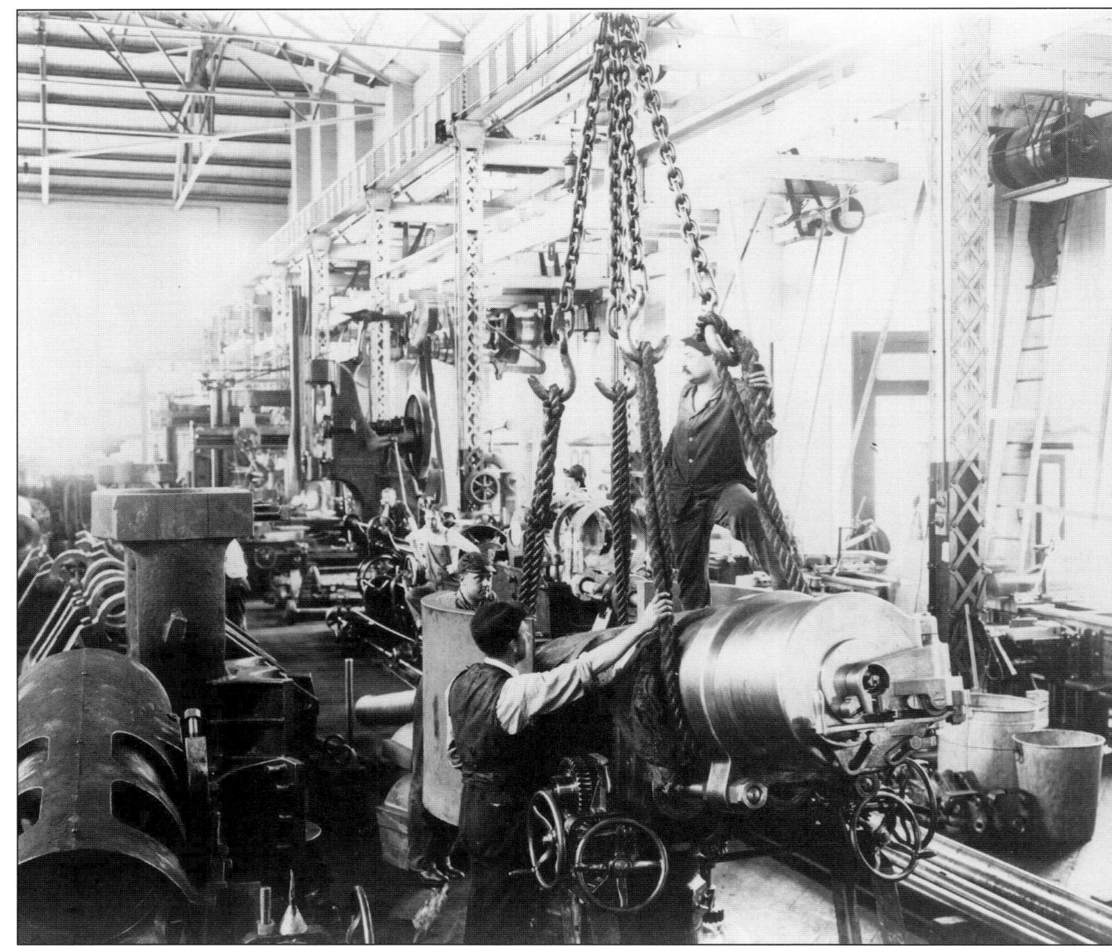

Navy Yard workers prepare to hoist a mounted gun, circa 1910, in this photograph by Frances Benjamin Johnston. While the bulk of government workers wore white collars after 1900, the government operated a number of industrial plants, the biggest of which was the Navy Yard. First created to build ships, the facility began to produce weaponry beginning in 1840. In 1876 it abandoned shipbuilding entirely for ordnance testing and manufacturing. It was known from its earliest days for employing skilled workers regardless of race.

The owner, staff and family of Anthony Magruder's tavern at 102 First Street, N.W., in the Swampoodle neighborhood, pose in 1908. The area near and including Union Station was densely settled with working-class Irish, Germans and Italians, most of them recent immigrants. Although Washington never experienced the waves of immigration of other more industrialized cities, its needs for construction and service workers made it attractive to immigrants, especially those skilled in the building trades.

The rural nature of much of Washington is underscored in this 1909 photograph of the W. L. Koontz Co. feed store at 1301 Good Hope Road, S.E. The store served farmers in Prince George's County and Southeast D.C.

William Henry Taft (no relation to the president) was photographed by his son, government electrician Henry Arthur Taft, enjoying a 1902 picnic at Chevy Chase Lake with his daughter-in-law and granddaughters. The Chevy Chase Land Company built the lake in the early 1890s where its Rock Creek Railway ended and its generator produced current to run the trolleys. The lake and its amusement park and bandstand drew potential home buyers, who rode open streetcars on hot summer days past the lots and houses of Chevy Chase Village. The lake was later drained, but its name persists on a road and shopping center on Connecticut Avenue just south of the Beltway.

The Tafts moved to a substantial new brick house at 4021 Kansas Avenue, N.W., (right) in 1903. The following spring Henry photographed his son and father as they built a fence for a vegetable garden. The rural area of North Columbia Heights was just beginning to be developed, and the Taft house cost $5,000; that year William Henry's salary was about $1,200, or 50 cents an hour.

Developer William F. Matteson pushed all the buttons in his 1910 advertising booklet for subdivisions in what would become Cleveland Park. Who could resist the horn of plenty's promise: piles of gold for whoever purchased lots and built substantial, tree-shaded dwellings, all within easy reach of downtown and the Capitol?

Bohemian artist and cultural champion Alice Pike Barney painted this self-portrait in about 1910. Alice and her husband Albert, both heirs to Midwest fortunes (hers from whiskey, his from rail cars), moved to Washington in 1888. Until 1927, Barney was the city's leading patron—and practitioner—of the arts. In addition to her own painting, she organized theatrical events, created Studio House on Sheridan Circle, helped develop the programs of Neighborhood House, a social settlement in Southwest, worked for world peace and women's rights and created the National Sylvan Theatre on the grounds of the Washington Monument.

Alice Barney's socialite friends appear in "Youth's Illusion of War," an anti-war tableau presented to a crowd of 6,000 by the Women's Peace Party of Washington at the foot of the Washington Monument in 1905. In this pre-movie era, the flamboyant Barney attracted spectacle-hungry audiences for her amateur and often political theatricals.

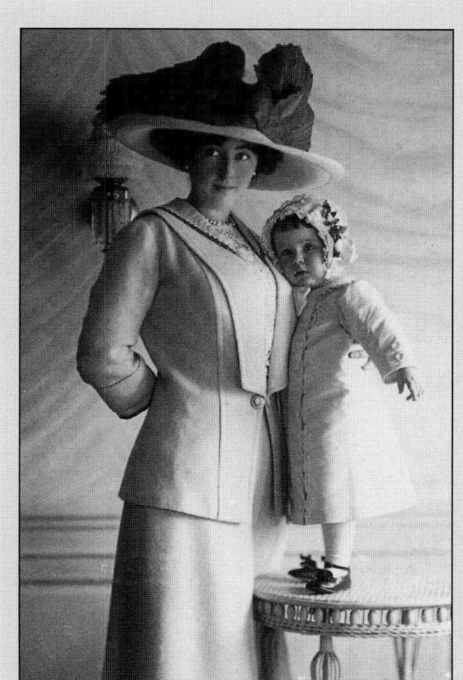

ALL YOU NEEDED WAS MONEY

Evalyn Walsh McLean, posing here with her son Vinson, was a representative descendant of the nouveau riche who flocked to Washington after the Civil War to lobby for advantages and who built mansions in the capital. The war had ruined most of the city's old elite families whose allegiance belonged to the South, leaving a vacuum in high society. Many of the rich who filled the void found a fluid and accepting Washington society. All you needed was money. As Evalyn Walsh McLean unabashedly wrote in *Father Struck It Rich*, her father, Irish immigrant Tom Walsh, abandoned work on railroad bridges in Massachusetts to search for gold out West. He found it in Colorado, became a millionaire and moved to Washington, where it was known that elected officials readily exchanged social access for campaign support. Tom Walsh built a 60-room mansion at 2020 Massachusetts Avenue, now the Indonesian Embassy. Daughter Evalyn married the equally rich Ned McLean, son of the owner of *The Washington Post* in 1908. Evalyn acquired the allegedly cursed Hope diamond in 1909; a decade later her son Vinson, then 9 years old, was killed by a car as he crossed Wisconsin Avenue at the gates to their estate, "Friendship," now McLean Gardens.

On July 14, 1911, aviator Harry Atwood takes off from the White House's South Lawn after President William Howard Taft presented him with a medal for his pioneering flights. According to news accounts, Atwood had landed by shutting off the motor of his biplane at treetop level and gliding to a safe stop. The previous night, Atwood had flown into the city from the College Park airstrip and circled the Washington Monument and the Capitol. He was among a handful of early aviator/exhibitionists who made daringly low flights in populated areas, cutting off the engine and then cheating death at the last moment by starting it up again. Days earlier, he had astounded Manhattanites by buzzing Wall Street.

Child labor contributed to Washington's economy, as it did elsewhere, during the early 20th century. Reformer/photographer Lewis Hine worked for the National Child Labor Committee documenting the exploitation of children. At upper left is 11-year-old Greek immigrant Gus Strateges, who sold celery at Center Market as well as newspapers and chewing gum. Above are boys employed in 1911 by the Old Dominion Glass Company of Alexandria.

A young man prepares to board a new Washington Railway and Electric Company trolley in 1908. The company began life in 1864 as a horse-drawn railway. In the boom years of electric railway growth (about 1890 to 1925), it acquired other rail companies, including the Washington and Rockville Railway, which by 1900 operated trolleys from Georgetown to the farming community of Rockville, hoping to spur suburban development.

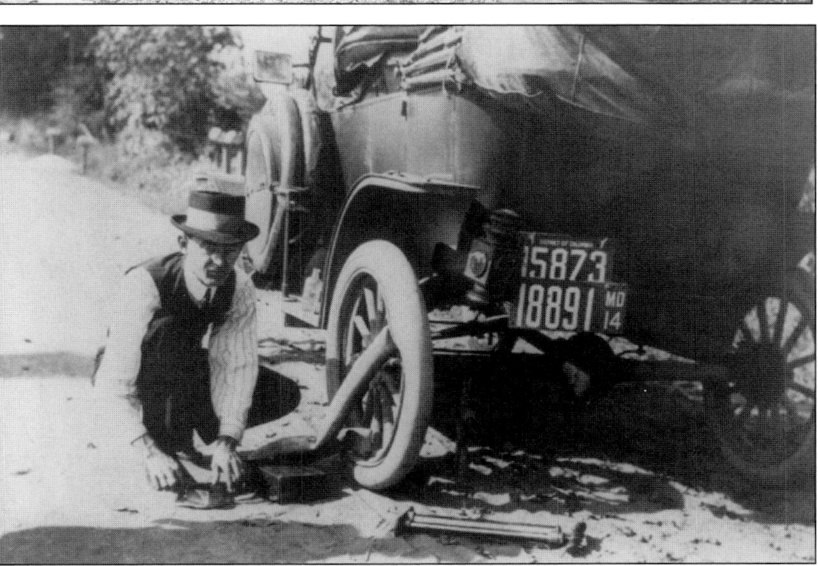

News photographer Herbert E. French attends to a flat tire in 1914. At the time, Maryland required outsiders to obtain license plates to drive in the state, which explains French's double plates. The District had reciprocity with Virginia for license plates but not with all states. Families driving long distances were often surprised by this rule, which forced the driver to leave his car and passengers along the District line while he hot-footed it downtown for the necessary tag. Standardized metal plates were first issued in 1907; before that, drivers created their own from any materials handy, choosing their own numbers.

A motorist crosses one of the many fords that carried vehicles through Rock Creek near the National Zoo, circa 1915. Until 1966, when a series of bridges was completed, drivers in the park had to ford the creek at several points. When Henry Ford's Model T made its debut in 1908, many Washingtonians bought them and went for pleasure drives. By the early 1920s, auto commuters were causing traffic tie-ups and trolley ridership was beginning to decline.

In October 1916, these two unidentified women participated in the 54th annual convention of former slaves, a "national reunion of ex-slaves and former owners," according to the *Evening Star*. News accounts described the reunion as a week-long revival during which former slaves were baptized and photographed for a memorial book. Such events were promoted in Southern cities by former owners intent on persuading the public that slavery had been a benign institution.

Soldiers of the First Division, just back from Germany, enjoy a watermelon feast near Union Station at the end of World War I. Patriotic citizens—especially young women—crowded the capital beyond capacity. Washingtonians, though, adapted to the inconveniences with patriotic good humor.

Hollywood film star Douglas Fairbanks exhorts spectators to invest in the third Liberty Loan, one of five bond drives that helped finance America's war effort. Each drive was launched with a new form of Hollywood hoopla, a parade from the White House to the Capitol led by movie stars whose appeal was unprecedented in American popular culture. On this day, thousands of government workers cut work to ogle Fairbanks, Mary Pickford and Charlie Chaplin.

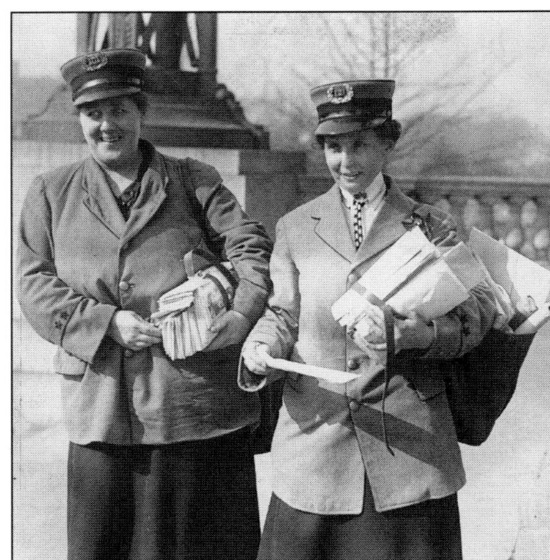

Two female letter carriers pose for the camera in 1917. As was true during the Civil War, white women stepped into what had been thought of as "men's jobs" during World War I. While black workmen found more work opportunities at better wages, jobs in the police department, public transportation and the upper reaches of the civil service were still closed to them despite manpower shortages.

Students of McKinley Manual Training High School present the four-inch shells they made as part of the war effort in 1917. At the time, both city schools divisions, white and "colored," offered a choice of curricula: manual training, business or academic.

Not to be outdone, these Girl Scouts break ground for a Victory Garden to be planted on the lawn of the Daughters of the American Revolution headquarters at 1776 D Street, N.W.

Cheering citizens waving American flags fill the streets to celebrate Armistice Day, November 11, 1918. Demonstrators were thankful not only that the war was over but also that they had survived the Spanish influenza epidemic, which, from September until early November, killed some 3,500 Washingtonians. The city's wartime overcrowding—young women commonly were housed four to a room and two to a bed—had helped spread the deadly virus.

Typesetters operate a linotype machine at the Goins Printing Company, 1344 U Street. Between 1890 and 1920, U Street and the Shaw neighborhood were the centers of African American economic development. Among U Street businesses were printers, a bank, real estate and insurance brokers, physicians, dentists, attorneys, beauticians and barbers, photographers, newspapers and a business college as well as restaurants and theaters. The designation "Shaw" for the neighborhood dates from 1966, when the National Capital Planning Commission borrowed the attendance boundaries of Shaw Junior High School for an Northwest urban renewal area. The school was named for Civil War hero Robert Gould Shaw, white leader of the 54th Massachusetts Regiment of U.S. Colored Troops portrayed in the 1989 film "Glory."

As Congress' favorite testing ground, Washington took on another federal policy before the rest of the nation when Prohibition was imposed on November 1, 1917, nearly three years before the 18th Amendment took effect. Soon speakeasies were everywhere, including the "lunch room" at 922 Pennsylvania Avenue (top), where revenue officers raided the basement storeroom in 1923. Newsmen dubbed this 500-gallon still (above) the "largest in captivity." It was raided in 1922 at 607 First Street, N.W., an easy walk from the Capitol. Rarely had so many flouted the law so flagrantly. The young woman at right models an ankle flask for ladies available at a fine jewelry store.

By the 1920s, Government Printing Office workers were racially segregated, with whites in higher-paying and higher-skilled jobs. Federal departments were not officially segregated until the arrival of the Woodrow Wilson administration in 1913. But segregation had taken hold of the city, mostly through custom. Although Washington did not have Jim Crow laws, it generally operated as if it did, partly because schools were legally segregated and race-restrictive housing covenants were enforced.

This government driver (right), posing by the State, War, and Navy Building (now the Eisenhower Executive Office Building) circa 1920, was typical of the growing black middle class, many of whose members moved to Washington to get stable, well-paying government jobs.

The nation's efforts to aid its war veterans dates from 1636, when Plymouth Colony provided support for soldiers disabled in the war with the Pequot Indians. By the early 1920s, when these Veterans Bureau workers were calculating bonuses owed to World War I vets, the government was providing pensions to veterans and their widows and dependents, as well as medical care, housing, disability compensation, insurance and vocational rehabilitation for the disabled.

Every 10 years an army of census takers attempted to interview every citizen in the nation. This young woman juggles files, forms and pen in 1920.

By the 1920s, the Georgetown waterfront had changed from a working port to a site for activities shunned by "better" neighborhoods. A catastrophic flood in 1889 had ruined the C&O Canal, which had supplied Georgetown's waterfront businesses with wheat, coal, lumber and other materials. The B&O Railroad, the canal's chief rival, held a majority of canal bonds and saw no reason to hurry to fix the damage. The canal went bankrupt, reopened briefly and closed for good in 1924. When this photo was taken, the flour and paper mills (powered by canal water) and coal/ice trade (schooners brought ice from Maine and took back coal from Cumberland, Md.) had given way to "industrial" uses: electric power and heat generation, construction-material storage and meat rendering.

A delegation of Native Americans, probably in town to negotiate claims with the Bureau of Indian Affairs, takes time out for sightseeing, circa 1920. Thousands of tribal delegations came to Washington seeking treaties and assurances of government protection. Many went home with empty promises.

A Peoples Drug Store baseball team poses in 1920. By the 20th century, the city had essentially divided into the government workforce and those whose goods and services tended to them. At the time of its purchase by CVS in 1990, Peoples was the city's largest drugstore chain.

A vendor sets up tents rented by the family in South Potomac Park's tourist camp, probably in 1921, the year the camp opened. According to the *Book of Washington*, many patrons were "itinerant travelers" moving from one part of the country to another. Others were vacationers in need of affordable shelter. A congressional appropriation provided 60 acres of land, streets, sewage, tents for rent, hot showers and food services.

Central High School students Grace Hurd, Evelyn Harrison and Corinna DiJulian, with Grace Wagner under the car, learn auto mechanics in 1927.

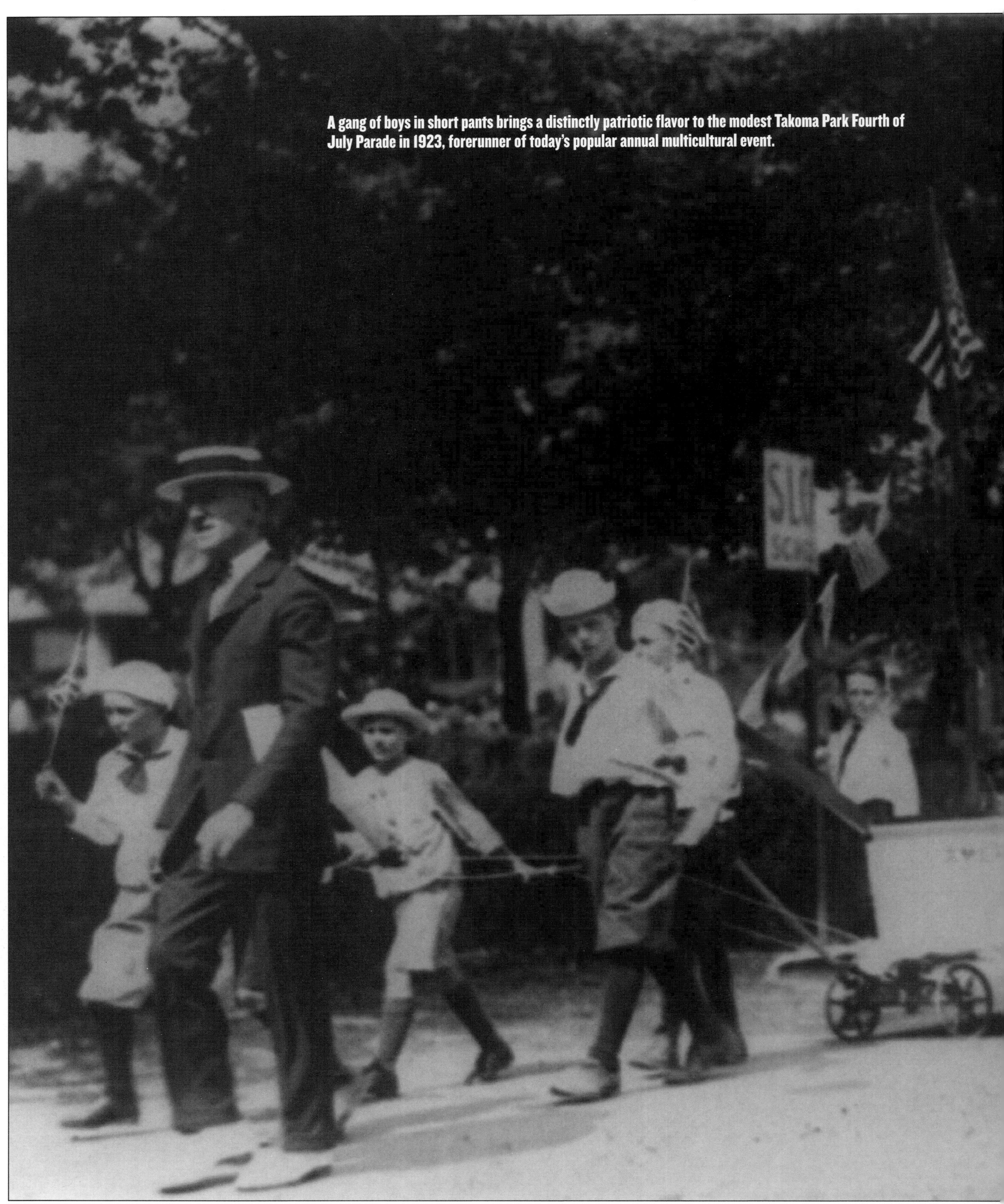

A gang of boys in short pants brings a distinctly patriotic flavor to the modest Takoma Park Fourth of July Parade in 1923, forerunner of today's popular annual multicultural event.

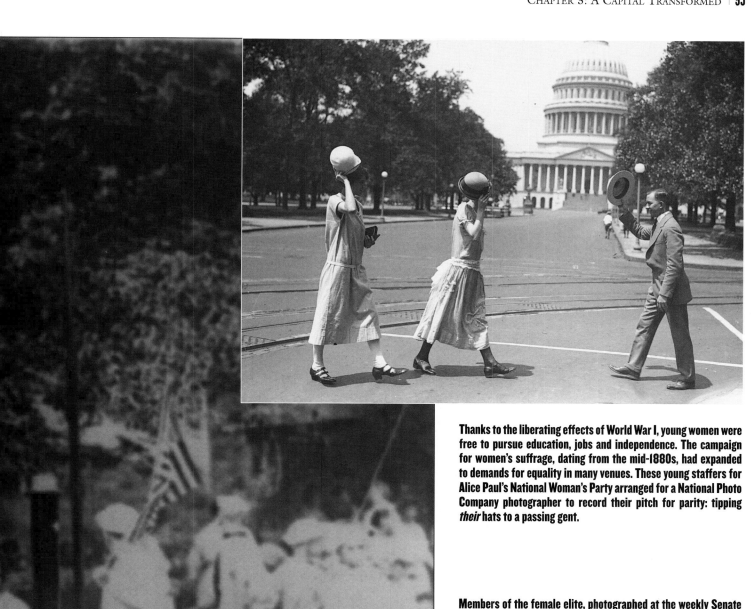

Thanks to the liberating effects of World War I, young women were free to pursue education, jobs and independence. The campaign for women's suffrage, dating from the mid-1880s, had expanded to demands for equality in many venues. These young staffers for Alice Paul's National Woman's Party arranged for a National Photo Company photographer to record their pitch for parity: tipping *their* hats to a passing gent.

Members of the female elite, photographed at the weekly Senate Ladies Luncheon in May 1925, followed more traditional roles. Enjoying their ice cream cones (eaten with a spoon!) at Edgemoor, the Bethesda home of Postmaster General Harry New, are the wives of Senators William N. Butler (Mary) and Frederick Gillette (Christine) of Massachusetts and Oscar Underwood (Bertha) of Alabama.

In the 1920s, Washington's Board of Trade promoted the capital as the perfect place for national conventions. Much to its chagrin, among the first takers was the Ku Klux Klan, 25,000 of whose members held a march on August 8, 1925. They wore hoods but no masks, to "show the world" that the Klan was "not ashamed of itself," according to the *Evening Star*. The marchers, including some 400 D.C. members, paraded down Pennsylvania Avenue to the National Sylvan Theatre.

In 1927, Special Assistant to the U.S. Attorney General Perry W. Howard, fourth from right in front row, hosted this dinner at the Whitelaw Hotel, then the city's best hotel owned by, and catering to, African Americans. To his right is Mary Church Terrell, educator and civil rights activist. The dinner appears to be a gathering of prominent black Republicans (African Americans were loyal to the party of Lincoln until the New Deal in 1933). Howard's father had represented Mississippi during Reconstruction, and Howard served as a Mississippi Republican National Committeeman from 1912 until 1960, attending each national convention despite continuous challenges from the whites in the Mississippi delegation. He moved to Washington in 1921 to take the Justice Department post and eventually practiced law with Cobb, Howard & Hayes.

Washington Senators pitcher Walter "Big Train" Johnson holds his daughter in a giant glove. For most of the 70 years that they played in the capital, the Senators were lampooned as "first in war, first in peace, and last in the American League." But when Johnson led the fight, the team won the 1924 World Series. At right is Josh Gibson, star of the Negro Leagues 1931 champions, the Homestead Grays. The Grays split their home games between Washington and Pittsburgh, using the stadiums of the Senators and Pirates when those teams were on the road.

In the spirit of the Roaring Twenties, a National Photo Company photographer caught "society girls" at play on the Potomac near the 14th Street Railroad Bridge in March 1927. Gardiner Orme is at the wheel of his new mahogany speedboat on opening day of the Corinthian Yacht Club's season. His passengers are Sally Hew Phillips (daughter of a physician), Fanny Dial (daughter of a former senator), Frances Gore and Georgiana Joyes (daughter of a general).

Scantily clad joggers making noontime circuits of the Mall were far in the future in 1923 when President Calvin Coolidge (right) took time for fitness, swinging clubs in the White House basement.

CHAPTER 4

CRISES AND CONFIDENCE

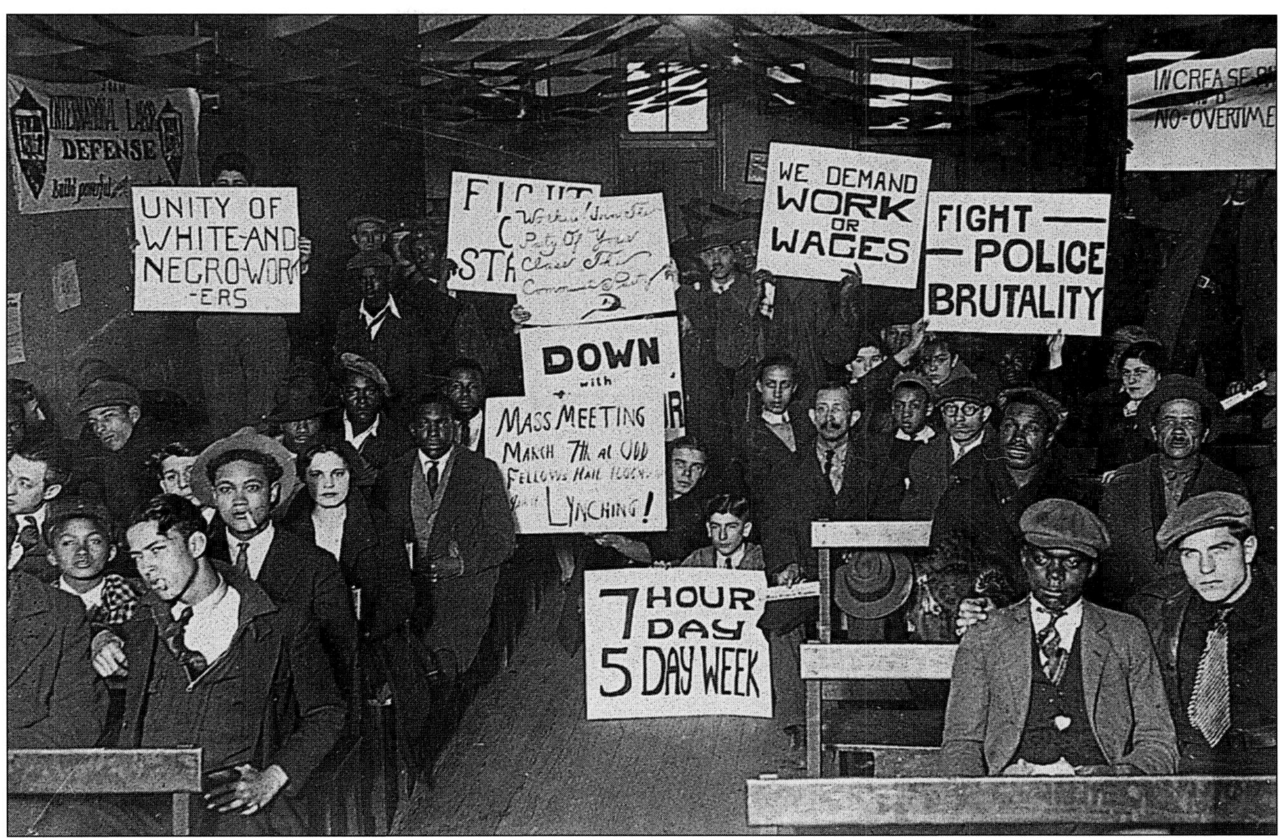

Members of the Washington Communism Society gather during the Great Depression for "Red Day," an "international unemployment day." Police used tear gas and clubs on March 6, 1930, to disperse the 106 demonstrators in front of the White House. Part of the communist message, spread in larger demonstrations in other cities as well, was interracial solidarity, a radical position at a time when even labor unions generally discriminated against African Americans. The communists were so identified with the issue that even after interest in American communists had abated, the FBI and others suspected civil rights advocates of any race as having communist sympathies.

Over the years, Americans have turned increasingly to Washington to protect them from life's risks—military attack, bank panics, farm price swings, depressions, pauperism in old age, disease, discrimination, tainted foods and drugs, monopoly power, perilous products and workplaces and much more. Then many have grumbled that Washington does too much, spends too much and benefits too much from the nation's woes, something akin to muttering that firefighters benefit from blazes or police from crime.

Never was demand more urgent for Washington's help than during the reign of President Franklin D. Roosevelt, spanning both the Great Depression and World War II, and never did Washington expand more.

The Great Depression had been preceded by an array of mishaps. Farms and factories had overproduced, pushing down prices. Farmers had defaulted on mortgages, causing small bank failures. A get-rich-quick frenzy had hit the stock market, only to end with the crash of

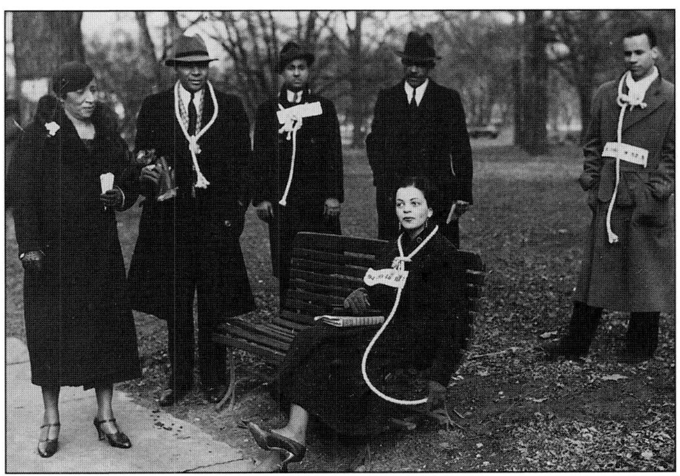

Crime Conference in 1934. Speakers decried gangsters, narcotics (especially the "mariihuna" craze, reported the *Washington Post*) and underage criminals—but they refused to support anti-lynching legislation.

October 1929. But it was a tightening of the nation's money supply that is generally blamed for the prolonged disaster that followed—thousands of banks shuttered, depositors' savings lost, factories closed, with the industrial heartland hit particularly hard. By mid-1932 in Ohio, for example, unemployment in Cleveland had soared to 50 percent and in Toledo to 80 percent. To make matters worse, a prolonged Midwest drought created the Dust Bowl, forcing more farm families to roam the nation in search of work.

Although Washingtonians were better off than others, bread lines, unemployment queues and soup kitchens sprang up in the capital as elsewhere. In early 1931, according to journalist Chalmers Roberts, false rumors of an impending failure of the Perpetual Building Association started a run on that institution. The president of Riggs National Bank personally rushed $500,000 to Perpetual and opened the bag full of cash to the public's view, stemming the panic.

To avoid government layoffs, President Hoover ordered federal pay cuts or furloughs (in 1932 Hoover himself took a voluntary 20 percent pay cut). From 1932 to 1937, only one member of a family was allowed to hold a civil service job.

By mid-1932, private construction in Washington had nearly stopped. White workers in the private sector turned to service jobs traditionally held by African Americans, throwing many blacks out of work. That

Amid the gloom of the early 1930s came a bright moment for many: the end of Prohibition. These patrons of the Silver Spring Liquor Dispensary belly up to the counter for $3 bottles of rye and other liquor on the first day of sales in December 1933. Thanks to Methodist temperance groups, Montgomery County endured 53 years of Prohibition, quadruple the 13 years of national Prohibition.

The Ford Motor Company's Alexandria assembly plant was one of the few national industrial facilities to operate in or near Washington. The plant was the successor to Ford's District facility, which assembled up to 25 cars a day at 451 Pennsylvania Ave., N.W., from 1917 until 1930. That year, the building became part of the parcel on which the Municipal Center was built. The Alexandria waterfront plant, at South Union Street, opened in 1932, but it ceased operations less than a year later, a victim of the Great Depression. The building was demolished in 1996 for the Ford's Landing townhouse development.

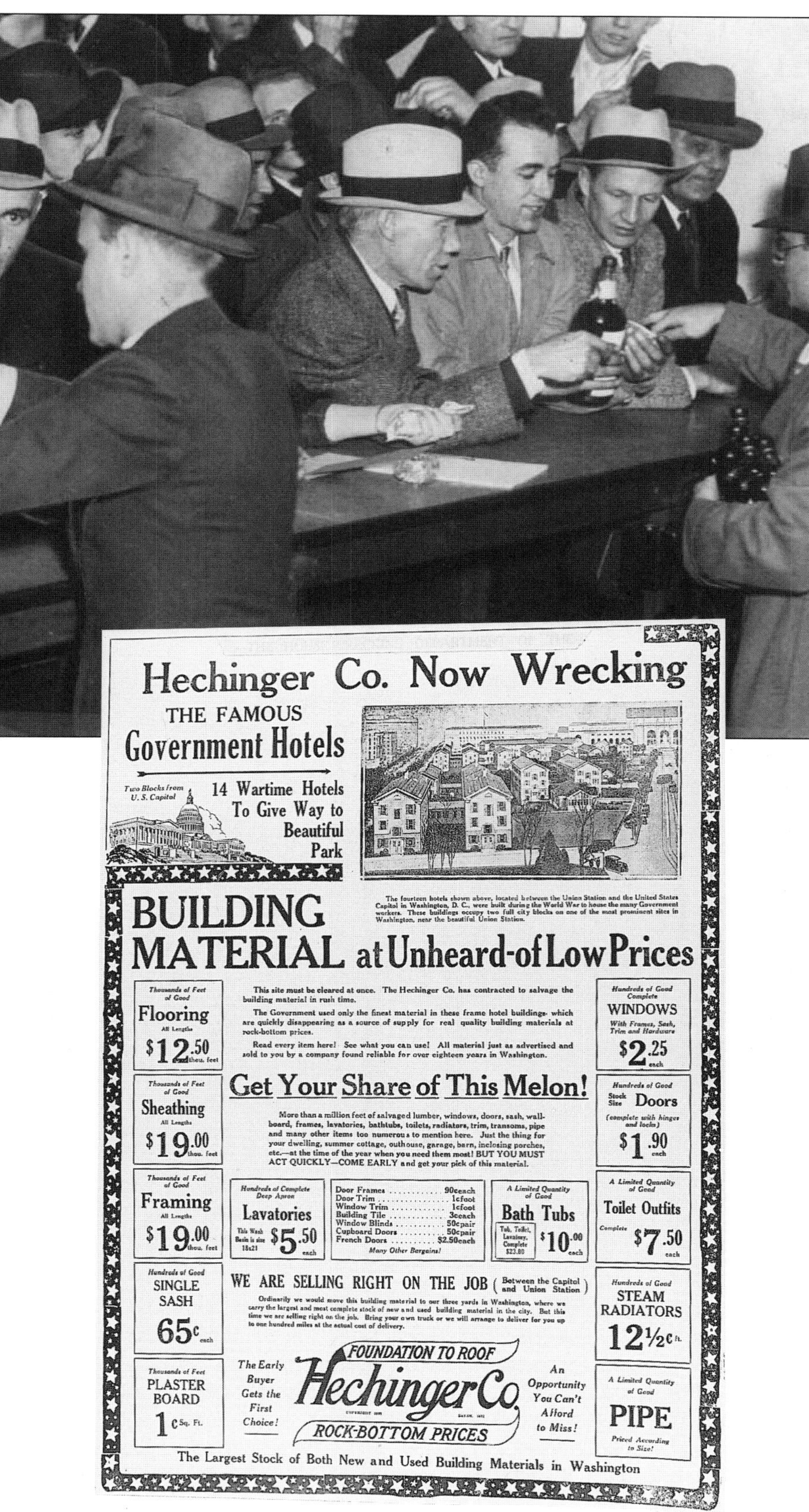

Hechinger Co. in 1931 advertises used building materials about to be salvaged from World War I-era dormitories. Sidney Hechinger's business, begun in 1911 as a wrecking company, branched into selling salvaged as well as new building materials from its first store at 5912 Georgia Ave., N.W. The company participated in major government construction projects before leaving the salvage business to concentrate on hardware and building materials for homeowners. By 1986 it owned 55 stores in six states and the District. The family sold the business in 1997, and two years later the new owners declared bankruptcy.

summer one-sixth of Washington households were receiving help from charitable agencies.

In June the nation's suffering arrived in the capital in the form of some 20,000 World War I veterans and their families. Congress eight years earlier had approved a $1,000 bonus for veterans, but it was not payable until 1945. The veterans needed the money now. When Congress refused, the bonus marchers stayed on, camping downtown and on the Anacostia Flats. An embarrassed President Hoover finally sent the U.S. Army, led by General Douglas MacArthur, to drive them out. MacArthur resorted to tear gas, violence and burning to achieve his mission.

By March 1933, when President Franklin D. Roosevelt was inaugurated, the nation was suffering from an acute crisis of confidence. He immediately closed banks that were still open, to reorganize them, and soon developed federal deposit insurance. After initial deflationary missteps—reductions in veterans' payments and federal salaries—he and his "Brain Trust" began creating an alphabet soup of New Deal programs that drew an army of new people to the capital—economists, lawyers, captains of industry, bankers, social scientists, reformers and intellectuals as well as clerks and typists. Most were white men, but those influencing policy included unprecedented numbers of women and African Americans, including Secretary of Labor Frances Perkins, the War Production Board's Robert Weaver and the National Youth Administration's

Mary McLeod Bethune.

The New Deal began a wave of growth in federal employment and in Washington's population unlike any before. In March 1933, about 63,000 people worked for the federal service. The number climbed to 93,000 just 21 months later and to 104,000 by the end of 1939. Overall, Washington's population expanded from 487,000 in 1930 to 663,000 in 1940. Private home construction resumed, fueled by the need to house the New Dealers, and after the government restored the pay Hoover had cut in 1935, local businesses profited.

In addition to the New Deal policymakers, the newcomers included African Americans leaving an increasingly hostile South for job opportunities. African Americans found employment in the Works Progress Administration and the Civilian Conservation Corps, though they worked in segregated units. WPA and CCC workers built roads and bridges in Rock Creek Park, laid water and sewer pipes for new residential sections, cleared paths for local parks on Roosevelt Island and laid out the grounds of the National Arboretum. White women were invited to work on massive government sewing projects; a training center for domestic workers, begun for both races, quickly became a blacks-only facility. Unemployment lines disappeared, only to return briefly in 1937 when an overconfident FDR cut the WPA in half, laying off 1.5 million relief workers nationwide and triggering a recession.

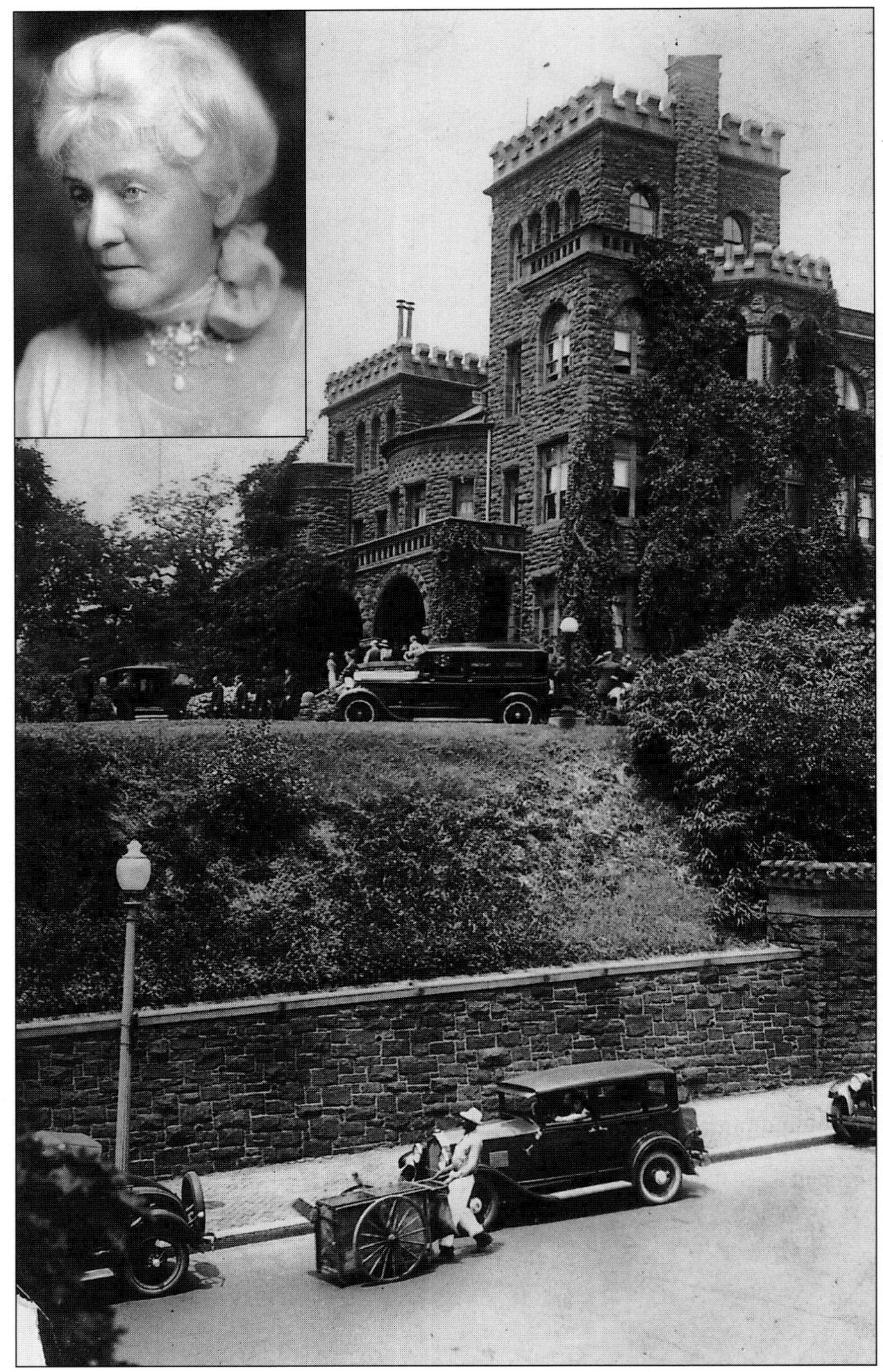

A casket with the remains of Mary Foote Henderson is carried from her red sandstone "castle" on 16th Street, north of Florida Avenue, in 1931. Henderson, wife of a Missouri senator, was prominent during her husband's term in the 1860s. In the late 1880s, the couple returned to Washington, built their fabulous mansion and entertained lavishly. Mary's ambitions to live in a grand neighborhood left a lasting impact: To build Meridian Hill Park, she forced a settlement of blacks dating from the Civil War from the crest of Meridian Hill. In addition, she bought nearby lots and built more than 12 mansions that she rented to embassies and aristocrats. Henderson's Castle was razed in 1949. Part of the estate was redeveloped In 1975 as Beekman Place. All that remains of the castle today is the crenellated red sandstone retaining wall along 16th Street.

Washington's children bore much of the brunt of the Great Depression, and social activists of the 1930s focused a good deal of attention on their needs. Above, poor kids playing with a rudimentary truck on a Georgetown sidewalk are captured by government photographer Carl Mydans for a 1935 series documenting child poverty. As part of a 1936 campaign to persuade the city to build public swimming pools, the *Evening Star* ran the photo, left, of children clambering into an old water-filled horse trough on First and F streets, N.W. Below, boys rest at the Easter Seals' Camp Bald Eagle Hill for children with tuberculosis at 4900 Nichols Avenue, S.E. (now Martin Luther King, Jr., Avenue).

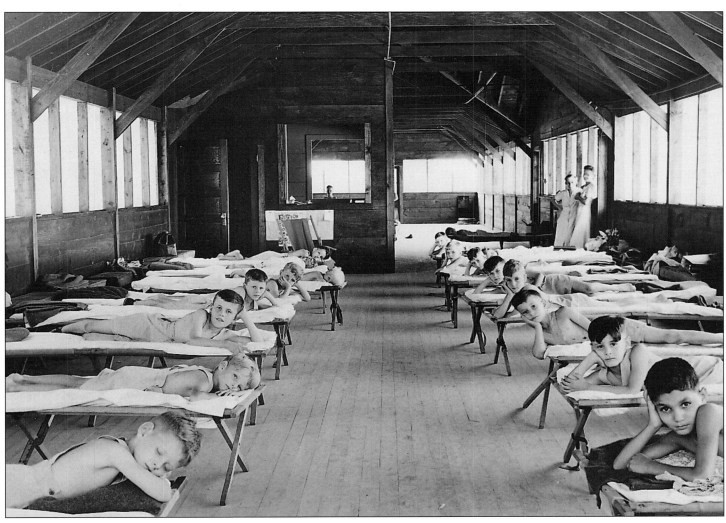

The influx of the early 1930s coincided with an unmatched spate of federal construction that had been recommended in 1901-02 in the McMillan Plan, the major effort to turn the capital into an architectural showplace. This helped bolster the local economy and attracted the unemployed as well as local laborers and craftsmen, who completed at least a dozen major government buildings. Among them: the Department of the Interior, the Department of Agriculture, the Supreme Court, the Library of Congress Annex and the Longworth House Office Building

Residential housing construction continued to boom. New Deal financing innovations helped reduce the risks of private home loans. In 1938, Greenbelt, Md., about 13 miles northeast of the White House, became the Washington area's only federally planned community.

Harry Wardman, the most prolific of the city's many pre-World War II developers, best known for thousands of typically Washington rowhouses, had gone bust in 1930. But after the dust settled, he still owned some lots, so he returned to building middle-class housing, in the Fort Stevens area. At the time of his death in 1938, according to historian James Goode, more than 80,000 residents of the District of Columbia lived in his buildings. Thanks largely to Wardman and his fellow builders, by 1940 the bulk of the metropolitan area's 1 million residents were generally well housed. Their confidence, like most of the nation's,

An unidentified worker in October 1935 displays his first paycheck from the New Deal's Works Progress Administration.

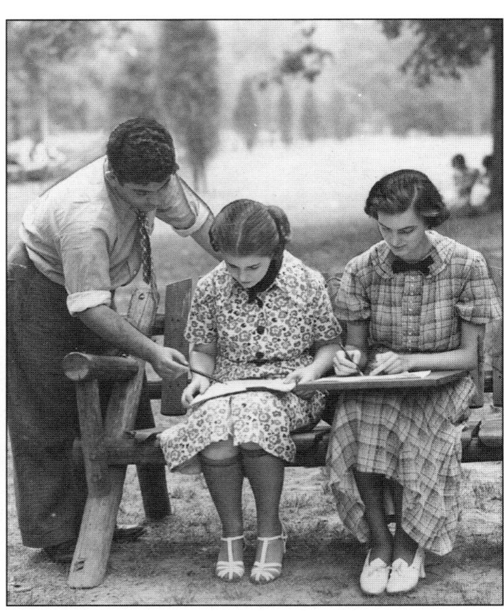

Artist Nelson Rosenberg helps students Mary Louise Kivgia and Eleanor Smith during a 1936 WPA Federal Art Project class in Rock Creek Park.

WPA workers lay new sewer pipes in 1936 at 36th and Albemarle streets, N.W.

Civilian Conservation Corps youths help pull down a tree on Roosevelt Island in 1935 to make room for hiking and riding trails.

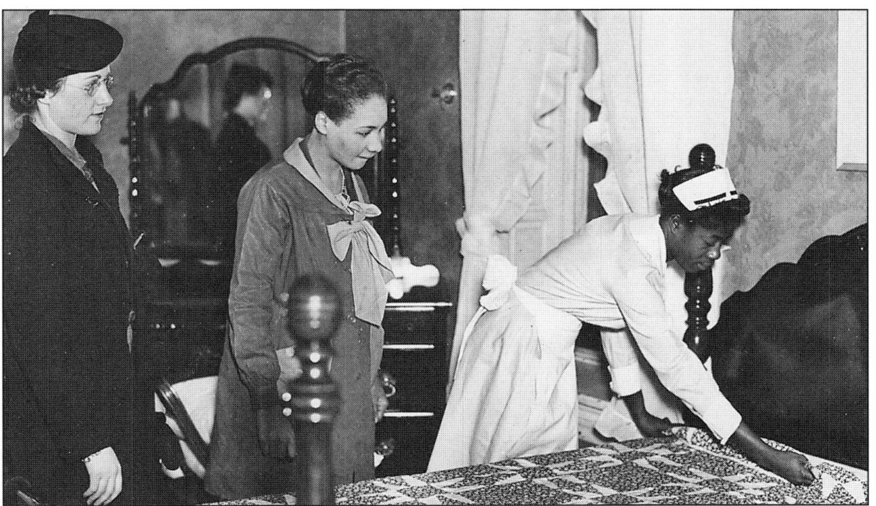

Instructor Thelma Craig, center, watches student Ola Tucker demonstrate bed-making in 1938 at the WPA's Household Workers Training School at O Street, N.W., where "colored" girls were trained for domestic work.

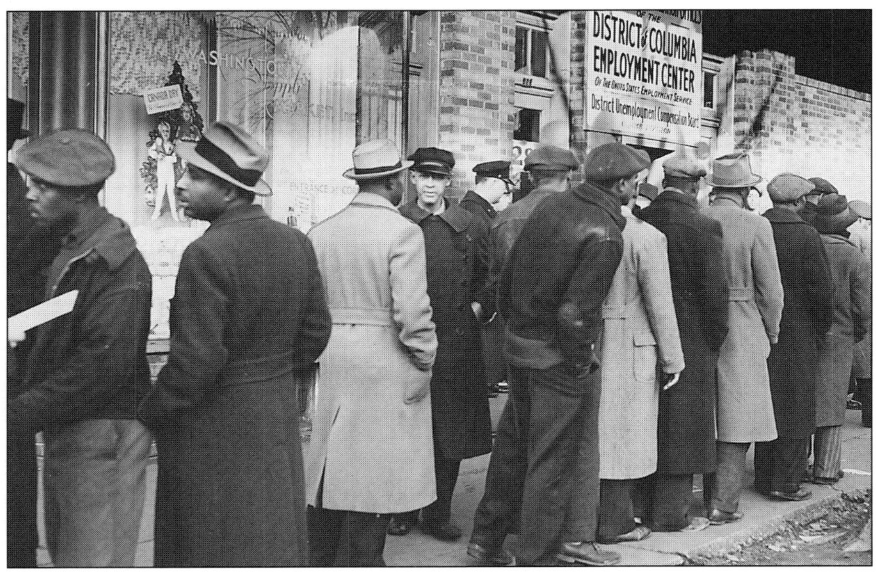

Hundreds of jobless Washingtonians line up in 1937 to file for unemployment compensation.

had been restored.

But poverty was still a stark reality for many, especially migrants from the South. In 1937, more than 11,000 District families still did not have indoor plumbing, and 9,000 homes were lighted by oil lamps. Most of the poor lived in the city's notorious alley dwellings, crowded behind more substantial streetfront houses in the oldest downtown sections.

A byproduct of the New Deal was the displacement of hundreds of poor blacks and whites in Georgetown and Foggy Bottom. Young newcomers, many single with comfortable incomes, saw opportunities in the rundown housing there. Landlords saw a way to unload substandard units to young people eager to live near the action and willing to renovate. Bargains were struck, and the poor tenants were forced to move to already crowded sections of the city. Those who owned their often tiny homes also found the prices offered too good to pass up. As a consequence, communities fractured, and alleys became even more densely populated.

Local politics remained rather docile during the period leading up to World War II, in part because the three presidentially appointed commissioners ran the city, as they had since 1874. There were no local elective offices, and national politics was off limits to federal workers after the Hatch Act (passed in 1939 and in effect until 1993) barred them from partisan political activity. Yet another wet blanket was the requirement that federal workers sign loyalty oaths. With widespread suspicion of the Communist Party—whose radical social agenda was attracting some support—even non-partisan local activity by non-federal workers in the name of social change was relatively risky.

Nonetheless, some worked for racial change. Students and faculty at Howard University's law school set the stage for the great post-war civil rights victories by developing the legal arguments that would overturn legally sanctioned segregation. In the 1930s, Howard students experimented with non-violent tactics, including sit-ins, to desegregate theaters, restaurants and retailers. Other young people worked with the Urban League and the New Negro Alliance to pressure white businessmen to employ African American workers in black neighborhoods. By 1940, they had met with more victories than defeats, gaining jobs for African Americans at Hechinger's, A&P, Heurich Brewing Co., the O Street Market, Washington Laundry and others.

Blacks and whites occasionally socialized together and worked side by side in both the private and federal sectors. But life generally remained rigidly segregated well into the 1950s.

Just as Washington was adjusting to the massive expansion of the 1930s, World War II unleashed another wave of population growth. By 1943, federal employment had climbed to 276,000, four times what it had been just a decade earlier.

The growth actually dated from 1939, when President

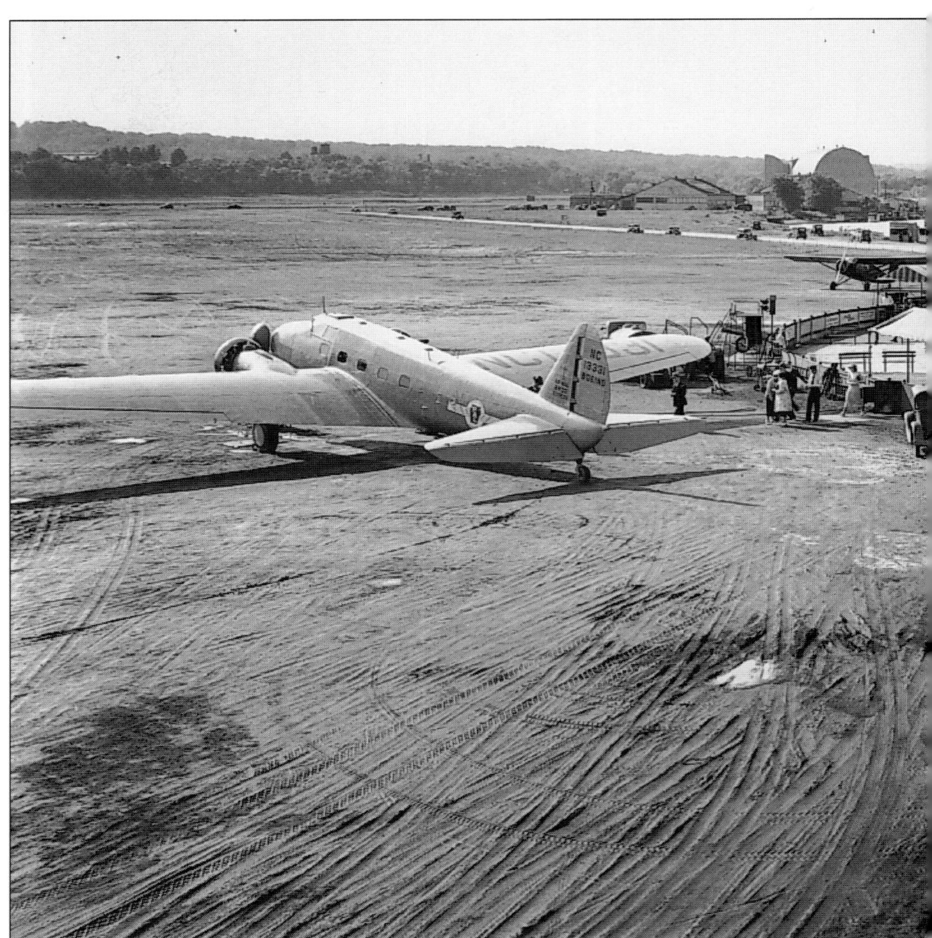

A gentle and hardworking millionaire, Treasury Secretary Andrew Mellon indulged in art and autos. He is pictured in 1928 with his unique "all-aluminum" car. Eight years later, construction began on his gift to the nation: the National Gallery of Art (facing page). Completed in 1941, the gallery was designed by John Russell Pope after the Roman pantheon and was seeded with 121 Old Masters collected by Mellon. His gift gave Washington major standing as a cultural center.

Washington-Hoover Airport, seen here in the mid-1930s, was located where the Pentagon complex is today. The airport still had sod landing strips long after other airports' runways had been paved, and its main runway was bisected by Arlington's Military Road. When a plane was ready to take off or land, the control tower signaled private guards, who dragged chains across the road to keep out traffic. National Airport replaced it in 1941.

Roosevelt quietly began to prepare the nation for conflict. After Great Britain and France went to war with Germany in September, Roosevelt declared a limited national emergency and created the Lend-Lease program to provide military aid to the Allies. The defense buildup grew in the spring of 1940 after the fall of France, with the government advertising nationwide for clerical workers. Construction began on the Pentagon in the summer of 1941, and a host of new agencies were created, including the War Production Board and the Office of Price Administration.

Most new government workers were young women, as men were needed in the military. The women came to type, and by 1942, according to journalist Willard Kiplinger, waste paper was Washington's number one export. Overcrowding, legendary during World War I, was even worse now. Houses and apartments were subdivided into offices. Dormitories were hastily constructed. Boarding houses were jammed. One "government girl," ousted from her Dupont Circle apartment, found herself back in her former bathroom working as a typist, according to *The Washington Post.* World War I-era temporary office buildings, still standing along the Mall, now had similar new neighbors.

Right after Japan attacked Pearl Harbor, Washingtonians prepared for the capital's defense, in case Hitler launched a bombing campaign similar to his air attacks on London. Guards patrolled the bridges and scanned the horizon from atop buildings. Citizens installed blackout curtains and practiced air raid drills. D.C. public school teachers briefly took turns guarding their school buildings at night.

Rationing of food, fuel oil and shoes was particularly frustrating in Washington, where average household income had climbed to $5,000 a year, 25 percent greater than New York City's. Residents had more money than ever to buy fewer goods than ever.

So they spent some of their cash on entertainment. Professional sports began to attract huge crowds as the Washington Redskins, which had moved from Boston in 1937 and won the world championship that year, became the preeminent team in town. Dances and movies (largely to keep up the morale of troops) were nightly occurrences. Young women outnumbered young civilian men, but not the constant crowds of men in uniform. When government agencies shut down in late afternoon, wrote journalist David Brinkley, "the streets looked like a women's college campus between classes." War agencies tried to help the young women through their loneliness and dislocation. They were trucked to military bases and welcomed at the Stage Door Canteen. Local churches and synagogues organized picnics and parties for them.

When the war ended, Washington had its new Pentagon (finished in 1943), several new highways and bridges and a large influx of returning

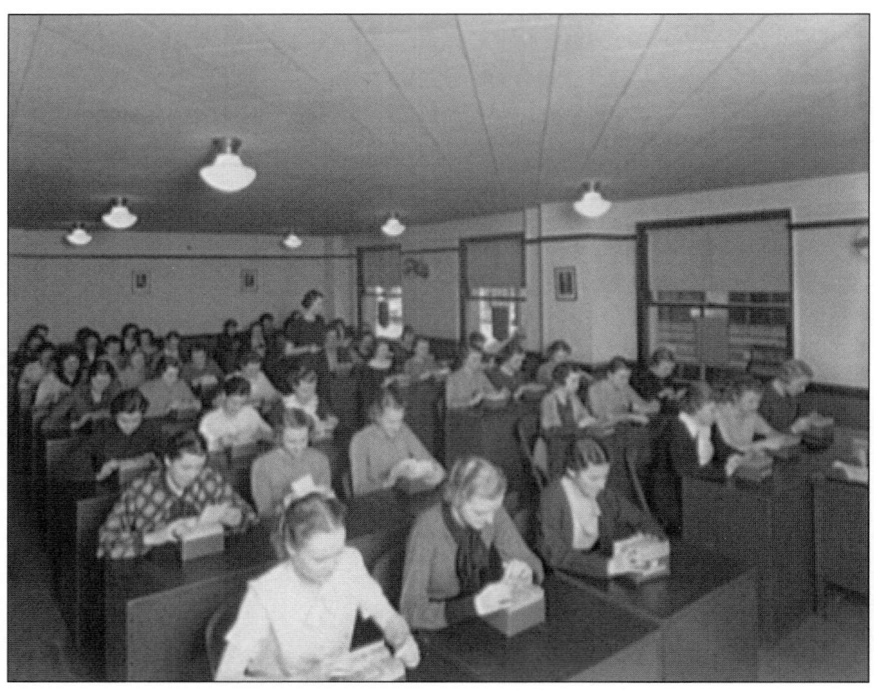

Despite a new acceptance of professional women by New Deal leaders, the capital of the 1930s was a bastion of traditional women's roles, with choices for most women ranging from secretary, teacher or nurse to mother/housewife. Young women of the Washington School for Secretaries practice filing cards in a mid-1930s class.

The Electric Institute of Washington, organized to persuade consumers to use electric appliances, holds a 1938 cooking class at the Boro Theatre (now Bethesda Theatre Cafe).

With a return to relative affluence thanks to New Deal programs and growing federal employment, Washingtonians enjoyed small pleasures. Above, a Sanitary Grocery (later Safeway) chain official signals the start of the 1935 Sanico Bowling league tournament, pitting the Peas Division against the Superintendent's Office. At top right, Vendor Harry Reynolds hawks school pennants and badges at the 1937 citywide drill competition for high school cadets, where 20,000 filled Griffith Stadium to see Western (now Duke Ellington) High School win first place. At right, Ninth Street, N.W., north of E, offers cheap drinks and cheap thrills at Jimmy Lake's nightclub and strip-teasers and off-color comedians at the Gayety. (The capital never developed a New York-style "cafe society," according to journalist Willard Kiplinger, because Washingtonians preferred socializing at each others' homes, where the "favorite indoor sport is conversation.") At bottom right, 1938 Christmas shoppers clog the intersection at 12th and F streets. Below, skaters take to the ice in 1941 at the Chevy Chase Ice Palace on Connecticut Ave. at Yuma St., N.W.

GIs who wanted to study at local universities under the GI Bill. The ironies of fighting the racism of Hitler's Germany were not lost on local African Americans and others working for full civil rights. A new energy brought a series of high-level studies and publications decrying the racism that denied African Americans their full American rights. New veterans organizations, such as the left-leaning American Veterans Committee, took up the crusade for social justice.

As GIs returned to what was now the capital of the free world, more families sprouted and the suburbs continued to boom. There was a sense of contentedness, almost complacency, among most white Washingtonians. But the unmet promises of the American dream, the cause for which so many fought overseas, left many African Americans and others poised for new battles.

An unidentified clerk at the Standard Drug Store, at 1748 7th St., N.W., helps a customer in 1938. The white-owned store was one of many in black neighborhoods that were boycotted or pressured by the New Negro Alliance to hire or promote African Americans. The Alliance's slogan, "Don't buy where you can't work," was adopted by similar groups in other cities. Between 1933 and 1941, the Alliance persuaded the *Evening Star* to hire black newsboys and convinced Hahn's Shoe Store, Woolworth's and High's Ice Cream stores, among others, to add black clerks. The group's nonviolent tactics were adopted by succeeding generations of civil rights activists.

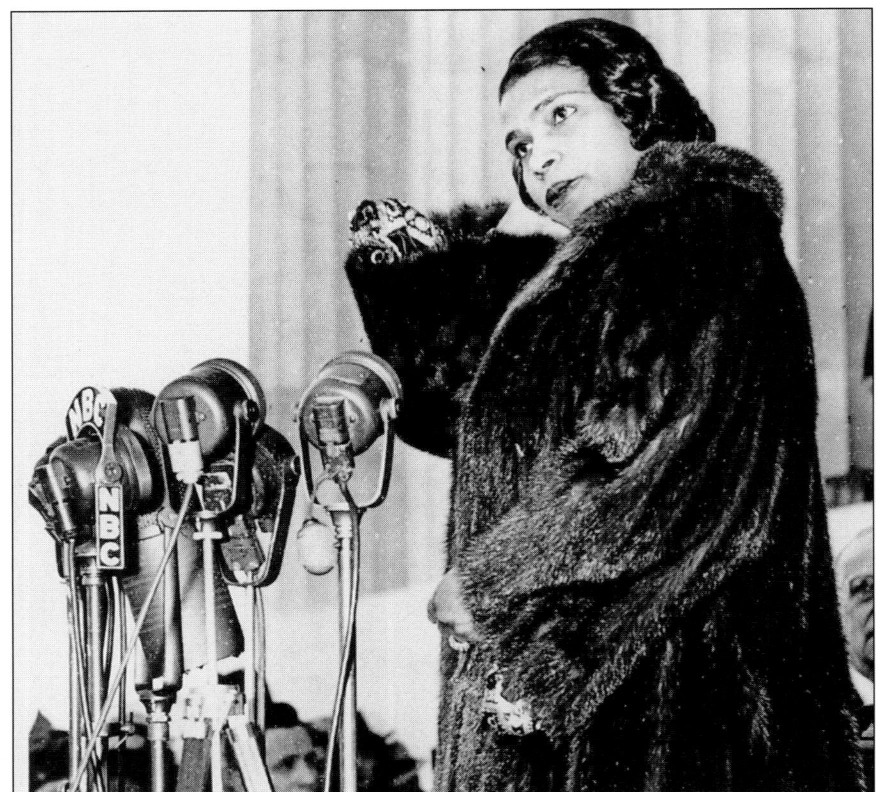

Celebrated contralto Marian Anderson surveys the thousands who came to hear her 1939 concert at the Lincoln Memorial. Washington discrimination became a national embarrassment that year when the Daughters of the American Revolution refused to let Anderson sing in Constitution Hall. The white school board said she could use Central High (now Cardozo) School's auditorium, but only as an exception to its whites-only policy. Secretary of the Interior Harold Ickes immediately authorized Anderson's use of the Lincoln Memorial.

The Agriculture Department was long home to an array of farm operations despite its location on the Mall. In 1940, it still had chicken pens and greenhouses at 12th and Constitution, N.W.

Specialists prepare cotton standards in 1939.

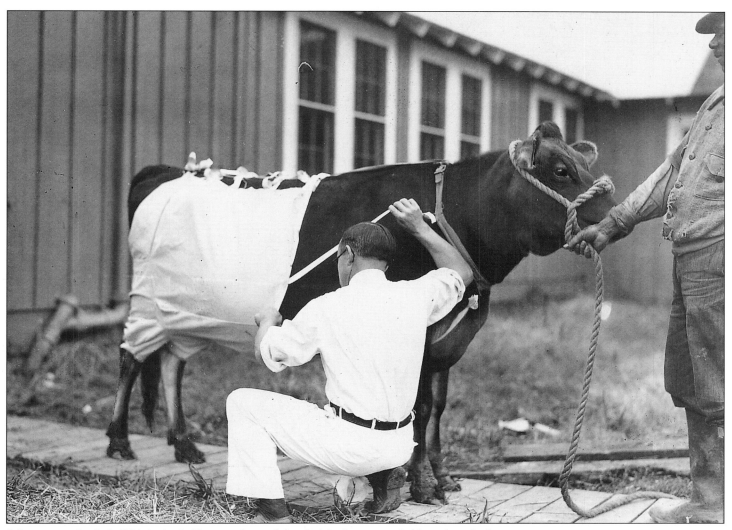

A department scientist in 1934 checks the bloomers of a cow for cattle ticks that were needed for an investigation.

J. Edgar Hoover, right, chats with Harvey's Restaurant Manager Julius Lully during a 1937 breakfast for the American Restaurant Association. Born and bred in Washington, the FBI director was a popular local figure, eating lunch at the Mayflower Hotel and dinner at Harvey's virtually every day and betting at Maryland's Laurel and Bowie racetracks. According to journalists Jack Lait and Lee Mortimer, Hoover was a prankster who once printed up "wanted" flyers with a photo of Lully, a friend, in his World War I uniform. He had them posted near Lully's country place, prompting the local sheriff to arrest Lully. When Lully gave Hoover as a reference, Hoover denied knowing him.

RCA introduces its "new, simplified radio facsimile receiver-printer," or fax machine, to Washington in 1938. The device, developed in the 1920s, was intended to "flash pictures, news bulletins, and other text through the air and into the home." Soon after, RCA made the machines available to radio broadcasters, who proved more receptive than home consumers.

Contestants in the 1940 Soap Box Derby prepare to race down a 1,000-foot course on Pennsylvania Ave. at Texas Ave., S.E. William F. Jennings, 15, was the fastest of the 205 racers. His car "Stuff" cost $9.75 to build and covered the distance in 29.3 seconds.

Traffic clogs the intersection of 14th St. and Pennsylvania Ave., N.W., in August 1941. The nation was not at war yet, but President Roosevelt's preparedness work and support for the Allies had added even more men and women to a city swollen by New Deal agencies.

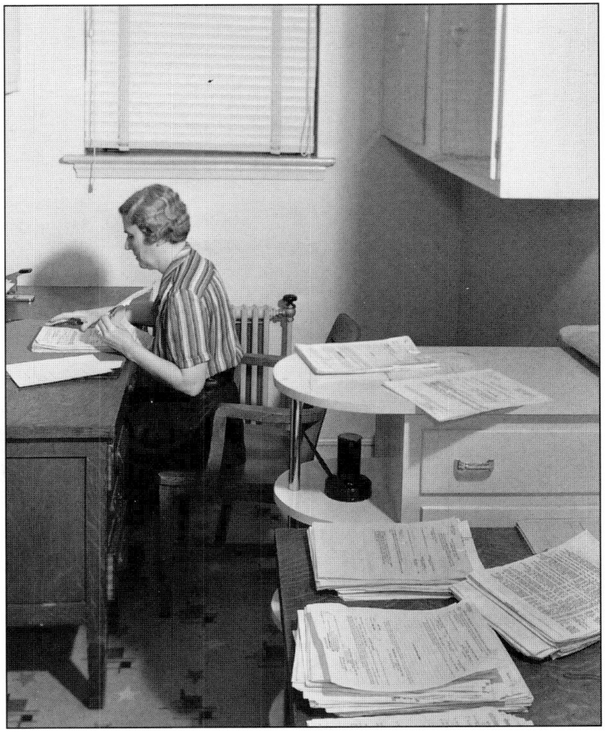

The Office of Lend-Lease Administration, which provided military aid to the Allies, jammed desks, files, phones and workers into every available nook of a commandeered apartment, even in the kitchen at right.

The tight housing situation spurred government experiments in practically instant shelter. In late 1941, the metal trailer at right, with its homey interior (center right), provided 380 square feet of living space in two rooms and a kitchenette designed for a married couple. Below, Federal Loan Administrator Jesse Jones sprays concrete on metal mesh supported by inflated balloons at an experimental defense housing project in Falls Church, Va., in late 1941. Once the concrete dried, the balloons were deflated, leaving a hemispheric shelter. The finished house (bottom) was made of two balloons joined at the center. The interior was divided into two bedrooms, living room with fireplace, kitchen and bathroom. According to news reports, consumers clamored for the houses, but poor financing shut down the project.

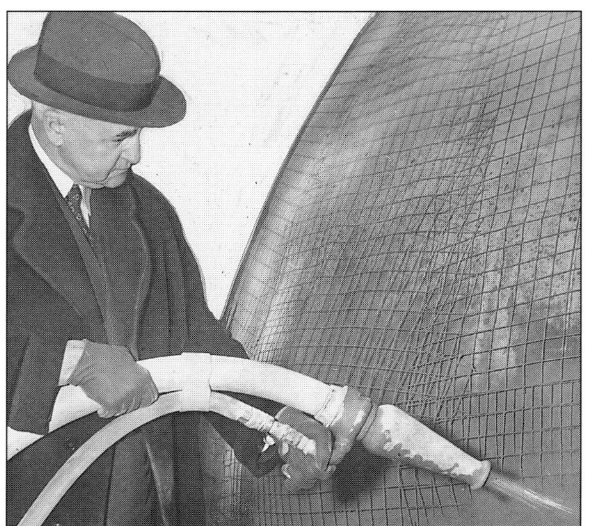

This 1941 view from atop the Washington Monument shows a few of the World War I-era "temporary" buildings that remained on the Mall and other open spaces well beyond the end of that war and into the next. Angling away from the "tempos" is Virginia Avenue.

When Tokyo attacked Pearl Harbor on December 7, 1941, and President Roosevelt declared war on Japan, Washingtonians feared for the city. U.S. Army scouts (left) protect the Rosslyn, Va., entrance to Key Bridge from saboteurs on Dec. 8, 1941. Area citizens (right) are sworn in as fire wardens, part of a large number of volunteers loosely organized by a retired colonel into a Civilian Defense Committee. With reports of London during the Blitz fresh in their minds, Washingtonians began hoarding food and weapons and scanning the skies and their neighborhoods for enemies.

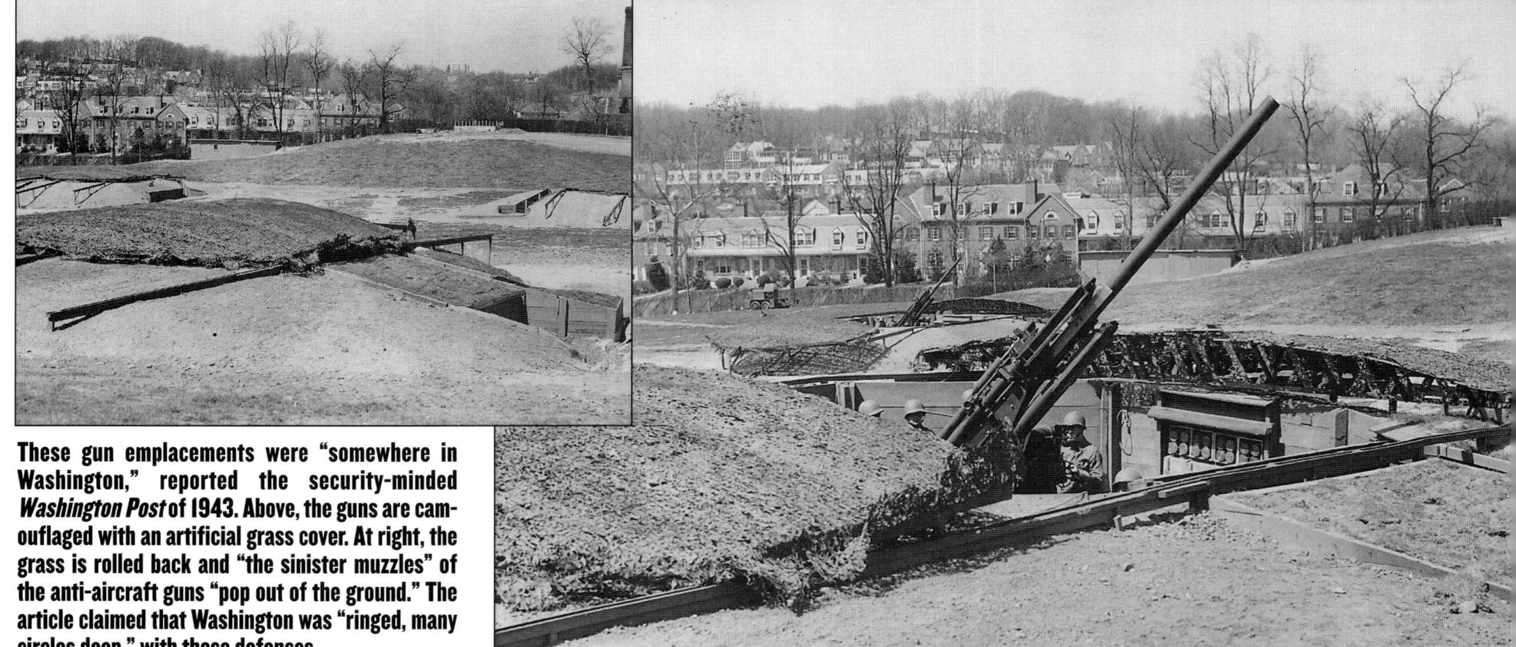

These gun emplacements were "somewhere in Washington," reported the security-minded *Washington Post* of 1943. Above, the guns are camouflaged with an artificial grass cover. At right, the grass is rolled back and "the sinister muzzles" of the anti-aircraft guns "pop out of the ground." The article claimed that Washington was "ringed, many circles deep," with these defenses.

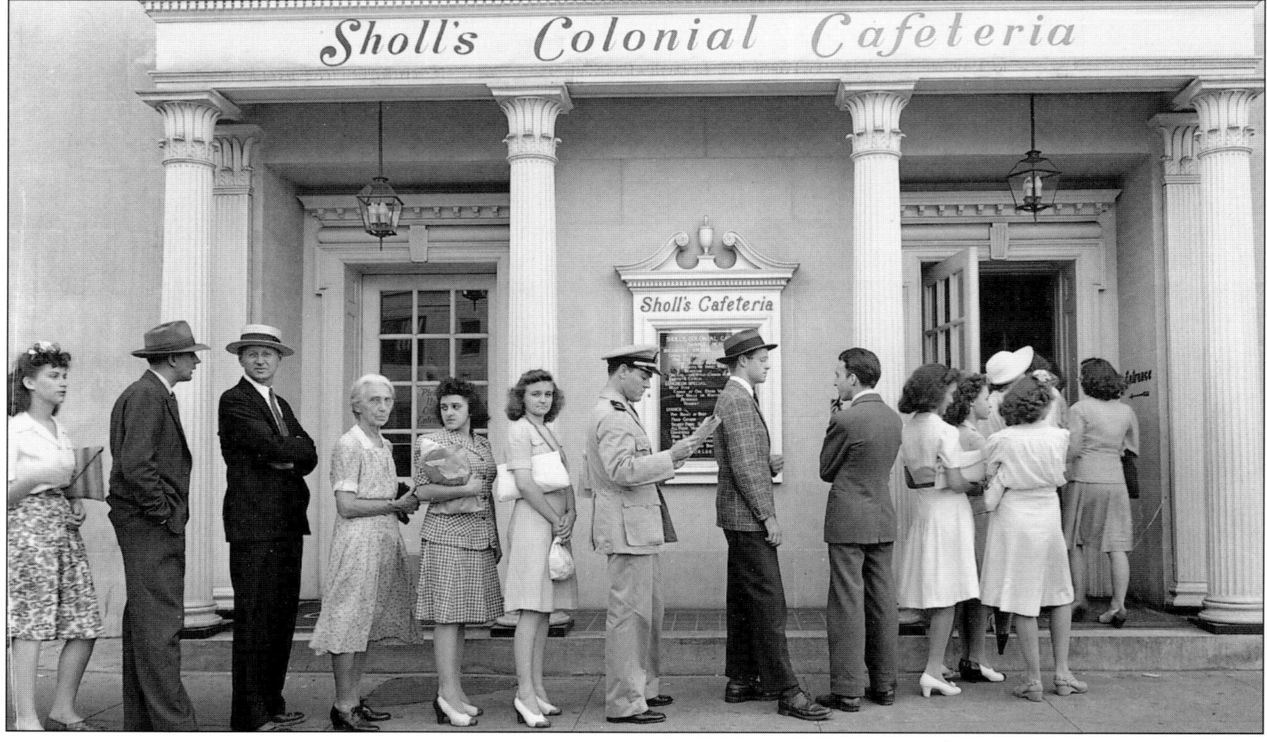

Wartime in Washington meant even more crowding and more lines. Dinner seekers queued up at Sholl's Colonial Cafeteria on Connecticut Avenue reportedly are served at a rate of one a minute.

At right are some of the nearly 300 phone operators and supervisors who handled the Pentagon's switchboard in September 1942, shortly after War Department personnel began moving into the still unfinished building.

Among the first commodities declared essential for the war effort—and thus strictly rationed—were rubber and building materials. As a result, the driver above for Tru Blu Beer Corp. returns to an earlier era by using an old beer wagon and a pair of sturdy dray horses in February 1942. At left, women line up outside a downtown shoe store in 1943 on the last day that a shoe ration coupon is valid.

Living and breathing space proved even more elusive after Pearl Harbor. In July 1943, a young mother and son (at top) find living space on a houseboat anchored in the Potomac. Above, infant Joey Massman sleeps in the bureau drawer of his parents' efficiency apartment in 1943. For the thousands of young and single "government girls" drawn to the war effort, the scarcest commodity was privacy. At right, two young women in 1943 "entertain" their guests in the card room of a government residence for women.

With so many government girls and transient servicemen, the city experienced a surge in nightlife. Above, Washington-born actress Helen Hayes (hand raised) tells young women about the program of the National Stage Door Canteen, seen at left on its opening night in 1942.

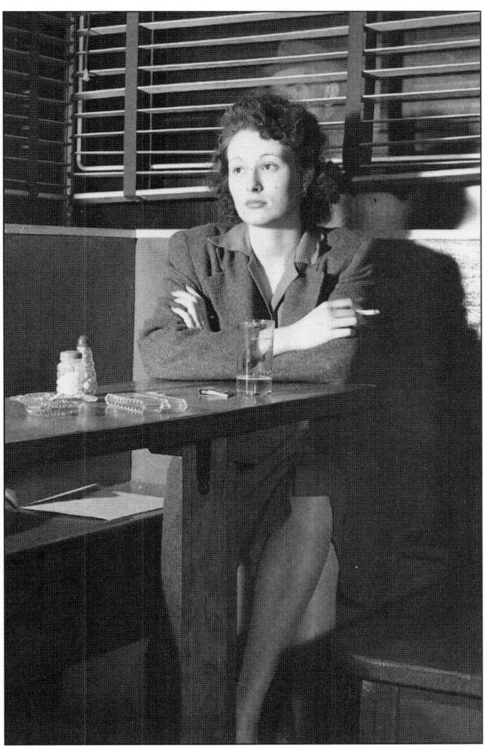

Young "jitterbugs," at left, take the floor at an Elks' Club dance in 1943. The young woman above, reported government photographer Esther Bubley, has come to the Sea Grill to be picked up: "I come in here pretty often . . . mostly with another girl. We drink beer and talk, and of course we keep our eyes open. You'd be surprised at how often nice, lonesome soldiers ask Sue the waitress to introduce them to us."

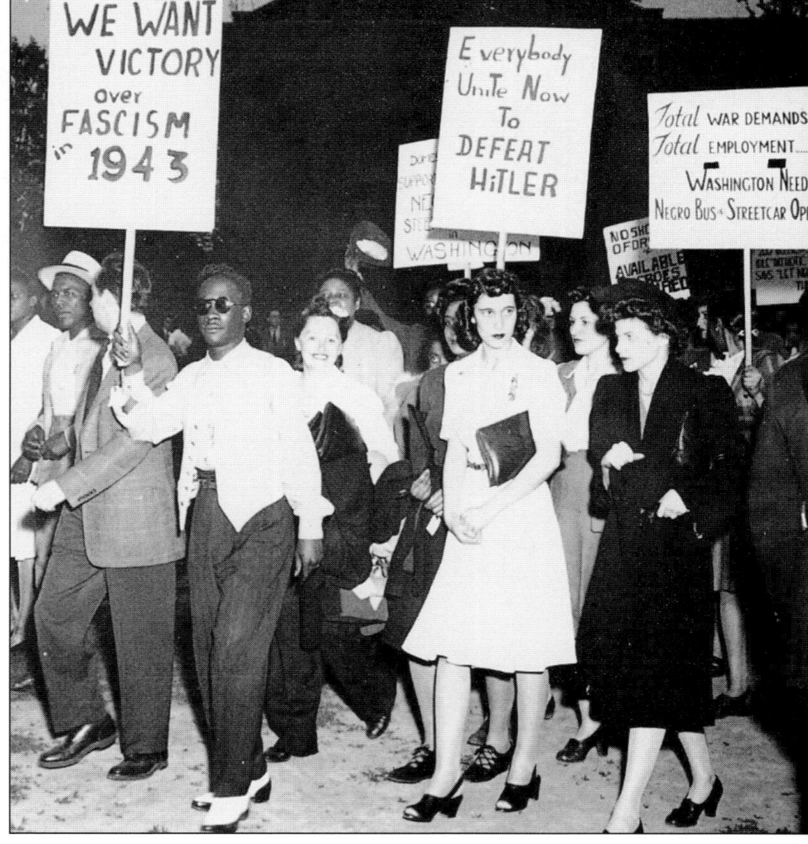

Despite the fact that we were fighting a war infused with racism, Washington remained strictly segregated. As seen in the mirror above the Peoples Drug Store lunch counter (top left), only whites were served in 1942. As in World War I, white women such as Mary Mills (top right) of the Arnold Operated line in suburban Virginia benefited when white men left for the military. At right, an integrated group of demonstrators protests Capitol Transit's refusal to hire African American bus drivers and streetcar operators as replacements. African American families, however, were not discriminated against when it came to accepting shortages and sacrificing family members. The Southwest resident above poses by her 1943 Victory Garden; the stars in her window represent two family members away at war.

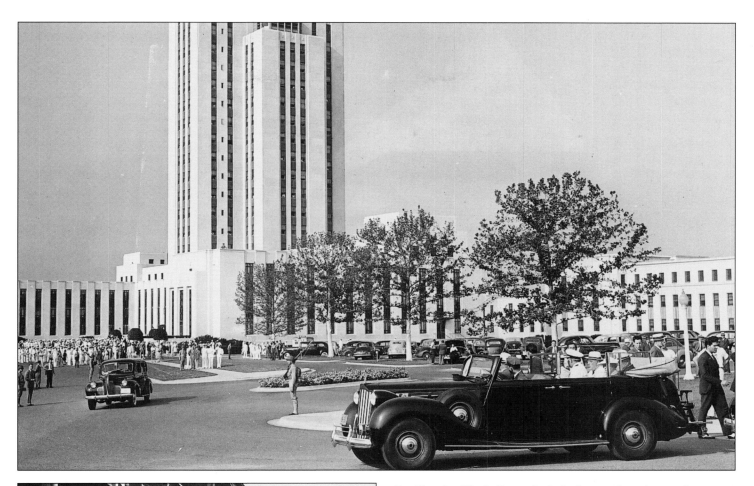

President Franklin D. Roosevelt, in back seat of touring car, leaves Bethesda after dedicating the Naval Hospital in 1942. With the National Institutes of Health's first installations built just across Wisconsin Avenue four years earlier, Bethesda was among the first suburbs to absorb a large federal facility. During the war, the government relocated 11 civilian agencies—the Securities and Exchange Commission, for example, moved to Philadelphia, the Patent Office to Richmond—but the city still could not find space for all of its war-related workers.

Members of a 1943 Senate subcommittee inspect "Washerwoman's Row" in Logan Court, an alley community near the Capitol. New Deal reformers had formed the Alley Dwelling Authority in 1934 to rid the city of such substandard housing in interior alleys of old downtown blocks. The original deadline for demolishing them was July 1944, but the crushing need for housing led to an extension to 1955, and some slum-like alleys lingered through the 1970s.

The Water Gate barge, a floating bandshell for public performances moored beside Arlington Memorial Bridge, is the venue for a National Symphony Orchestra Concert featuring a young Frank Sinatra. Below, Sinatra signs autographs for a mob of young female admirers.

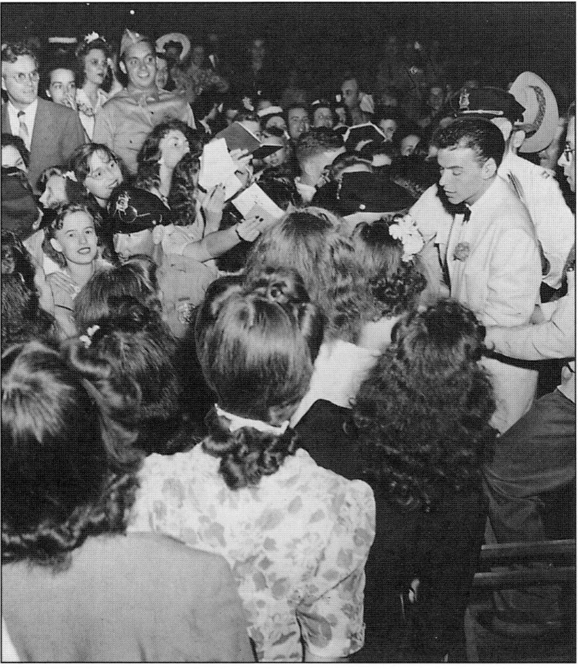

After the longest series of presidential terms in U.S. history, Franklin Roosevelt died in April 1945 in Warm Springs, Ga. Thousands of mourners watched his casket make its way from Union Station to the White House. A month later the war in Europe was over and the war in Asia was nearly won. World War II also had ended the Great Depression.

V-J (Victory in Japan) Day, on August 14, 1945, sent cheering crowds into Washington streets.

Two hours after his separation from the Army on December 26, 1945, former Corporal Robert R. Russell arrives at his home at 230 15th Street, N.E., where his slightly skeptical son greets him. From left are the ex-soldier's sister, parents and brother. The toddler's mother was unable to be there because she worked as a telephone operator on the late shift.

CHAPTER 5
THE LURE OF THE SUBURBS

Private Charles Vessels of Fort Belvoir gives Marion Merriman of Arlington Farms a ride on the handlebars of his bike near the Tidal Basin in 1946.

When World War II ended, the capital held joyous celebrations and then sought to return to normal life—to provide jobs and education for returning veterans, to snap up formerly scarce goods, to enjoy a movie or bowling or jazz. But in small ways and large, from the decline of the trolley to Cold War fears of atomic attack, what was "normal" would soon change.

Some of the changes were long overdue, especially those involving racial justice. When President Harry Truman desegregated the armed forces in 1948, African Americans gained a new structure for personal advancement centuries after they had proved their ability as soldiers. That same year the Supreme Court ruled that race-restrictive housing covenants could no longer be enforced, though it would take more time, and more official prodding, before Washington's real estate and banking barons would open housing to all.

Perhaps the broadest change, however, was the move to the suburbs. New federal agencies went up beyond District lines. Many white war workers chose to continue working in Washington but to live beyond its boundaries, while retailers and other service businesses moved with their clienteles. As a result, a sprawling Washington area would focus more on huge shopping malls and cars. It would experience unprecedented demand for suburban housing, schools and roads. In part because most suburban builders refused to sell to African Americans, the suburban exodus left most blacks behind in a decaying city, changing the District's racial complexion more sharply in the 1950s alone than in the previous 150 years.

A few government agencies had already gone suburban. The Pentagon, which would shortly have a war in Korea on its hands, had been built in Arlington, Va., during World War II. The National Cancer Institute had gone to Bethesda, Md., shortly before the war, to be followed by the

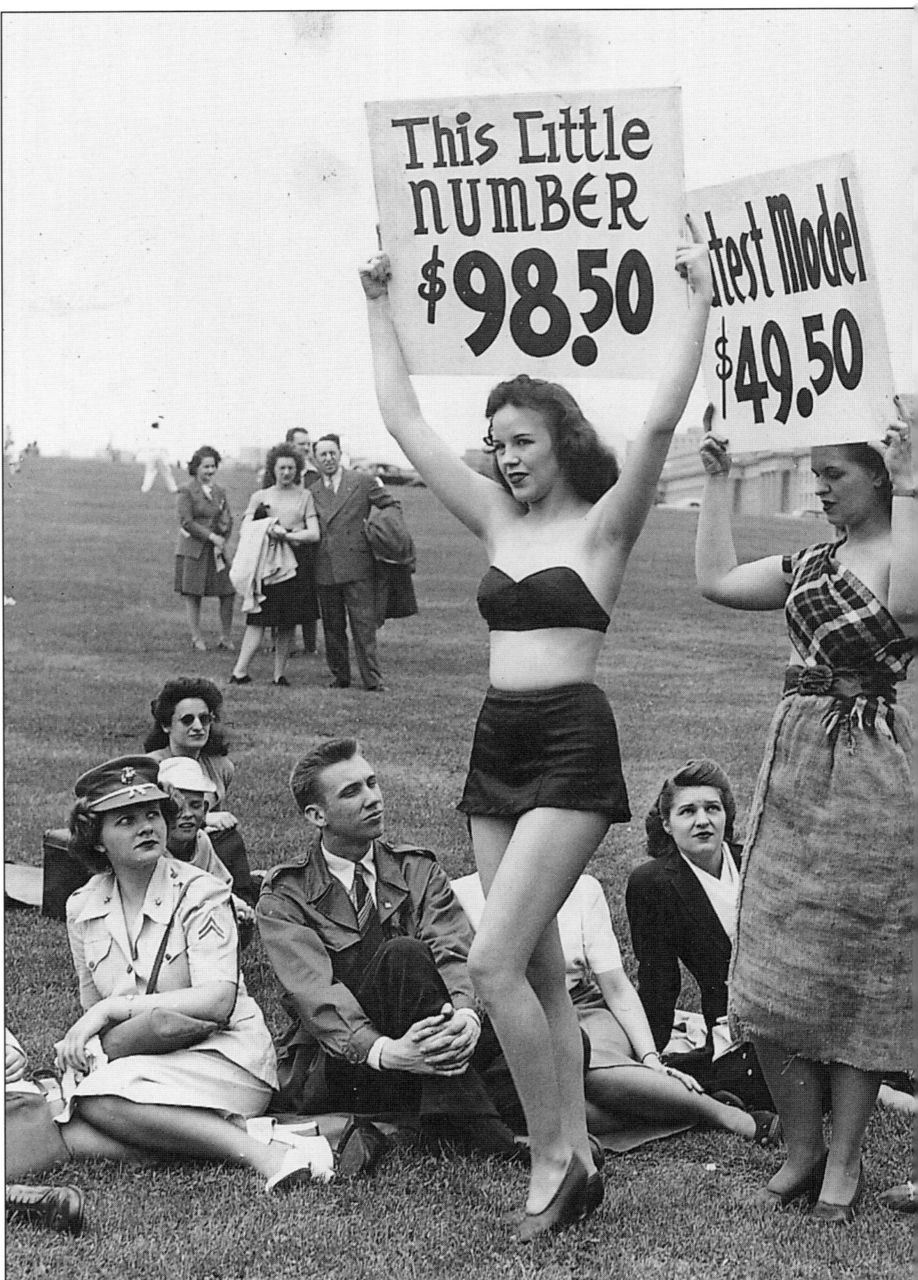

Soon after V-J Day, the city began returning to a more normal life, though one that was not problem-free. Sharon and Lynn Terry and Chad and Timothy Paterson (above), fearful of runaway inflation as consumer goods finally become available again, demonstrate to save wartime price controls—lest a bathing suit suddenly cost $98.50. At upper right, a float of homeless veterans leads a May 1946 parade sponsored by the Commissioners' Veterans' Housing Committee to urge citizens to rent or sell living space to GIs. The continued scarcity of building materials and the reluctance of many war workers to give up Washington life left returning vets with few options. To conserve cloth needed for military uniforms, the War Production Board in 1942 had prohibited women's all-around pleats, balloon sleeves and long skirts. At right, Stanley Marcus, chief of the WPB apparel section and son and eventual successor to Neiman-Marcus co-founder Herbert Marcus, explains the rules. In 1947 the restrictions were lifted, and women thrilled to the luxurious lengths and drape of the "New Look," as seen in the 1948 Garfinckel's fashion shoot at far right by photographer Toni Frissell.

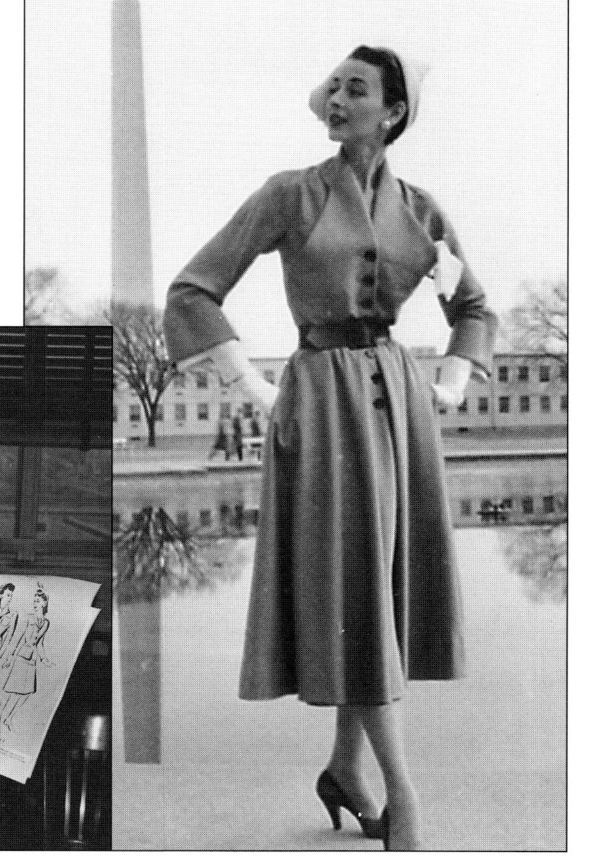

Bethesda Naval Hospital in 1942 and by 10 more National Institutes of Health research units and the National Library of Medicine in the post-war era.

Now, with the advent of the Cold War, three major new agencies geared up—the Central Intelligence Agency, the Atomic Energy Commission and the National Security Agency. By 1962, all three were in the suburbs, and dozens more would follow. As a result, the Washington area's new normality included "edge cities" that developed around the Beltway where Washingtonians worked, lived, ate, slept, played, shopped, procreated and recreated without ever entering the District of Columbia.

Following their customers, Hecht's and Woodward & Lothrop, the city's two largest department stores, opened their first suburban branches in the late 1940s. Washington's first suburban shopping mall, developer Theodore Lerner's Wheaton Plaza in Montgomery County, opened in 1960 and was followed by many others, including another Lerner project, Tyson's Corner, developed at a former country crossroads in Fairfax County, Va., named for a farm once owned by William Tyson.

The auto and the Capital Beltway made important differences in suburbia's growth. The last run by a Washington trolley was made in 1962, but cars had won the transportation fight more than a decade earlier. By 1950, the Washington area had the highest average number of cars per household—2.1—of any city in the world. When the Capital Beltway, the circumferential highway built eight miles from the White House, opened in 1964, it was hailed as a solution for local and through traffic alike. In fewer than 10 years, however, "Washington's Noose" was jammed during rush hours, and area officials had long since drafted plans to add lanes and build a subway/rail system as well to relieve the congestion.

Racial issues also played a role in the flight from the city. District parents watched as suburban development lured whites away while another wave of black migrants flocked to the capital. White schools remained open, even though enrollments tumbled and neighborhoods changed complexion. Black schools, often older and smaller to begin with, became overcrowded and ill-equipped—clearly no longer "equal" to the white schools, as mandated by the prevailing "separate but equal" doctrine.

Black parents wanted to send their children to comfortable, well-equipped neighborhood schools that happened to be designated "white." They brought a lawsuit, *Bolling v. Sharpe,* that was folded into *Brown v. Board of Education,* the landmark case in which the Supreme Court in 1954 outlawed officially segregated schools. Washington was one of the first jurisdictions to desegregate. Although there was only modest initial resistance, over the next few years white parents increasingly opted for whiter public schools in the suburbs.

Education, moreover, was just one of several arenas for Washington racial controversies. Protestors of both races organized

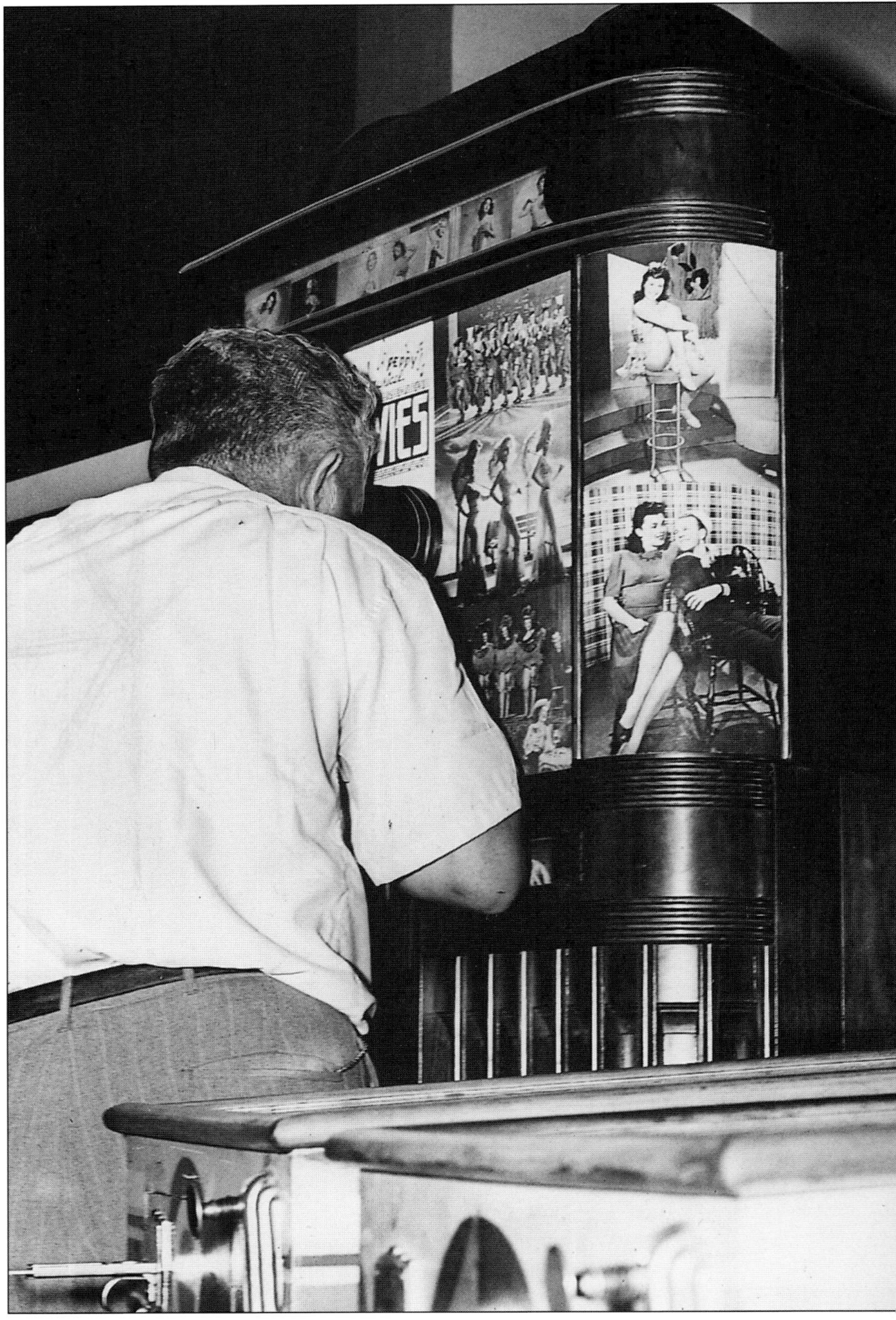

A customer enjoys a peep show on Ninth Street, home of cheap and quick entertainment. This picture accompanied an August 1946 *Washington Post* story by Dorothea Andrews on the return to everyday life. Among now-vanished city sounds that she noted: "the cry of newshawks, the shrill policeman's whistle . . . the clang and sighs of streetcars, the click of typewriters echoing from office buildings . . ."

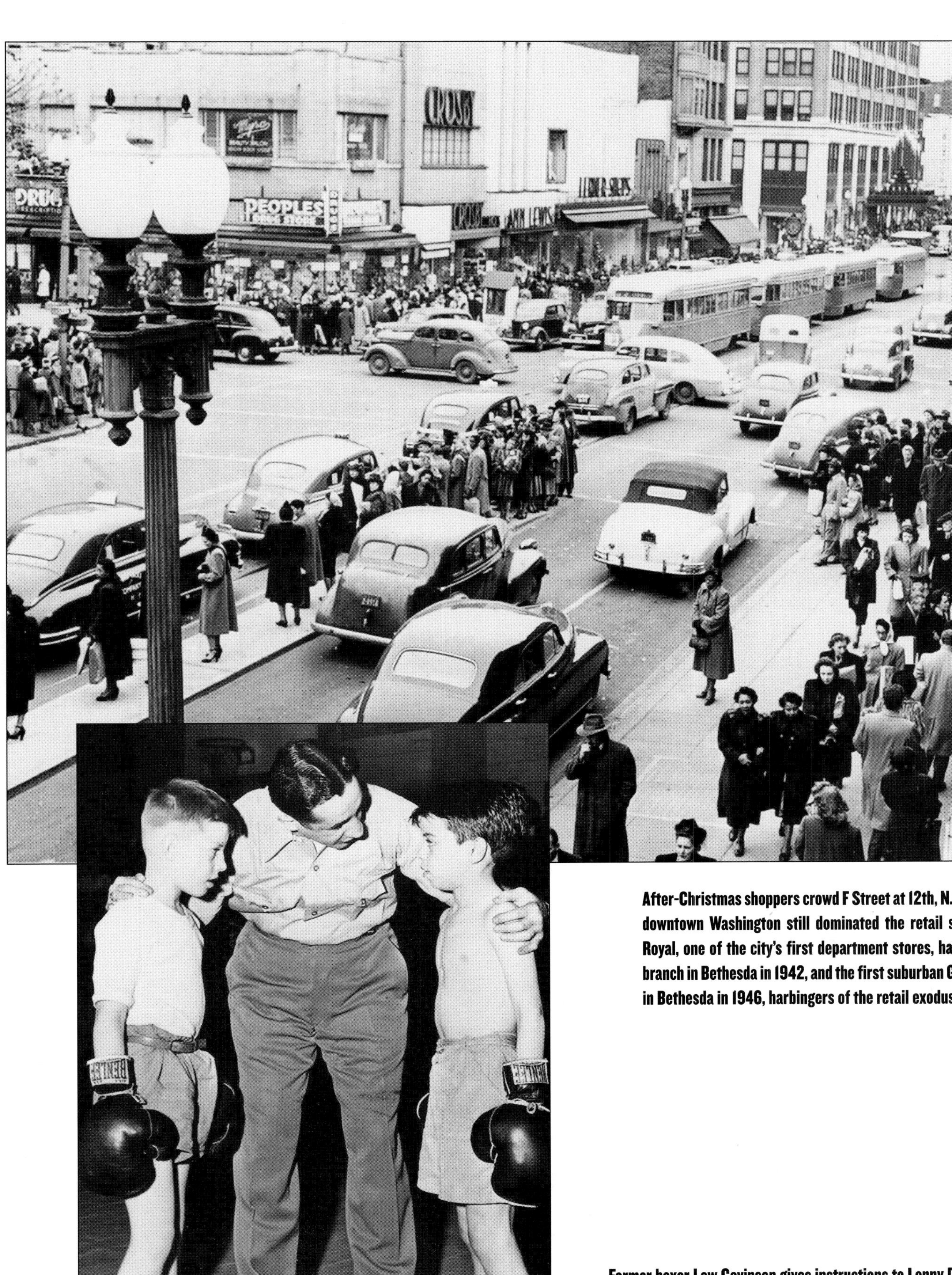

After-Christmas shoppers crowd F Street at 12th, N.W., in 1946, when downtown Washington still dominated the retail scene. But Palais Royal, one of the city's first department stores, had opened a small branch in Bethesda in 1942, and the first suburban Giant Food opened in Bethesda in 1946, harbingers of the retail exodus from the city.

Former boxer Lew Gevinson gives instructions to Lenny Davis, left, and Lee Ganey at the Boys Club of Washington in 1946. Returned GIs helped restore a sense of normality to such city youths as a new social problem called juvenile delinquency had begun to take hold.

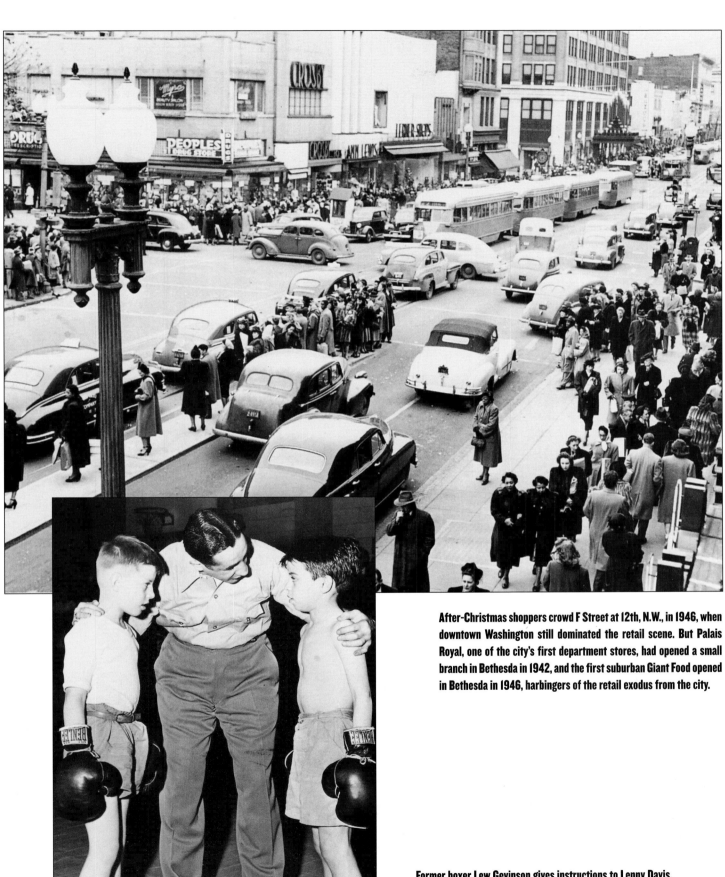

civil rights demonstrations that were larger and better publicized than those of the pre-war years. The National Theatre, under intense pressure to desegregate, turned itself into a movie house in 1948, only to reopen four years later under new ownership without racial restrictions. In 1953, the Supreme Court ruled in the Thompson's Restaurant case that 19th century laws guaranteeing access to public accommodations by all "well-behaved persons" regardless of race were still in effect, despite their having mysteriously disappeared from the D.C. Code of 1901. Now, thanks to pioneering sit-ins led by law student Pauli Murray in the early 1940s and to protests later headed by Mary Church Terrell and her multiracial committee, African Americans could expect to be served at any downtown restaurant, to try on clothes at any downtown store and to attend any movie theater. A few years later, they won the right to ride roller coasters at Glen Echo Amusement Park in suburban Montgomery County and to be served at suburban lunch counters.

But discrimination in housing persisted despite the 1948 Supreme Court ruling. The seeds of that discrimination had been firmly planted when the New Deal created the Home Owners Loan Act of 1933 to bail out mortgages in danger of default, according to historian Kenneth T. Jackson. Subsequent legislation and regulations creating low-cost guaranteed loans for veterans and others required lenders to minimize risk. Bureaucrats of the Federal Housing Administration helpfully

defined minimizing risk as favoring white families in white neighborhoods and steering clear of "inharmonious racial or nationality groups."

FHA appraisers created secret "Residential Security Maps" of cities, including Washington. Top-rated areas, where the housing was new and the residents were "Americans of the better class"—i.e., predominantly white Protestants—were color-coded green. Blue areas were still desirable but had "reached their peak." Yellow was reserved for housing in decline because of age, obsolescence or change of style, with lower rents attracting "an undesirable element." Finally, areas where blacks lived, or where housing was deteriorated, were colored red (the origin of the term "redlining").

Although the last such maps apparently were made in 1942, the reasoning behind them lingered much longer. In the 1950s, real estate firms and banks still quietly colluded to prevent—or sometimes to provoke—racial change. "Blockbusting"—a new twist on an old game—cropped up: Real estate agents panicked white homeowners into selling by whispering that black families were about to buy, or had just bought, a house down the block. By 1960, white subdivisions in Fairfax, Prince George's, and Montgomery counties had received seven times as much FHA financing as the city. Like other metropolitan areas, Washington was becoming a largely chocolate city with vanilla suburbs.

Just as powerful was the de facto segregation caused by economics. Although both races

Above: Tenor saxophonist Ben Webster, whose long career included stints with Duke Ellington's orchestra and as leader of his own band, greets patrons at U Street's Club Bengasi in 1947. Then a "mecca for café society," according to Fitzpatrick & Goodwin's *Guide to Black Washington,* the Bengasi welcomed everyone. U Street's nightlife outclassed that of the seedier, whites-only Ninth Street strip.

Above left: A Georgetown Local freight train sits on the B&O tracks at Dempsey's boathouse in Georgetown in 1947. The rail spur was still delivering supplies to Georgetown's remaining mills, power plant and construction yards. Completed in 1910, the line ran from Silver Spring west through the Columbia Country Club golf course, under Wisconsin Avenue in Bethesda, through Kenwood, Somerset, Green Acres and Dalecarlia Reservoir, and then down along the C& O Canal. Today it is the Capital Crescent bike and walking path.

Left: Thanks to L'Enfant's original vision and "Boss" Shepherd's tree-planting campaign, the city was well shaded by the 1940s. But traffic demands would uproot much of the "City of Trees." These elms on New York Avenue, between Ninth and Thirteenth streets, N.W., were slated for removal, as were the Benning streetcar tracks they framed in 1948. Bus service replaced the streetcars, and shade eventually was provided to some degree by taller buildings.

enjoyed unprecedented prosperity in the 1950s, whites enjoyed much more of it. They tended to move as far from town as they could, pulled by new schools and new homes as large as they could afford, and pushed by decaying older neighborhoods.

In the 1950s alone, the District of Columbia lost 300,000 whites and gained 300,000 blacks. In 1957, Washington became the first major city in the United States to have more black residents than white. Far more significant was the decline of the middle-class tax base that left with the new suburbanites and the businesses that followed them. As the civil rights victories of the 1960s began to have an impact, the city's African American middle class grew, but so did the numbers of low-income families trapped by economics in the older areas of the city and large portions of Southeast.

In the early 1960s, as residents increasingly left the city center's older housing, Washington "grew" more downtown office buildings. Where yesterday a gas station occupied a street corner, today a boxy high-rise opened for business. Its occupants were mostly white-collar professionals—law firms, accountants, lobbyists. The result was a "new downtown" stretching east and west from the corner of Connecticut Avenue and K Street, N.W. At the same time that other cities were losing jobs to the suburbs in droves, more than two-thirds of working adults in the Washington metropolitan area still commuted to desks downtown. City leaders, like those in other large metropolitan areas, called for a commuter tax to support the

HELP BREAK THE COLOR BARRIERS IN THE WASHINGTON THEATRE!

SIGN THE PETITION! **SIGN THE BOYCOTT PLEDGE!**

DID YOU KNOW THAT

Negroes are permitted on the stage at The National but not in the audience?

Negroes are permitted in the audience at Constitution Hall but not on the stage?

Yet—in the first decade of this century—at a time when there were no bars against Negroes in the theatre, Washington had five or six theatres for an infinitely smaller population!

DID YOU KNOW THAT

Negroes have free and complete access to all recreation facilities under the jurisdiction of the federal government. Negroes may attend concerts, operas and anything else at the Watergate and Sylvan Theatres, but when these same productions go indoors in the Fall whether Negroes can go or not depends on who happens to control the buildings and how the building owners feel—and generally Negroes are barred!

Yet—this is supposed to be the seat of world democracy!

DID YOU KNOW THAT

Most of the good plays are now by-passing Washington because so many playwrights and stars will not be a party to jim crow in the Nation's Capital?

Close to forty playwrights have signed a pledge requiring a non-discrimination clause in all future Washington contracts, and Actor's Equity is considering requiring a similar clause for all actors?

As a result of the public protest the color bar has been lifted at George Washington University's Lisner Auditorium for public meetings, and although the Board has announced they will not take commercial plays the principle of non-segregation of the public has been established at Lisner.

Yet—the officials of The National continue to insist that you are not a good enough American to sit alongside Negroes in the theatre, as you do in the ball parks, the trolleys, and so many other places?

DOES THAT MAKE SENSE?

SIGN THE PETITION! SIGN THE BOYCOTT PLEDGE!

Help Break the Color Barriers in the Washington Theatres!

COMMITTEE FOR RACIAL DEMOCRACY IN THE NATION'S CAPITAL

1944 9th St., N. W., Washington 1, D. C.

roads and services used by those commuters. The Congress refused.

But Congress consistently did the bidding of the highway lobby and proposed an extensive network of freeways for the city, most honeycombing the downtown core. Planners thought the freeways would keep commuters coming downtown as well as ease traffic congestion in a city in love with its autos. To build the eight-lane Inner Loop Freeway alone—encircling the White House at a distance of one mile—would have required demolishing 65,000 building units, about one-fourth of the city's total. Plans sharpened in 1956 after passage of the National Highway Act, which raised the federal share of construction costs from half to 90 percent. By 1959 a regional planning report recommended 329 miles of new superhighways in the city, including an eight-lane bridge across the Potomac River into Georgetown and a six-lane freeway that would have replaced the heavily commercial Wisconsin Avenue corridor in Maryland and the District. In the same report, a mere 33 miles of rapid rail were recommended.

The racial implications were easy to read. As early as 1952, a report by the Committee of 100, a local business group, noted that city residents might object to the planned freeways. It did not bother to point out that African Americans occupied the vast majority of homes that lay in the path of the planned roads, although some white areas such as Cleveland Park also would have been badly compromised. The report warned that without the

DISCRIMINATION DRAMA

The battle to desegregate post-war Washington was fought on many fronts: schools, restaurants, housing and even theaters. By 1948, student pickets had forced George Washington University to stop operating Lisner Auditorium on a segregated basis. The National Theatre, the city's oldest continuous theatrical venue (it opened in 1835), came under heavy fire. Playwrights pledged to require a non-discrimination clause in their Washington contracts, and Actor's Equity refused to allow its members to perform before segregated audiences. Hundreds of local activists picketed the theater and handed out flyers (facing page, bottom). The owners, rejecting the protesters' demands, announced that the theater would be converted to a movie house. The national touring company of *Oklahoma* (above) sings "Auld Lang Syne" after its final performance in July 1948. The following October, the theater reopened (facing page, top), with *The Red Shoes* as its first film. In response to the lack of a professional theater, Zelda Fichandler and Edward Mangum (below) organized the racially unrestricted Arena Stage in an old movie house in 1950. After the National was sold, it reopened in 1952 as an integrated, legitimate theater.

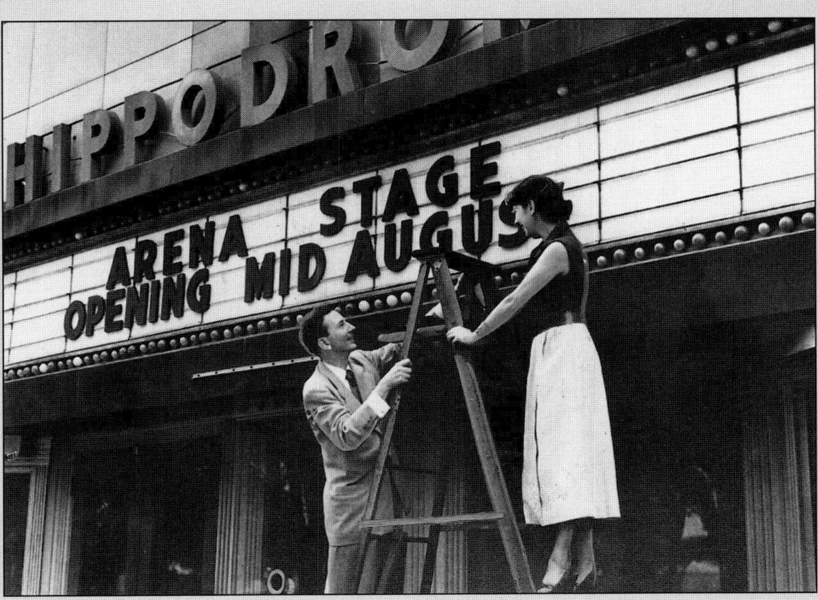

new highways, the "city's economic and cultural life will dry up."

The freeway struggle continued until 1971. Much of the skirmishing centered on Rep. William Natcher, a Kentucky Democrat who chaired the House District Appropriations Subcommittee. He was determined to withhold subway construction funds until freeways were built. The situation provoked unprecedented grass-roots resistance, coupled with back-channel maneuvering by influential local lawyers.

The eventual compromise provided funds for a 103-mile subway system—nearly complete today—and only fragments of the original freeway plan. A planned Three Sisters Bridge spanning the Potomac was never built. The Inner Loop was cancelled after its southern leg (the Southeast-Southwest Freeway, which ends abruptly at Pennsylvania Avenue, S.E.) was completed. Similarly, a remnant of the Center Leg Freeway stops at New Jersey Avenue, the E Street Expressway ends at 19th Street, N.W., and Interstate 95 does not continue south from its junction with the Beltway just north of Takoma Park. A plan for freeways became a collection of freeway stubs, reminders that the voteless citizens of Washington actually could thwart their congressional overseers.

While post-war Washingtonians earned attractive livings, they did not always trust themselves to spend their money wisely or stylishly. Woodward & Lothrop offered lessons to housewives on how to entertain and how to dress. According to *The Washington*

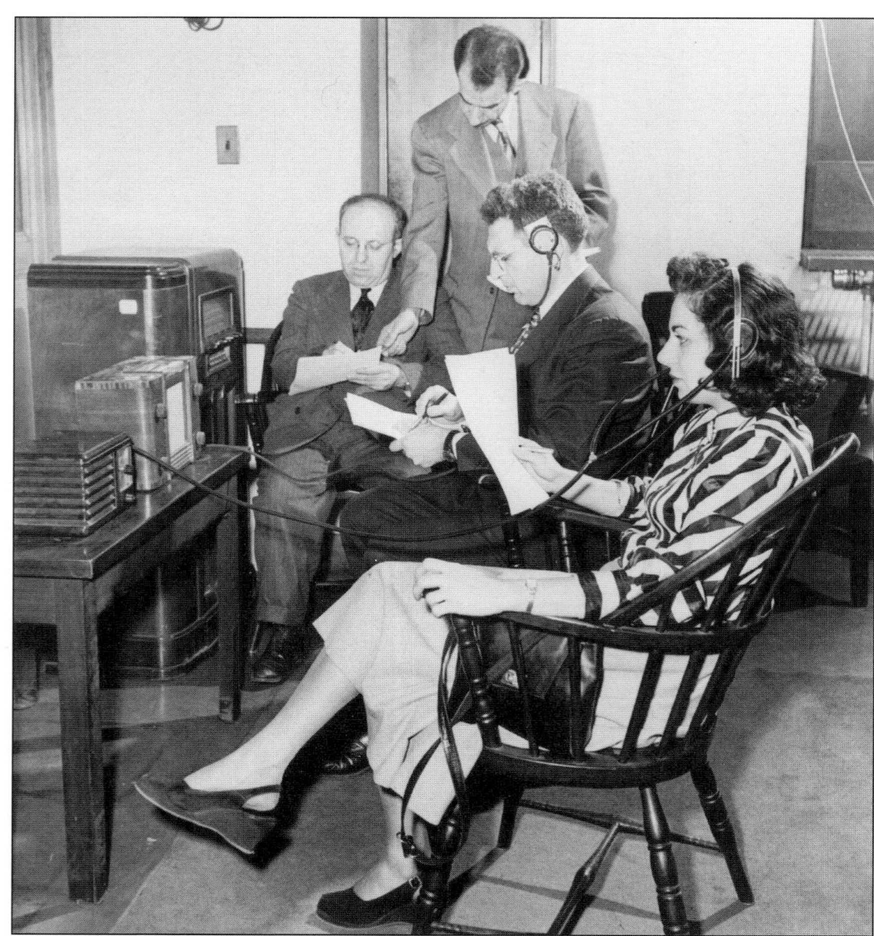

Government watchdogs tune into the audio portion of 1949 television programs in search of false or misleading advertising. TV had arrived in Washington in early 1946 when W3XWT (later WTTG), Channel 5, began broadcasting for one or two hours, three days a week. Commercials started appearing that November.

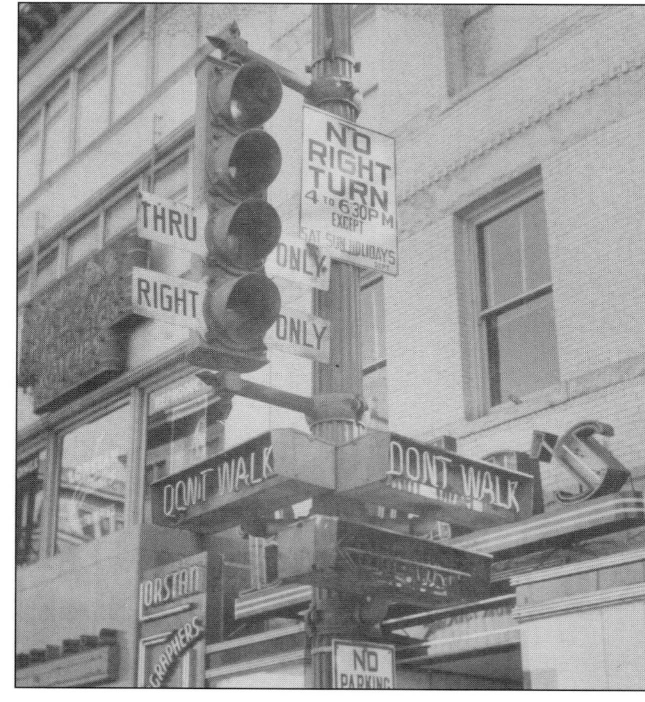

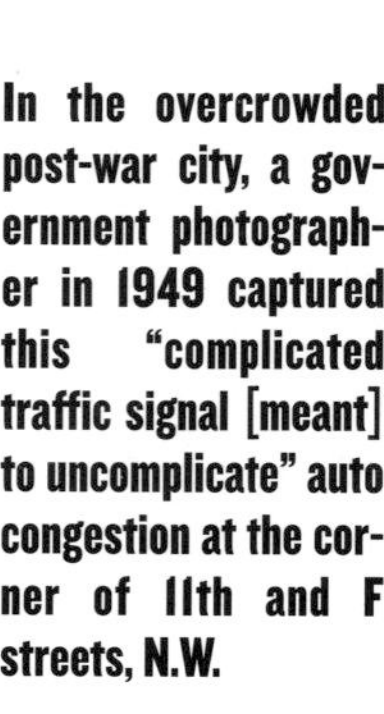

In the overcrowded post-war city, a government photographer in 1949 captured this "complicated traffic signal [meant] to uncomplicate" auto congestion at the corner of 11th and F streets, N.W.

In the era of fedoras and big cigars, patrons shop in 1950 at Morgan's Pharmacy at 30th and P streets, N.W., in Georgetown.

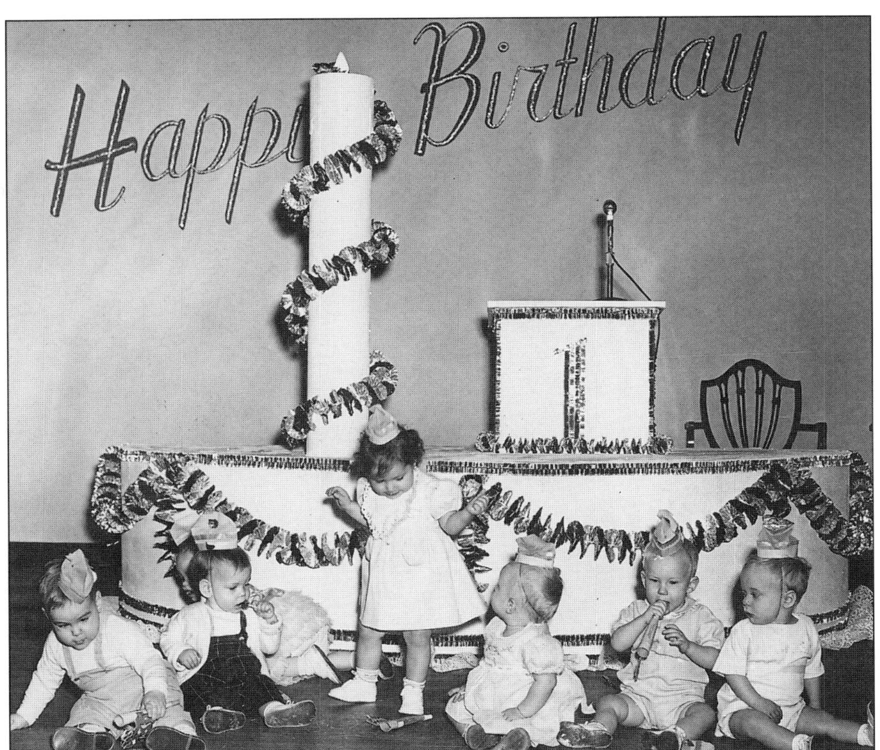

To celebrate its first year at Wisconsin and Western avenues in Bethesda (now considered Chevy Chase), Woodward & Lothrop invited babies born in the Washington area on November 3, 1950, to join the party. Fourteen babies and their families participated. The Hecht Company, though, was the first to build a full-sized store in the suburbs, opening its Silver Spring branch in 1947.

Post's "1946 Brand Survey," compiled for prospective advertisers, District households preferred predictable products like Wonder Bread, Lipton Tea, Coca-Cola and Del Monte canned peaches. The 1953 version of the same study reported that Ritz Crackers (found in 66 percent of Washington homes) and Crisco (found in 62 percent) were the two most popular food products. Clorox bleach (83 percent) led all products.

Restaurants tended to serve meat and potatoes or Chesapeake Bay-style seafood, and grocery stores generally stocked the safe and the pedestrian. Speaking of that period, comedian Mark Russell said that if you wanted to find Velveeta cheese spread in a Washington grocery, you looked in the gourmet food section.

The capital still cast envious glances at New York when it came to culture, and well-to-do women from Washington routinely shopped for clothes in Manhattan rather than at home. First-run theater seldom played in the capital. Washington audiences mainly saw tryouts of shows that were bound for Broadway, or hoped that they were. In 1950, two years before the National Theatre reopened as a live theater without race restrictions, Arena Stage opened its door, offering small-scale, homegrown professional productions to enthusiastic audiences.

Then came the administration of John F. Kennedy, and for a brief time Washington was Camelot. Many in the younger generation that had taken power were drawn to work in the new administration. Georgetown, the former working-class port city that had been gentrified during the New Deal, was seen as glamorous because the Kennedys had lived there at the time of the president's election. Jackie Kennedy patronized—and brought much attention to—a since-closed French restaurant at Wisconsin Avenue and M Street, N.W. called Rive Gauche. Painters and poets, filmmakers and musicians became regular White House guests or performers.

The Kennedys' celebration of the city and their refusal to compare it unfavorably to New York or Paris were contagious. Washington businesses and the remnants of its old elite society became enthusiastic supporters of the arts, foreign cuisines and international influences.

But when Kennedy was assassinated on November 22, 1963, the cultural flowering of Washington was incomplete. Five years later, in April 1968, the Rev. Martin Luther King, Jr. was murdered in Memphis, Tenn., triggering nationwide protests that included four days and nights of riots that engulfed downtown Washington—shattered store windows, looting, fires—and accelerated the city's population loss.

According to *Ten Blocks from the White House,* an analysis of the riots by the staff of *The Washington Post,* more than 20,000 people—many of them federal employees—took part in the rioting. At least 12 people died and at least 7,600 were arrested. More than 667 dwelling units were destroyed, and more than 900 businesses were damaged. Property damage ran to about $24 million. White merchants were driven out of town and in many cases out of business.

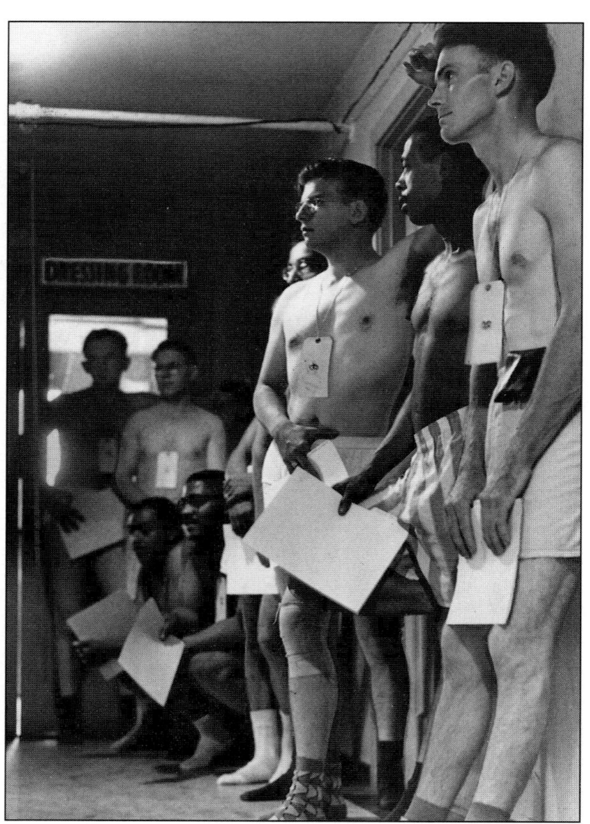

Recruits in skivvies and socks await medical exams at the Army-Air Force Recruiting Station at Arlington Farms in July 1950, a month after President Truman sent the U.S. military into the Korean conflict. As the "police action" turns nasty, D.C. Commissioner Gordon Young (below, at right) calls out the troops at home in the form of aircraft spotters, seen at the Nalle School, 50th and Bass streets, S.E. The school was one of 42 observation posts meant to "guard the city from air attacks," according to the *Washington Post.*

For many, the possibility of a nuclear strike against Washington became very real in 1949 when the Soviet Union developed an atomic bomb. D.C. Commissioner Young briefs reporters in 1951 on what officials believed would be target areas in Washington during an atom bomb raid. The unrealistically small circles are centered on the White House and Union Station.

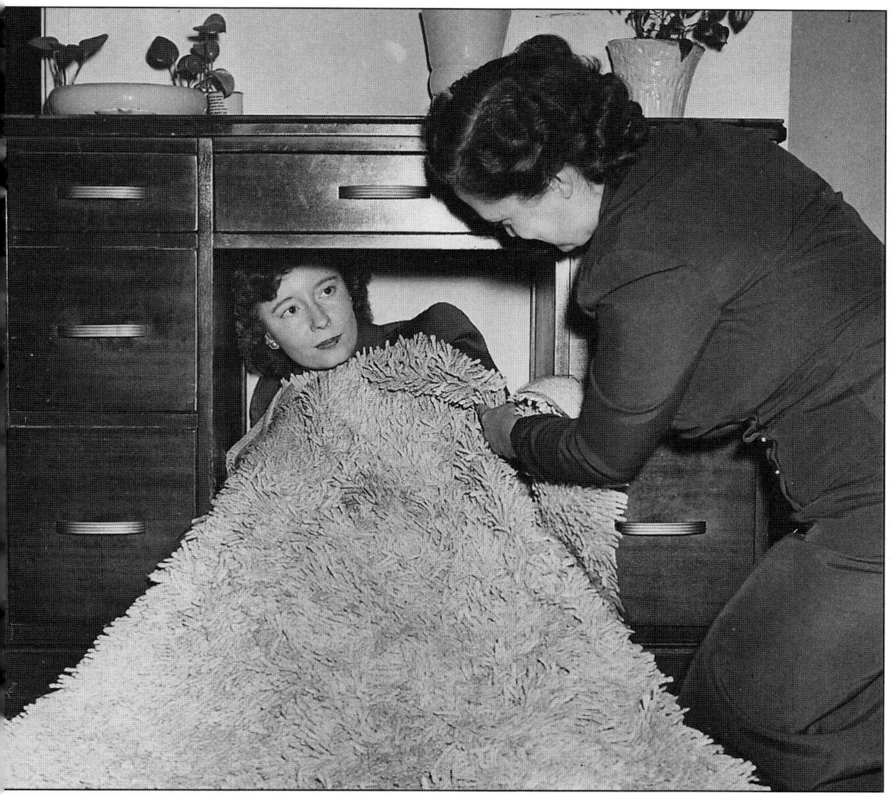

June Townsend, an instructor for the D.C. Business and Professional Women's Club's Civil Defense Course, demonstrates the thinking of the time on how Washingtonians could protect themselves from atomic attack: huddle under a desk. The rug "protects from deadly gamma rays," according to a *Washington Post* report.

Commercial life in the District of Columbia never fully recovered.

City officials instantly promised rebuilding, but for the most part it never took place.

Even when the city government made plans, they often were poorly targeted. As *Washington Post* reporter Eugene L. Meyer wrote in 1973, "The housing planned for all the three riot corridors [H Street, N.E., and 7th and 14th streets, N.W.] was mostly for moderate-income families . . . while most of those facing displacement were poor. In Shaw, where 60 percent of the 40,000 residents are poor enough for public housing, only 54 such units were planned. No public housing was planned in the other two areas." Some public housing has been built along H, 7th and 14th streets in the years since, but not nearly as much as there was before the riots.

It was not the first time that District redevelopment promises had not been kept. With the best of intentions, for example, the Truman and Eisenhower administrations had changed the face of Southwest Washington forever. Following plans laid out in the late 1940s and early 1950s, the homey quadrant of the city where Jews, Italians, blacks and Asians had lived for more than 100 years was razed in the name of urban renewal. To many, the renewal failed because it didn't replace the old sense of community. Low-income residents of Southwest had been promised that they would get help in relocating. They never did. They were scattered across the metropolitan area, adding more stress to the overburdened housing stock.

District residents did enjoy one notable gain in the 1960s: limited home rule. Under the leadership of President Lyndon B. Johnson, the city in 1967 was given a presidentially appointed mayor and City Council. Congress retained power over the local budget by keeping the right to set the annual federal payment (in lieu of taxes on federal properties) and also to veto local legislation. But the first taste of self-government in nearly a century whetted appetites for more. Statehood was seriously discussed, and a Statehood Party would soon be formed. Local politics began to look like politics everywhere else as Washington elected a school board for the first time in 1968.

But the city also endured more political turmoil as the Vietnam war began to shake the capital. The first massive antiwar protest, held in October 1967, brought more than 400,000 demonstrators to Washington. With the assassinations, these and other protests and the security required, the capital's sense of innocence (in the early New Deal years visitors could stroll unannounced into the White House) was gone forever.

However, life had never been better—or bigger—in Northern Virginia or suburban Maryland. By 1968, the exodus to the suburbs had resulted in Fairfax and Montgomery counties each surpassing the District of Columbia in population. These new suburbanites still called themselves "Washingtonians."

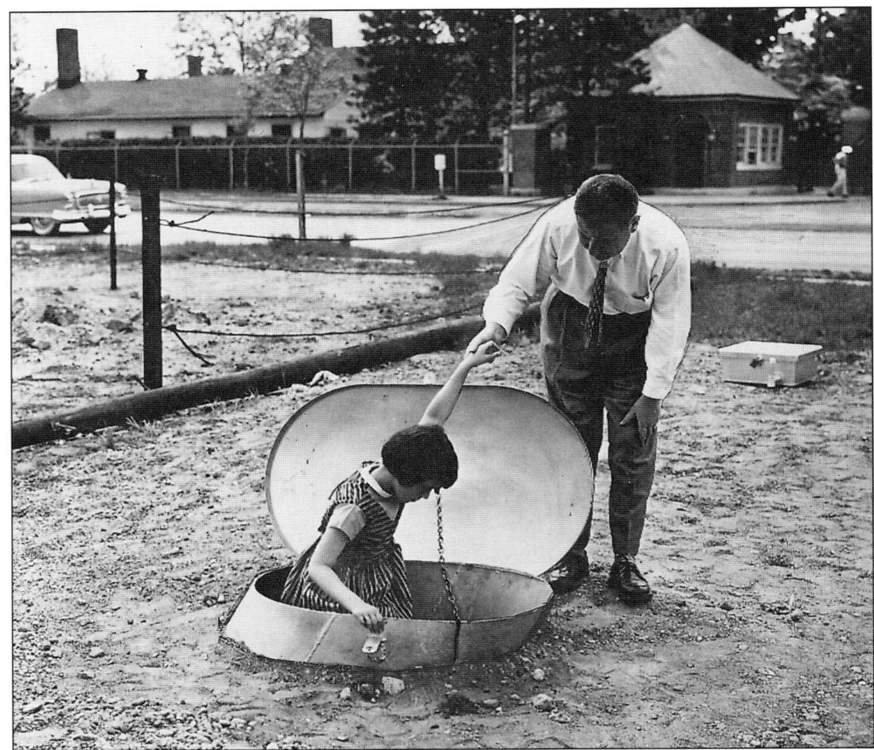

The Cold War turned hotter in 1955 as the Soviet Union exploded its first hydrogen bomb. The Defense Department had installed a Missile Master system at the first area Nike Missile site, at Fort George G. Meade, Md. (top), where members of the 35th Antiaircraft Artillery Brigade monitor "early warning information" at tracking consoles. In all, 13 sites ringed the city until the early 1970s, when intercontinental ballistic missiles rendered the Nikes obsolete. The fear of annihilation led to more dramatic citizen defenses. Above, a father helps his little girl down the hatch of the family's bomb shelter, a tank buried 10 feet below ground.

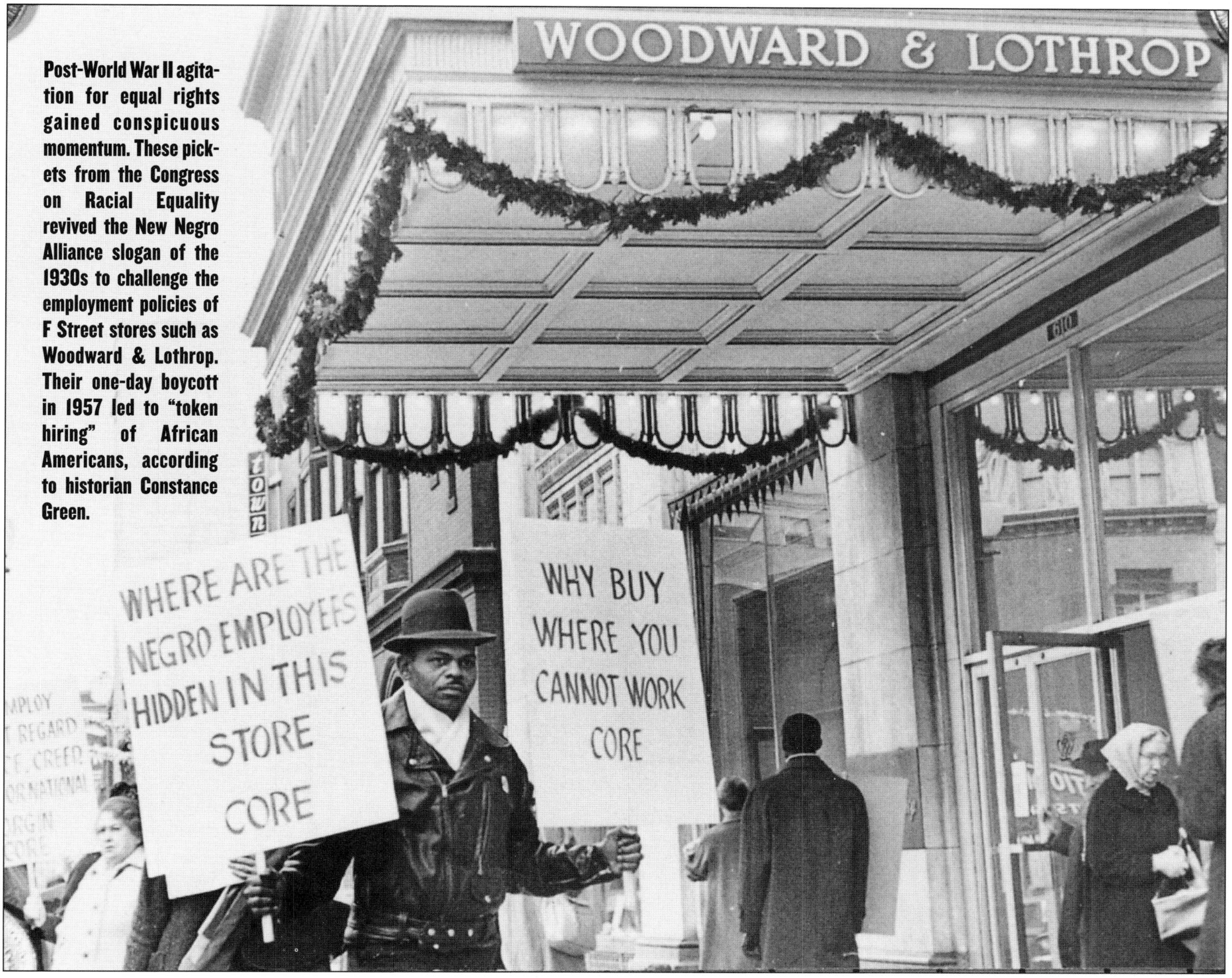

Post-World War II agitation for equal rights gained conspicuous momentum. These pickets from the Congress on Racial Equality revived the New Negro Alliance slogan of the 1930s to challenge the employment policies of F Street stores such as Woodward & Lothrop. Their one-day boycott in 1957 led to "token hiring" of African Americans, according to historian Constance Green.

Swimmers crowd the three-level pool at Glen Echo, Md., in 1947. In 1961, protests forced the privately owned amusement park to desegregate. In Washington, pools operated by the D.C. Recreation Department were long officially segregated, while de facto segregation prevailed at others run by the U.S. Interior Department. In the summer of 1949, when black teenagers sought to swim in Interior pools, white teenagers resisted during a battle at the Anacostia pool. The Interior Department closed the pool for the summer, and all pools were integegrated the next year.

THE COLOR OF SCHOOLS

At top, Anacostia High School students Nancy Neissen, Jim Stoner, Jack West, Pat Evans, Dick Penrod, Marilyn Raybould, Joan Talbott and cameraman Robert James party at an all-night formal dance for graduates in June 1954. Theirs would be the last all-white graduating class at Anacostia.

In middle, eighth graders at Terrell Junior High School on Wheeler Rd., S.E., crowd 44 to a classroom in Mrs. L.M. Hillman's history class in 1947. The rapid racial change in Washington had led to underpopulated "white" schools in neighborhoods that had shifted to majority African American and "colored" schools such as Terrell, where many students were crammed two-to-a-desk.

African American schools, once the pride of the community, now struggled as per-pupil spending shrank. Legal challenges by African American parents eventually were folded into *Brown v. Board of Education*. In May 1954, the Supreme Court declared school segregation laws unconstitutional and called for desegregation with "all deliberate speed." Despite some pockets of local disapproval, Congress ordered the immediate desegregation of Washington's schools as a model for the nation. Despite efforts by the schools and the American Friends Service Committee, some white students at Eastern, McKinley and Anacostia high schools went on an anti-integration strike in October 1954, but the protests were short-lived.

A year after the children at left were photographed in 1955 at the formerly all-white Burroughs School at 18th and Monroe streets, N.E., Assistant School Superintendent Carl Hansen called Washington's integration experience "a miracle of social adjustment."

A cafeteria scene at McFarland Junior High School in Petworth in 1957 (top) shows the immediate result of desegregation: By decade's end, the student body was almost entirely African American. Above, 1956 pickets in Poolesville, Md., protest desegregation. According to historian Jane Sween, rural Poolesville was the only Montgomery County community to demonstrate against desegregation. All of Virginia officially resisted desegregation; finally, in 1959, Michael G. Jones, Gloria Thompson, Ronald Deskins, and Lance D. Newman (left) desegregated the seventh grade of Arlington's Stratford Junior High.

MERCURY 10
Perhaps
E-723

The capital's African American community, like those in other cities, responded to segregation by building first-class institutions of its own. Warren "Billy" Brooks of Washington (facing page) wins the Labor Day Race at Columbia Beach, Md. in 1952. The resort on the Chesapeake Bay's western shore was one of a number of vacation communities that catered to Washington's African American upper class. Above, the Bachelor-Benedict Club of Washington presents a debutante class in this undated group portrait, circa 1950. The club was inspired by the Bachelor-Benedict Club of New York, an offshoot of the exclusive Society of the Sons of New York, founded in 1884.

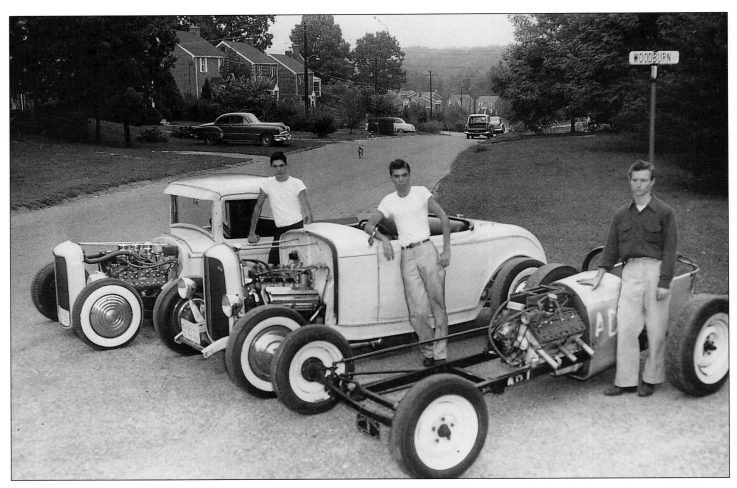

Members of the D.C. Dragons and Arlington Road Knights auto clubs pose in 1955 with their rebuilt 1932 Fords. As suburban life became the norm in Washington, unprecedented numbers of teenagers acquired driver's licenses and their own cars. Resentful of their image as irresponsible, the *Washington Post* reported, these "hot rodders" organized a campaign to aid motorists in trouble. They also held drag races at the Old Dominion Speedway in Manassas, Va.

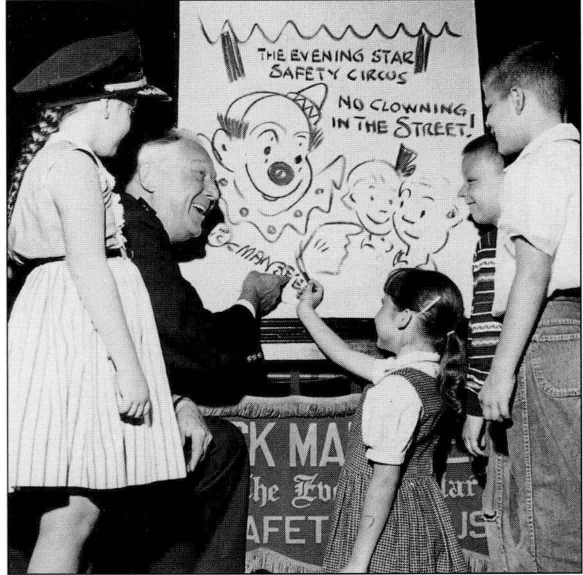

Dick Mansfield presents one of his trademark chalk talks on traffic safety, circa 1955. Well known to children from the 1930s through the 1960s, he was a prolific cartoonist as well as a D.C. police detective. His "Safety Carefuliers" club members memorized the creed: "We're Safety Carefuliers. We use our eyes and ears. We look both ways, we watch our step, we're safety carefuliers."

In 1966, these eager teens at Maryland's Bladensburg High School learned to drive using a car simulator and following instructions on a movie screen.

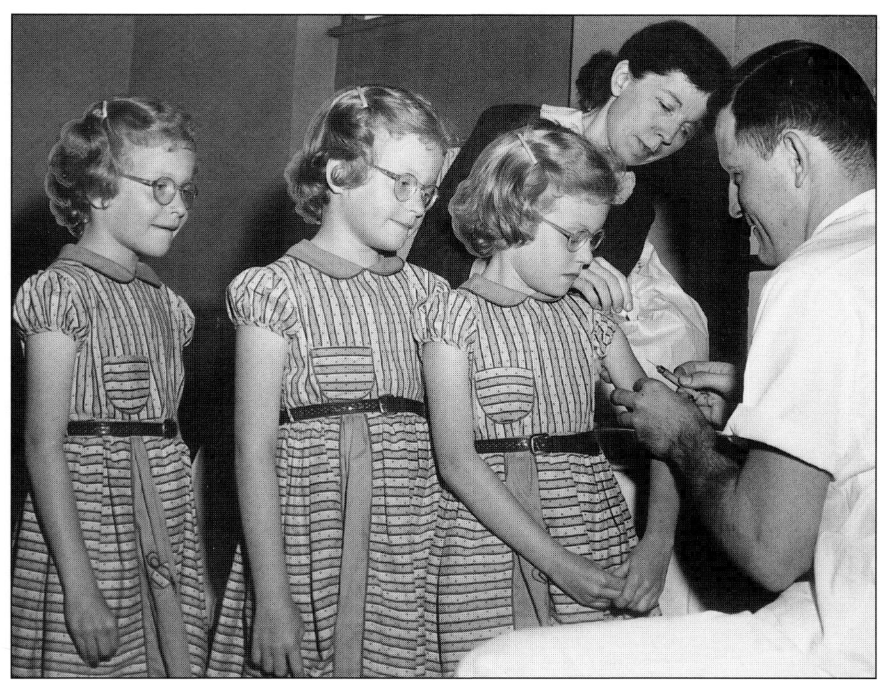

Cheryl, Claudia, and Carol Burroughs of Arlington, Va., get polio shots from Dr. Edward Novak at Patrick Henry School on April 26, 1955. Jonas Salk's vaccine freed millions from the deadly bacterium that had crippled President Franklin D. Roosevelt and condemned thousands to life inside iron lungs.

Doris Patterson instructs a dance class at her Washington dance school, circa 1950. As the U.S. economy soared during the 1950s, more baby boomers than ever were exposed to cultural and artistic training.

Only in Washington: Vice President Richard M. Nixon and 1955 Cherry Blossom Festival Queen Jeannine Raymond of Maine point to the wheel of fortune, which determined who received the crown. Cherry Blossom princesses were selected by state delegations, who often honored legislators' daughters. The wheel of fortune made sure the contest did not rely on beauty, brains, talent or influence.

Washington TV produced local stars and international heroes. Pick Temple and his dog Lady (left) were the kings of kids' shows in the early 1950s. Temple's "Giant Ranch" (named for its sponsor) featured cartoons, cowboy songs and audience participation in children's games. Jim Henson (right), circa 1958, poses with Kermit, Yorick, Sam and Harry of "Sam and Friends." The show began in 1954—the year Henson graduated from Northwestern High School in Hyattsville, Md.—as a five-minute lead-in to the "Tonight Show" on WRC-TV. It ran for eight years, winning a local Emmy.

In 1950, when Washingtonians celebrated the 175th anniversary of the city's founding, their present was the Carter Barron Amphitheater in Rock Creek Park. As seen in this 1957 season brochure, the amphitheater attracted topflight entertainment, from opera to Jerry Lewis, the American Ballet Theatre to Harry Belafonte.

Young women compete in a duckpin bowling match circa 1955. Born in Baltimore in 1900 and imported to Washington in 1903, duckpin bowling remained mostly a regional favorite. In the 1950s, alleys built glassed-in play spaces for preschoolers while their mothers showed their stuff.

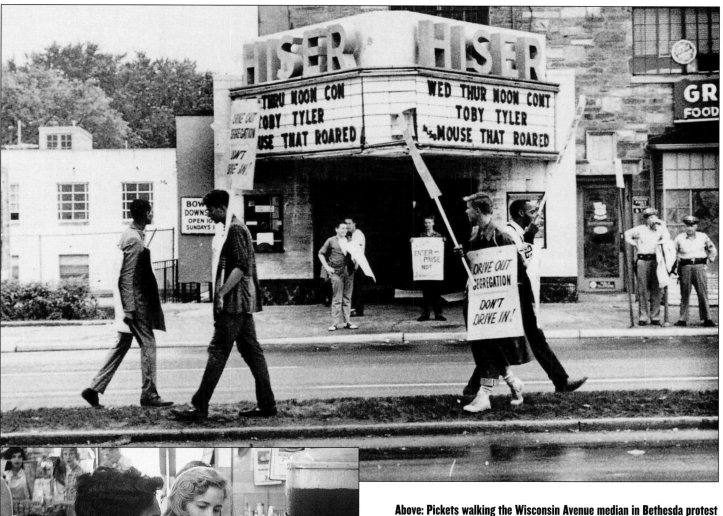

Above: Pickets walking the Wisconsin Avenue median in Bethesda protest the Hiser Theater's segregation policy in July 1960. Counter-demonstrators, at times including American Nazi Party leader George Lincoln Rockwell, show their opposition in the background. Owner John H. Hiser refused to desegregate, but protesters kept up the pressure until he sold the theater to the K-B chain. In October, the theater reopened as the integrated Baronet.

Middle: Duke University student Joan Trumpower of Alexandria sits at the Woolworth's lunch counter in Shirlington, Va., in June 1960, eating hot dogs with Gwendolyn Greene, a Howard University student. As a result, the whites-only lunch counter was closed. Three days later, after similar sit-ins in Arlington, Woolworth's, Drug Fair, Peoples Drug Store, Lansburgh's and Kann's announced that they would desegregate their lunch counters. The establishments received assurances that Virginia's segregation law—requiring segregation in places of public assembly—did not apply to private stores.

Left: In August 1963, Karl D. Gregory, middle, listens as a salesman for the Levitt Company of Levittown fame refuses to sell him a house in Belair at Bowie, Md. Despite the Supreme Court prohibition against race-restrictive housing covenants, developers, real estate agents and bankers routinely prevented African Americans from buying property in communities deemed white. Pickets pressured Levitt to change its policy, and a year later Belair's first African American family moved in.

Real estate practices—including, until 1960, newspaper policies of designating housing ads by race—kept Wheaton, Md. (above), seen in the 1950s, white for many years. While open housing became District law in 1963, not until the 1968 Civil Rights Act were suburbs forced to follow suit. Not all Washingtonians, however, sought segregated housing. In upper Northwest's Manor Park, black and white homeowners, led by journalist Marvin Caplan, established Neighbors, Inc., to foster an integrated community. At middle left, members of the group's Neighborhood Services Committee work on fencing in 1965.

Washington trolleys gave way to buses in 1962. Since the streetcar's heyday before World War I, the grandes dames of transportation had struggled for passengers and street space, first with autos and, beginning in the 1920s, with buses. The crews that removed trolley tracks and repaved streets, like the one pictured on 14th Street, were a familiar sight in the 1960s.

Marchers from local groups such as the Asbury Methodist Church, the Washington Board of Rabbis and the Baptist Ministers Conference join more than 250,000 others in the August 1963 March on Washington for Jobs and Freedom. Hailed as the largest demonstration for human rights in the nation's history, the event received intense media coverage. The country was especially moved when the Rev. Dr. Martin Luther King, Jr., delivered his "I Have a Dream" speech. Many Washingtonians, whose own civil rights revolution was well underway, opened their homes to visiting marchers.

Residents line up at the Jessie La Salle School in Northeast to vote in the 1964 presidential election, the first in which Washingtonians could participate since 1800. The District had struggled for the right to govern itself, elect representatives to Congress and vote in presidential elections since Congress wrote the first city charter in 1802. When Washington became the nation's first majority African American city in 1957, these issues became even more intertwined with the growing civil rights movement. While segregationists in Congress had long blocked home rule and voting rights, in 1960 Congress passed a constitutional amendment giving D.C. citizens the right to vote for president. Within nine months the requisite 38 states ratified the amendment.

A crowd of cars and spectators on August 17, 1964, awaits the opening of the final links in the Capital Beltway, seen here looking east, with the Riggs Road overpass in the background. Maryland Governor J. Millard Tawes and Bureau of Public Roads Administrator Rex Whitton officiated at the ribbon cutting. The Beltway, meant to be an urban bypass, instead became a high-speed, inter-suburban connector, the most important engine of local development since the first electric streetcars. Whitton called it a "huge wedding ring" for the suburbs. It was conceived as one of five concentric loops designed to ease traffic as it entered the city. Constructed eight miles out from the White House, the Beltway is the only one of the five to be built (the others would have been one, four, 15, and 25 miles from the White House and would have destroyed dozens of neighborhoods).

SOUTHWEST

When this picture was taken in 1969, Southwest Washington (above left) was a shining example of urban renewal — the wholesale clearing of a neighborhood deemed substandard, unhealthy and obsolete. Only a few "significant" old structures remained among Southwest's modern townhouses and apartments bordered by federal offices, including the new Department of Housing and Urban Development at center and L'Enfant Plaza to the left of center. Saint Dominic's Catholic Church, at right along the Southeast-Southwest Freeway, reflects the neighborhood's 19th century roots.

These other two views show the Southwest that disappeared when the bulldozers began their work in 1954. Reformers had long focused on rehabilitating the housing of slum dwellers near the Capitol and in other aging neighborhoods. But by the end of World War II, demolition and rebuilding was viewed as more efficient.

When federal and local agencies teamed with private developers, the need for adequate low-income housing was overridden by the imperative to protect developers' investments. Most housing was replaced with more expensive accommodations, and promises to help relocate Southwest's population—mainly African Americans, Jews and other ethnic whites—were not kept. A cleaner, more homogeneous Southwest was gained, but century-old communities were lost. This unidentified alley (middle) was typical of the area, as were the two boys shooting marbles in front of their alley homes, captured by noted photographer Gordon Parks. While lacking modern utilities and safe play spaces, many of the alley cultures offered modest churches and other community services.

Lifelong Southwest resident Joseph Owen Curtis photographed the corner of Fourth and I streets, S.W., in 1939 (bottom), showing the shops, movie theater and street life that had been at the heart of the area's small-town style.

The night the Beatles came to play the Coliseum in Washington, February 11, 1964, *Post* reporter Leroy Aarons planted tongue firmly in cheek as he wrote, "An 8,000-voice choir last night performed at Washington Coliseum in the premiere of what is likely to become an American classic. Call it Cacophony in B for want of a better name. The choir was accompanied, incidentally, by four young British artists who call themselves the Beatles. Their part was almost completely obscured by the larger choral group, but one imagines they'll be heard from again."

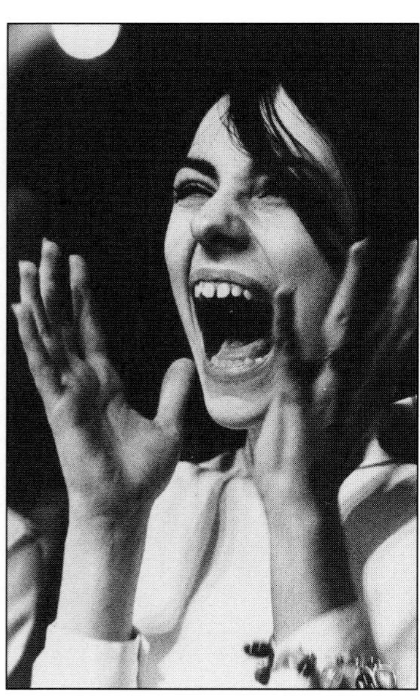

The imprint of the Griffith Stadium infield lingers like a bittersweet melody in Le Droit Park after the venerable stadium is torn down in 1966. Built on Florida Avenue, N.W., in 1914 by Washington businessman Clark Griffith to house his Washington Senators baseball team, the stadium's grandstand was one of the few integrated public places in Washington—although for many years its teams were not. Such local black baseball teams as the Washington Elite Giants, the Le Droit Tigers and the Washington Pilots played at Griffith, as did the National Negro League Homestead Grays. In 1937 the Washington Redskins took up residence there. The community also used the stadium regularly for religious revivals and for the high school Cadet Corps annual drill competitions. Its useful life was winding down in 1961 when D.C. Stadium (later Robert F. Kennedy Memorial Stadium) was opened by the National Park Service and the Redskins and Senators left for that bigger facility. Acquired by Howard University, Griffith Stadium was razed in 1966 and replaced by Howard University Hospital.

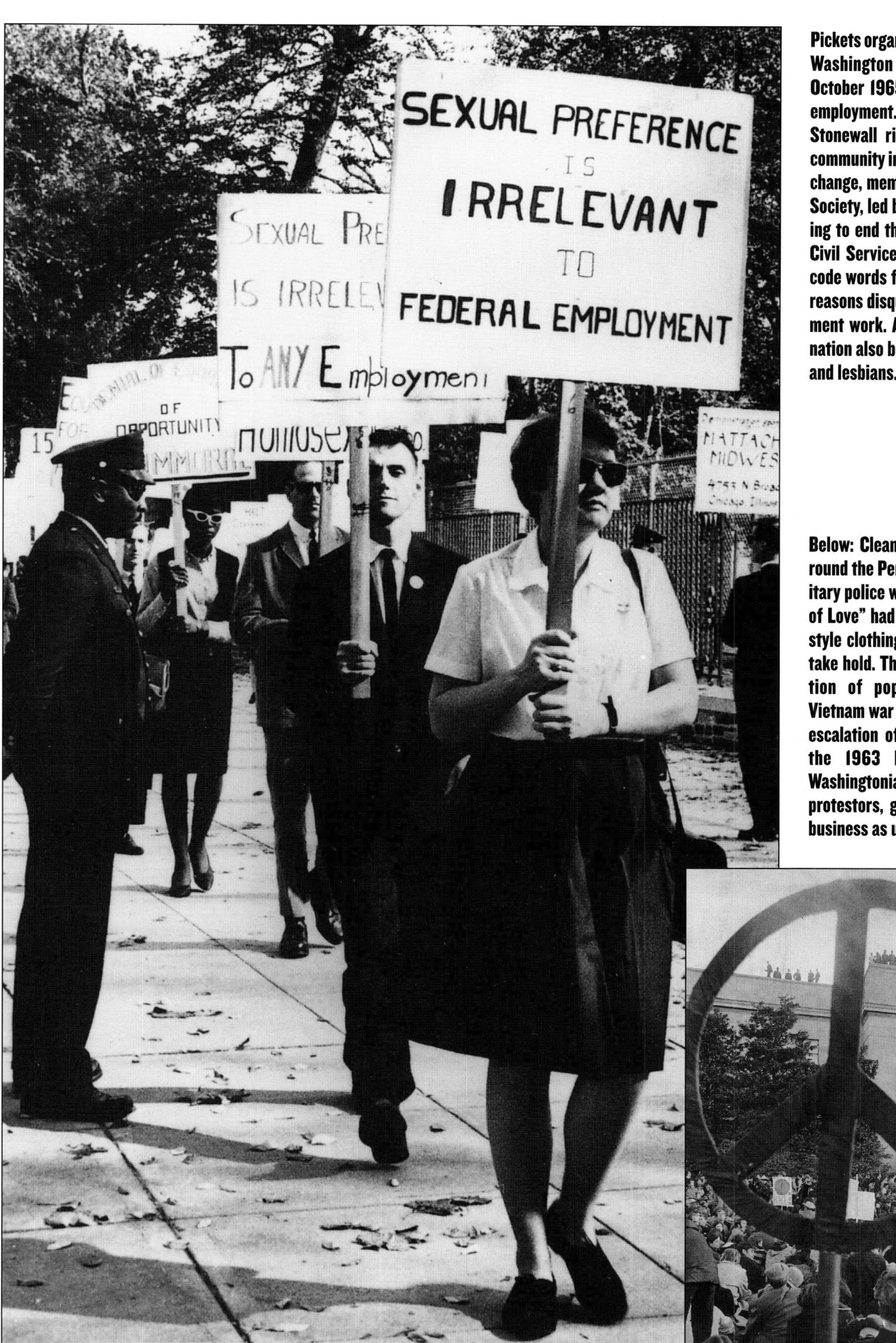

Pickets organized by the Mattachine Society of Washington march on the White House in October 1965, demanding the right to federal employment. In 1961, nine years before the Stonewall riot brought New York City's gay community into the open as a force for political change, members of Washington's Mattachine Society, led by Franklin Kameny, were organizing to end the government's ban. In 1975, the Civil Service removed "immoral conduct," its code words for homosexuality, from the list of reasons disqualifying individuals from government work. As a result, employers across the nation also began opening employment to gays and lesbians.

Below: Clean-cut antiwar demonstrators surround the Pentagon in October 1967 while military police watch from the roof. The "Summer of Love" had just ended, and long hair, hippie-style clothing and pacifism were beginning to take hold. This was the first mass demonstration of popular dissatisfaction with the Vietnam war and the Johnson administration's escalation of American involvement. As with the 1963 March on Washington, many Washingtonians opened their homes to visiting protestors, grumbled about the disruption to business as usual and joined the marchers.

MURPHY

THE FIRE THIS TIME

News of the assassination of Martin Luther King, Jr., on April 4, 1968 triggered three days of burning and looting by angry African Americans. On April 5, 1968, commuters fleeing the city (facing page, top) create gridlock on 15th Street, N.W. That afternoon, firefighters battle arson in a G.C. Murphy's Store on 14th Street, N.W., (facing page, below).

A lone soldier walks past smoldering ruins at Eighth and H streets, N.E. (top), and a National Guardsmen stand ready in front of a Safeway looted the previous night at Sixth and M streets, N.W. (right). At bottom, a mother and daughter walk past the debris of a Seventh Street building on Easter Sunday, 10 days after King's death. The riots accelerated the exodus to the suburbs and curtailed visits downtown by suburbanites for years to come. They also fueled the growth of African American political power in the city.

CHAPTER 6

SEARCHING FOR A NEW IDENTITY

President Lyndon B. Johnson, back to the camera, commands the attention of his newly appointed District mayor and City Council in 1967. Because Johnson spent much of his adult life in the capital, he considered it his adopted home. He hoped to restore home rule, but segregationist-dominated congressional committees refused to cooperate. So Johnson used his executive powers to reorganize the District government, abolishing the Board of Commissioners and appointing a single mayor-commissioner and City Council. To Johnson's left is City Council Chairman John W. Hechinger, Sr., and to his right is Mayor-Commissioner Walter E. Washington. Six years later, after Washingtonians went to South Carolina to help defeat John L. McMillan, head of the House District Committee, President Richard Nixon signed the District of Columbia Self-Government and Reorganization Act, allowing popular election in 1974 of the mayor and City Council. Congress, however, retained control over the city's budget, held veto power over its legislation, prohibited a commuter tax and denied the city voting representation in Congress.

During its first 175 years as the nation's capital, Washington struggled to become a center of commerce as well as of government, to deal with the never-ending issue of race, to compete with it sprawling suburbs and to gain the basic right to govern itself. Since then, while still grappling with these issues, the Washington area has been in the process of reinventing itself, a chore made more difficult by concerns about crime.

In the wake of the 1968 riots, Richard M. Nixon's presidential campaign included branding Washington as "the crime capital of the world." After he took office in 1969, he immediately adopted a policy for Washington (and nowhere else) of "preventive detention"—open-ended jailings of suspects deemed dangerous by a prosecutor, even if they had no previous criminal record and were not likely to flee.

Despite Nixon's prescription, crime continued to burgeon, even though the Metropolitan Police force swelled to its largest total ever, 5,200 officers, by the early 1970s. Crime became almost expected. In their 1975 look at daily life in Washington, *Washington Now*, authors Austin H. and Knight A. Kiplinger recount a typical day in the nation's capital. They almost casually report that "a Capitol Hill couple rise to find the back door has been forced open during the night, and the TV, table radio and stereo are gone."

As drug gangs competed for turf in the city beginning in the 1980s, drive-by shootings became regular events. For five years in a row, from 1992 to 1997, the city won the unwanted title of "Murder Capital of the United States." An average of 410 people were murdered in each of those years. All that bloodshed came on the heels of the 1990 arrest of Mayor Marion Barry, who was videotaped in a downtown Washington hotel smoking crack cocaine. Barry's arrest brought international scorn to the city.

By the end of the 1990s, however, the city's murder rate had fallen by 10 percent. Suburbanites who had shunned the city after the 1968 riots were returning to enjoy new theater productions and a growing array of restaurants, concerts, museums and sporting events.

This renewal can be traced in large measure to 1976, when the city's subway system first opened. Ground had been broken in 1969 for what was to be a 103-mile, multibillion-dollar system. Just blocks from the first planned stations, neighborhoods and commercial strips still lay in ruins, victims of the 1968 riots. It was going to be, said a congressional skeptic,

The Vietnam war made Washington the key destination for the politically motivated in the late 1960s and early 1970s. Vietnam veterans from Connecticut regroup in April 1971 at the end of a day of protesting the war.

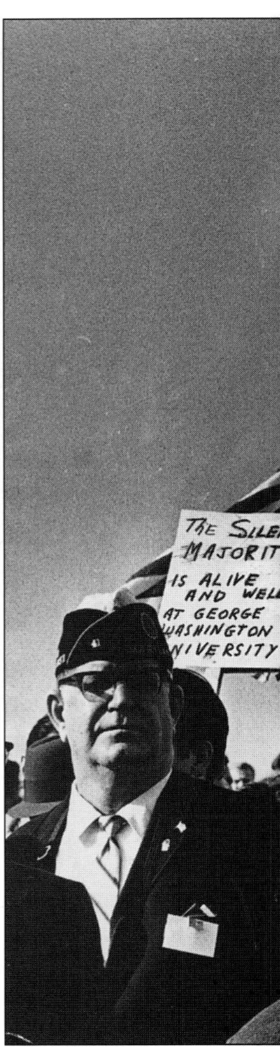

The John F. Kennedy Center for the Performing Arts, seen under construction, was separated from the rest of Foggy Bottom by its collar of highways. They were remnants of a planned system of freeways that, had it been built, would have destroyed portions of Brookland, Cleveland Park, Georgetown and the Mall. The Kennedy Center opened in 1971.

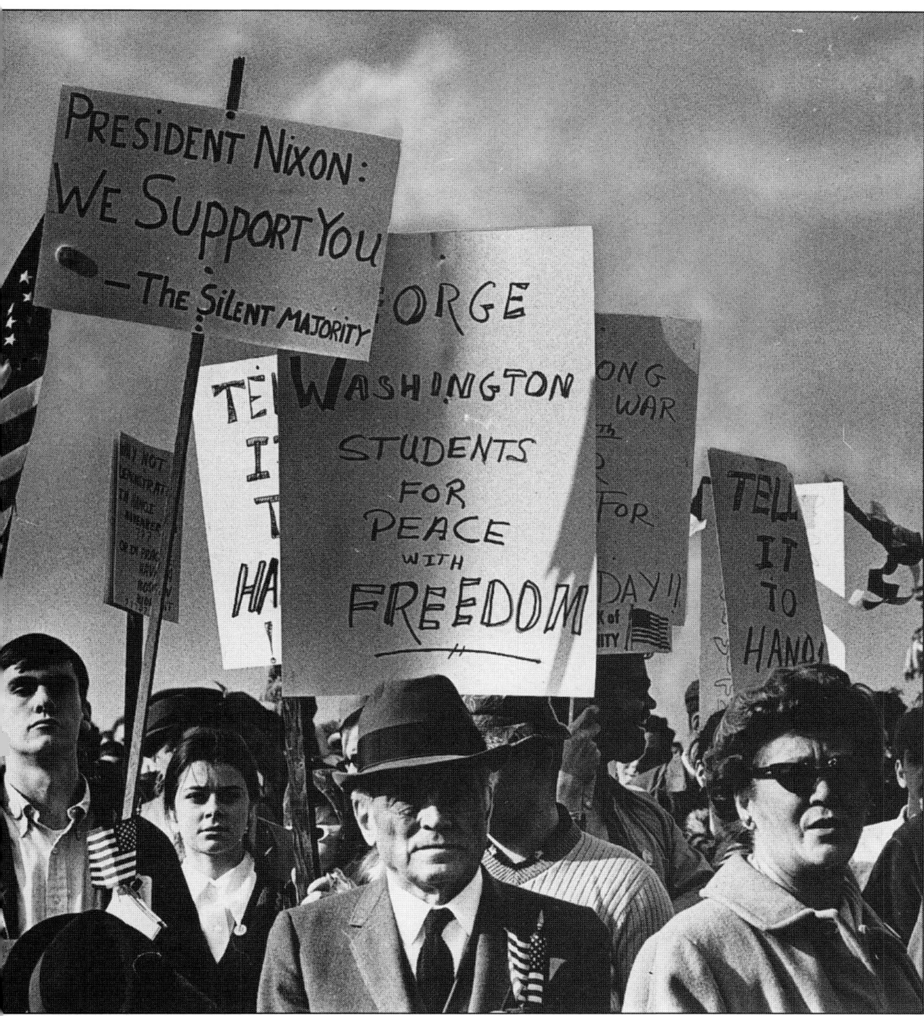

A gathering of what President Nixon termed the "Silent Majority," voters who elected him in 1968 and backed his Vietnam policies, stages a counter-demonstration during a November 1969 "Freedom Rally."

White House Police Private B.F. Jenkins models the White House uniform introduced by the Nixon Administration in January 1970 after Nixon had visited Western Europe. Derided by the public as more appropriate for a comic operetta and evidence of Nixon's ambitions for an "imperial presidency," the white suits were abandoned after one week. Ten years later they found a home as uniforms for a high school band in Iowa.

a subway to nowhere.

The skeptic could not have been more wrong. By 1985, nine years after the Metro opened, more than 400,000 people were riding it each weekday, even though more than a third of the system was not yet finished. By 1990, according to the D.C. Convention and Visitors Bureau, the subway itself—with its vaulted station roofs and technologically advanced trains—was the city's third most popular tourist attraction, outdrawing the Jefferson Memorial and Mount Vernon. Since 1980, according to the Metropolitan Washington Council of Governments, nearly half of all new commercial space in the metropolitan area has been built within walking distance of a Metro station. The great majority of that new construction has been inside the District of Columbia.

The subway was the key factor in bringing big-league winter sports back to downtown Washington from the suburban Capital Centre, in Landover, Md., where the Bullets (now the Wizards) had played basketball and the Capitals had played hockey since 1973. When MCI Center opened in 1997, it sat atop the Gallery Place subway station in the center of "old downtown." Droves of new restaurants and bars cropped up nearby, and developers jockeyed for the chance to erect entertainment complexes within two blocks of MCI. Perhaps most significantly, 60 percent of the people who attended games at MCI in 1998 and 1999 were suburbanites who came and went by subway—and 40 percent of them were females who cheerfully ventured into the supposedly crime-ridden District of Columbia at night.

However, at the same time that the basketball and hockey franchises were moving from the suburbs to the city, the Washington Redskins were moving from the city to the suburbs. Many musical and theatrical events already had moved—to Wolf Trap Farm Park, in Vienna, Va., producing some hard times at the world-famous Kennedy Center in Foggy Bottom.

In the meantime, local retailing in the city had taken a nosedive with the outside takeover and subsequent closing of Garfinckel's department store in 1990 and Woodward & Lothrop in 1995. Such distant discount mega-malls as Potomac Mills, in Dale City, Va., had opened in 1985 to immediate success. National chain retailers like Macy's and Nordstrom became instantly popular when they opened in the suburbs in the 1980s. That proved the economic vibrancy of the area, but it also proved that local residents did not value local companies simply because they were local. Above all, the financial health of national-brand suburban retailing showed that the suburban dollar was what counted most. In their tastes and shopping habits, the Washington suburbs increasingly looked like other American suburbs.

The metropolitan area's population was almost 800,000 greater in 1970 than it had been in 1960. But all of that growth had occurred in the suburbs. In just 10 years, the city fell from 39.4 percent of the area's population to 26.4 percent. Yet by many mea-

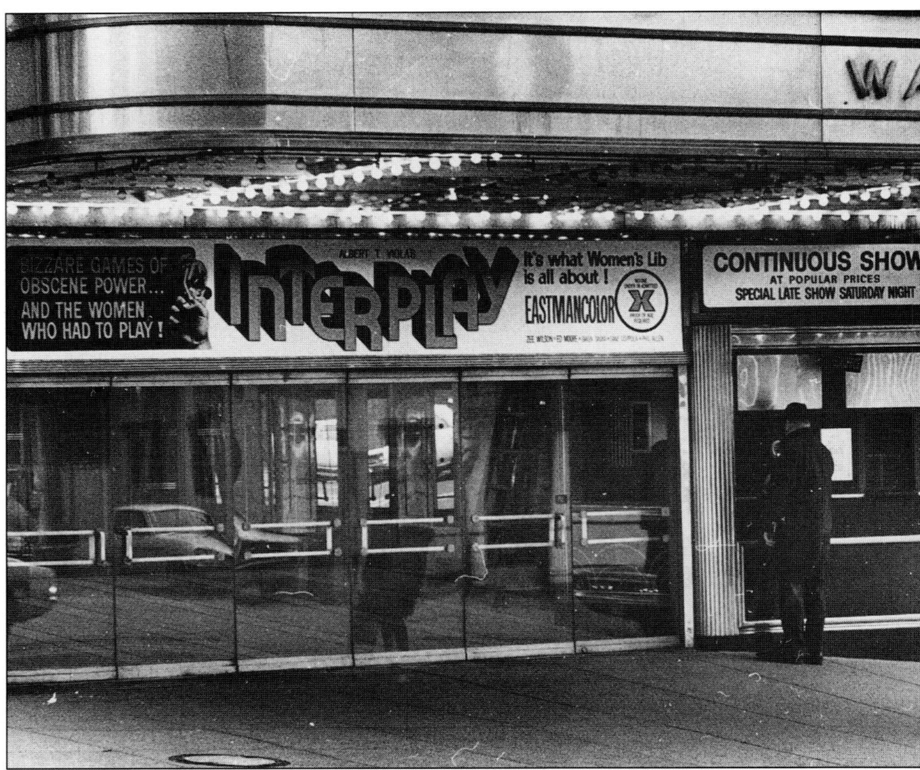

It was not easy to find popular entertainment downtown after the 1968 riots and the acceleration of suburban flight. Venues such as the Warner Theater, once a premier movie palace, were relegated to showing supposedly topical X-rated movies, as seen here in 1971.

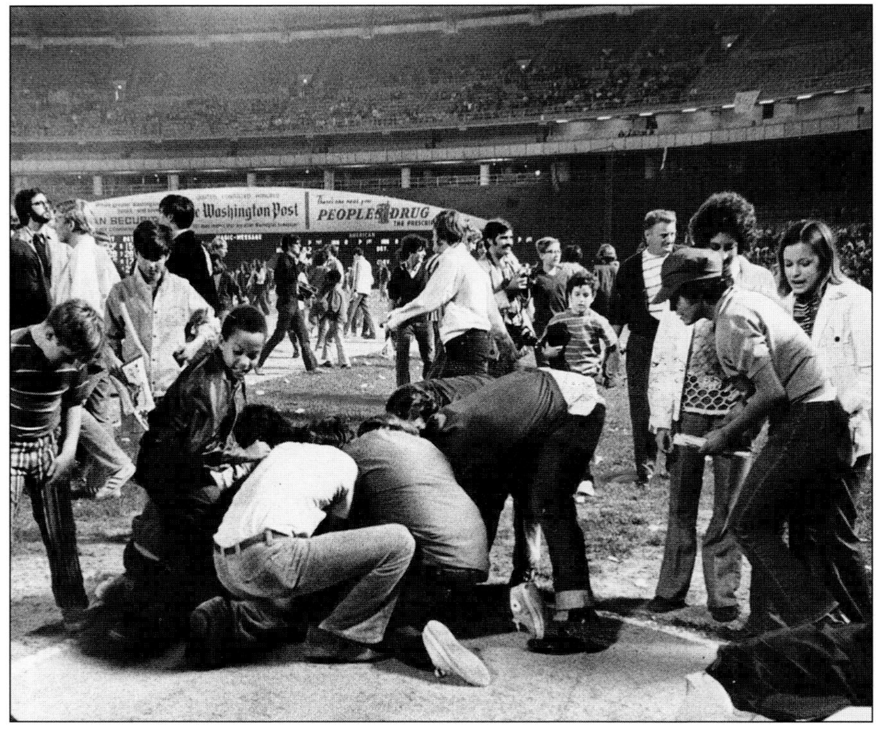

Washington Senators owner Robert Short moved the team in 1971 to Arlington, Texas, where he was offered a rent-free stadium. Unlike Washington, Arlington was a place where fans supposedly would be "safe at night." The move ended 70 years of local American League baseball. The last game was forfeited to the New York Yankees when, despite a single out remaining, fans streamed onto the field to grab souvenirs and order could not be restored.

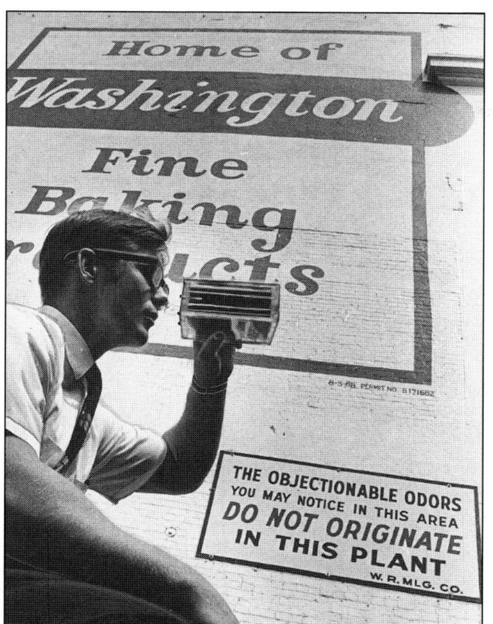

James Morgan uses a "scentometer" in 1969 to trace the origin of Georgetown's objectionable odors. Washington Flour, dating from the 19th century, was understandably sensitive to implications that the smells from the Hopfenmaier Rendering Plant might be associated with its milling company.

With the addition of the Whitehurst Freeway to Georgetown's waterfront in 1948, the industrial nature of the area seemed fated to remain indefinitely. But by 1975, when this photo was taken, developers were beginning to reclaim most of the rundown waterfront for upscale office and residential uses.

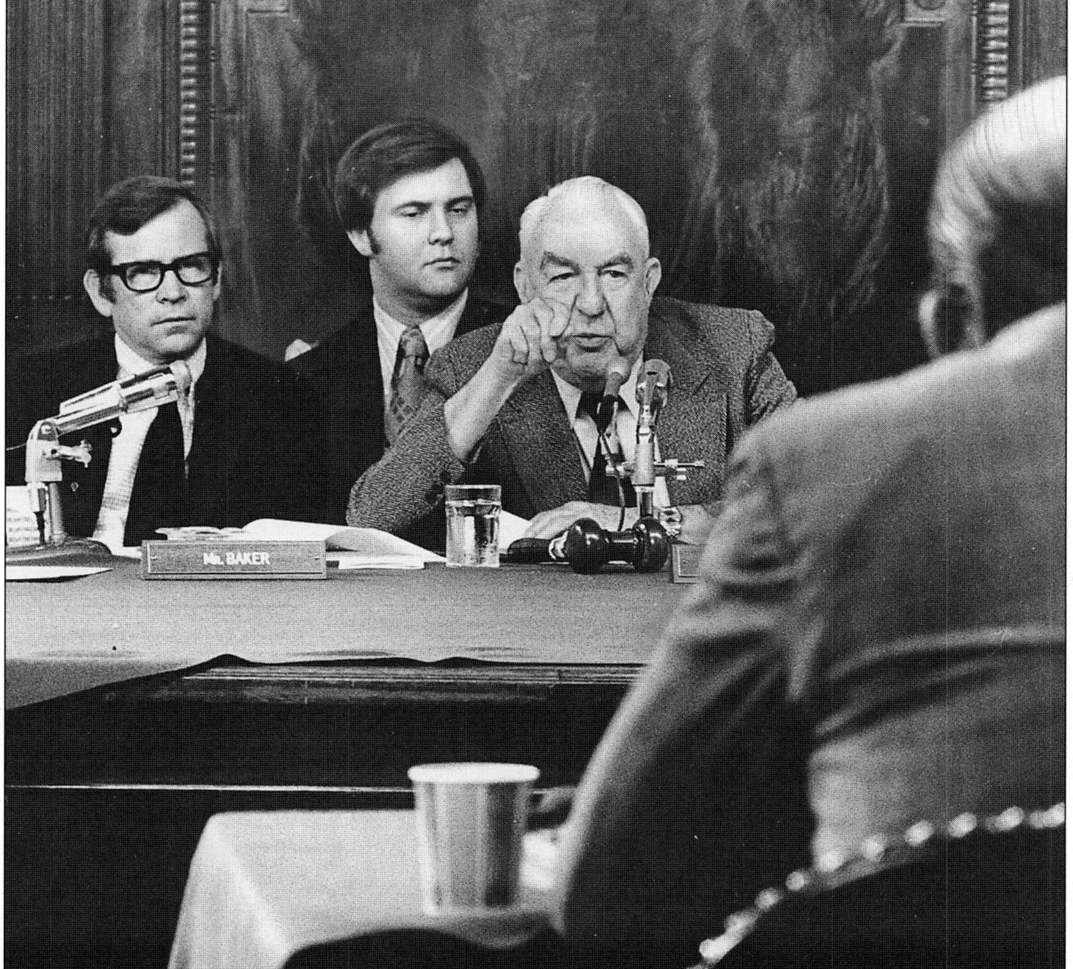

In 1972, burglars employed by President Nixon's re-election committee were caught breaking into the headquarters of the Democratic National Committee in the Watergate Office Building. By the summer of 1973, the Senate Judiciary Committee, under chairman Sam Ervin (D-N.C.), center, held riveting hearings into illegalities in the president's campaign. Downtown employees brought miniature TVs to work to catch a few moments of testimony during lunch.

sures, the District was doing very well indeed, despite constant racial friction. Government salaries for all races, which had been twice the national household average in 1940, have never fallen below that average. George Grier of the Washington Center for Metropolitan Studies observed that becoming largely African American did not mean that the city had become entirely poor. The number of African American families with middle-class annual incomes above $15,000 tripled between 1960 and 1970, Grier reported.

Elected city officials spoke long and loud about the need to retain the middle class in general and middle-class blacks in particular. But as early as the late 1970s, two-earner black families worried about the troubled D.C. public schools and began to desert the city, chiefly for the once-rural Prince George's County. At the same time, Mayors Walter E. Washington and Marion Barry strongly supported condominium conversion laws in such neighborhoods as Congress Heights, Capitol Hill and Dupont Circle. The effect was to shove out longtime tenants (often black) and replace them with richer owners (usually white), a process known as gentrification.

Marion Barry dominated city politics from 1978 to 1998, winning four terms as mayor by building a coalition of working-class blacks and D.C. government employees of both races. Barry was the symbol of a new, upbeat city—a prosperous, natty African American man breaking bread with white developers, insisting vigorously that blacks be given a large

In the 1970s, Washington society still consisted of the "cavedwellers," the power elite and ambitious newcomers. In 1979, Evangeline Bruce and Laughlin Phillips dance at the Viennese Waltz honoring donors to the Smithsonian's National Associate Program. Until 1992, Phillips ran the Phillips Collection, the nation's first permanent museum of modern art, opened by his father Duncan in 1921. Bruce, widow of diplomat and Virginia aristocrat David K.E. Bruce, was from an old New York family.

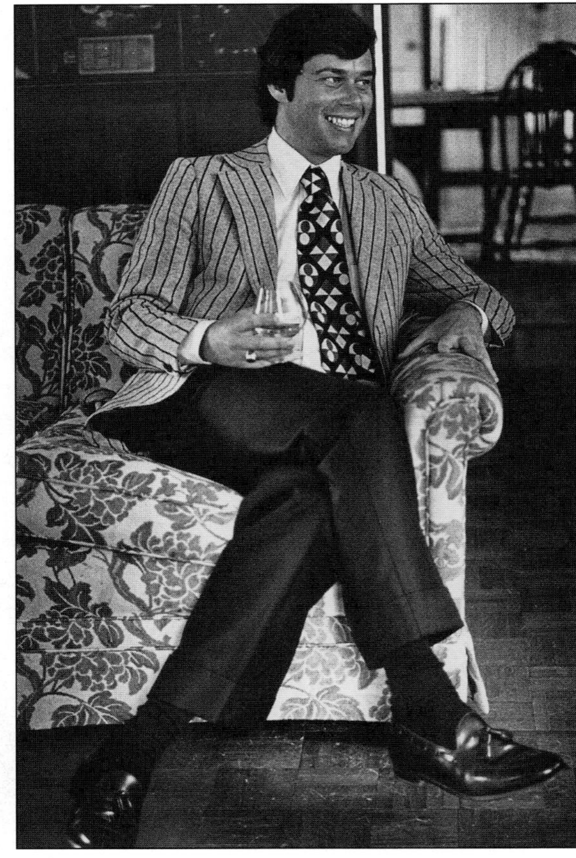

Steve Martindale, a flamboyant lobbyist from Pocatello, Idaho, photographed in 1974, turned political access into social success. In 1972, as a former Hill staffer, he burst onto the scene by holding a party for John and Yoko Lennon, who were seeking political patrons for their bid to establish U.S. residency. Martindale went on to create small parties where the powerful rubbed elbows with their peers. Press scrutiny of Martindale, however, soured his high-placed friends, and by the time of his 1990 death he had withdrawn from the party circuit.

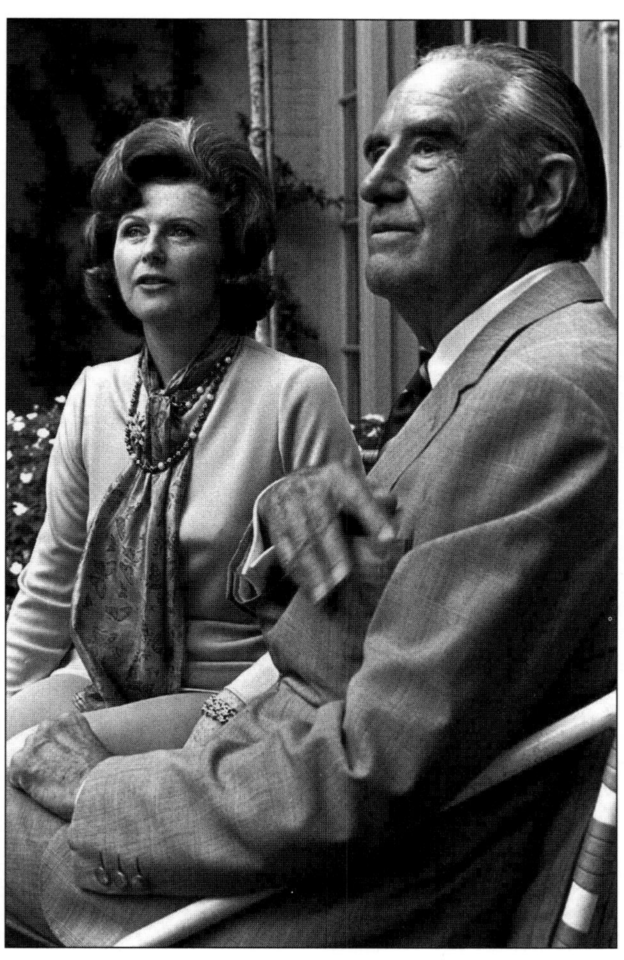

Pamela and W. Averell Harriman were the quintessential Washington power couple. Scion of a railroad family, he enjoyed a long career in Democratic politics and diplomacy. His wife, whose rise to high society began with her first marriage to Winston Churchill's son Randolph, was one of Washington's eminent political hostesses. After her husband's death in 1986, she came into her own as a major Democratic fundraiser and as U.S. ambassador to France.

Strollers on Wisconsin Avenue step into the street to avoid holiday shoppers crowding a sidewalk vendor in 1973. The "generation gap" of the 1960s continued to widen in the 1970s. For the young, Georgetown was the place to be. There, boutiques beckoned where hardware was once sold.

piece of the action. However, full home rule was the issue that wouldn't go away, and Barry was unsuccessful in making any headway on it. His drive for a constitutional amendment to give D.C. two elected senators and two congressmen in the early 1980s passed Congress, thanks to the support of Democratic Senator Edward M. Kennedy of Massachusetts, but it failed to win ratification by state legislatures.

A taste of political influence had already come in 1964 when, for the first time since 1800, Washingtonians voted in a presidential election. Then, in 1967, President Lyndon B. Johnson appointed a transitional mayor and City Council. The first mayor and council elected in the 20th century were chosen in 1972. The first mayor, Walter Washington, was African American, as was more than half of the original council. But Johnson was the last president to exert any serious political muscle on behalf of the city's residents. Local officials of the 1960s and 1970s believed (and said publicly) that they had best not rock the boat; change would come at some point, and it would only come more slowly if voices were strident. Others saw the struggle for full home rule as a natural outgrowth of the civil rights revolt percolating throughout the country at the time, especially since Washington had become majority-black in 1957.

Barry disagreed with the go-slow approach and alienated white supporters of home rule, even though whites had helped lead the charge for open public accommodations in the city from the 1930s to the 1950s. Barry's habit of "playing the race card"—blaming the white power structure for the city's problems—made it clear from the late 1970s on that whites were no longer welcome. Not a single white served in a key position in any Barry administration. After Barry's drug conviction, his race-baiting farewell remarks drove the two camps even farther apart. His final days were mired in disgrace. The Congress had installed a panel called the District of Columbia Financial Responsibility and Management Assistance Authority (known as the Control Board). It ran almost every facet of the city government. On his final day in office, Barry had direct authority over only one city agency—the Recreation Department.

Barry's successor, Anthony Williams, elected in 1998, was given back most mayoral powers before the Control Board was required by Congress to do so. At the same time, real estate values in all city neighborhoods rose at the end of the 1990s, for the first time since the 1970s. The reason was strong demand from single people, from childless couples and from families weary of long suburban commutes.

But Washington's suburbs continued to stretch and expand to new heights—even into new states. At the end of the 1990s, the metropolitan area contained nearly 4.5 million people and stretched more than 80 miles to the north and west. The Bureau of the Census now considered Jefferson County, W. Va., and Adams County, Pa., part of the D.C. area, along with once-rural counties like Stafford

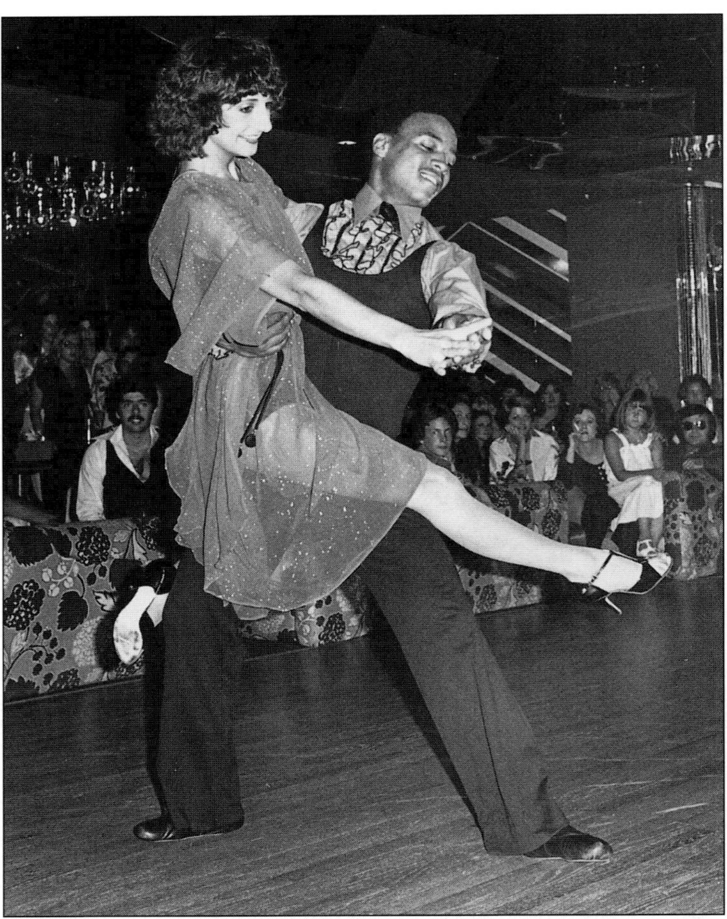

By the end of the 1970s, disco seemed to have everyone clad in slinky polyester doing the "Hustle" in local clubs such as the Plum on 21st Street, N.W., where Annette Filippini and Marvin Thomas compete in a 1978 dance contest.

Police cadet Janetta Winters employs some moves of her own as she directs traffic at Connecticut Avenue and K Street, N.W., during a bus strike in 1974.

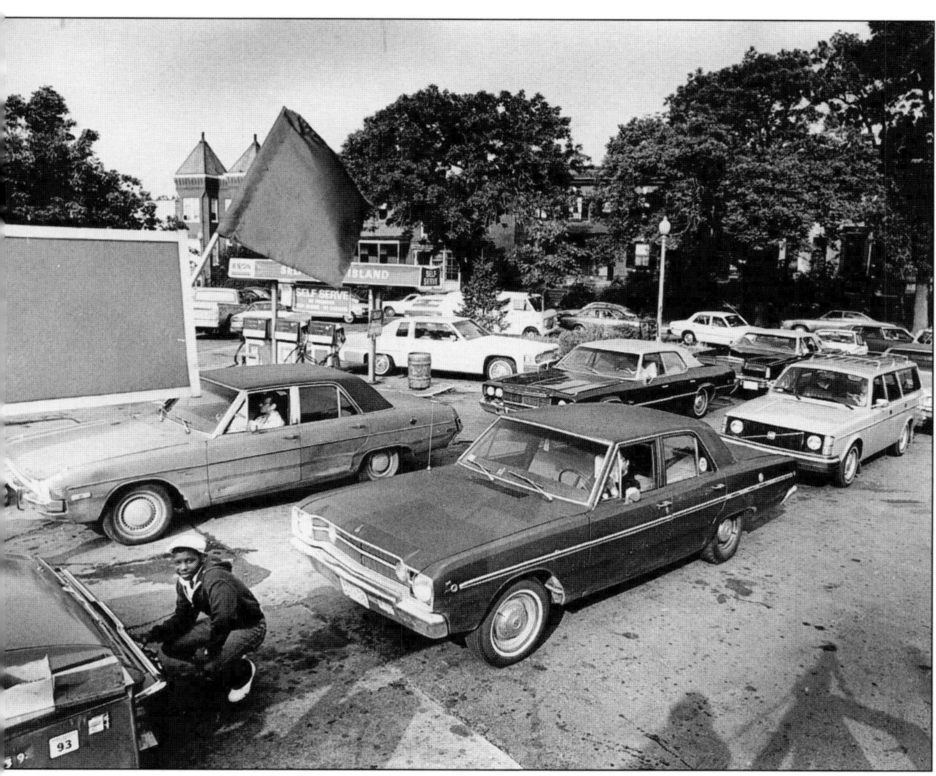

Drivers line up to purchase gasoline at an Exxon station on Pennsylvania Ave., S.E., in July 1979. Gas lines first appeared in Washington in 1973, when Arab nations began a one-year oil embargo against the United States in retaliation for U.S. support of Israel. For the first time since World War II, Washingtonians resigned themselves to rationing. When gas prices reached $1 a gallon in 1979 after another price hike, gas lines—and short tempers—returned.

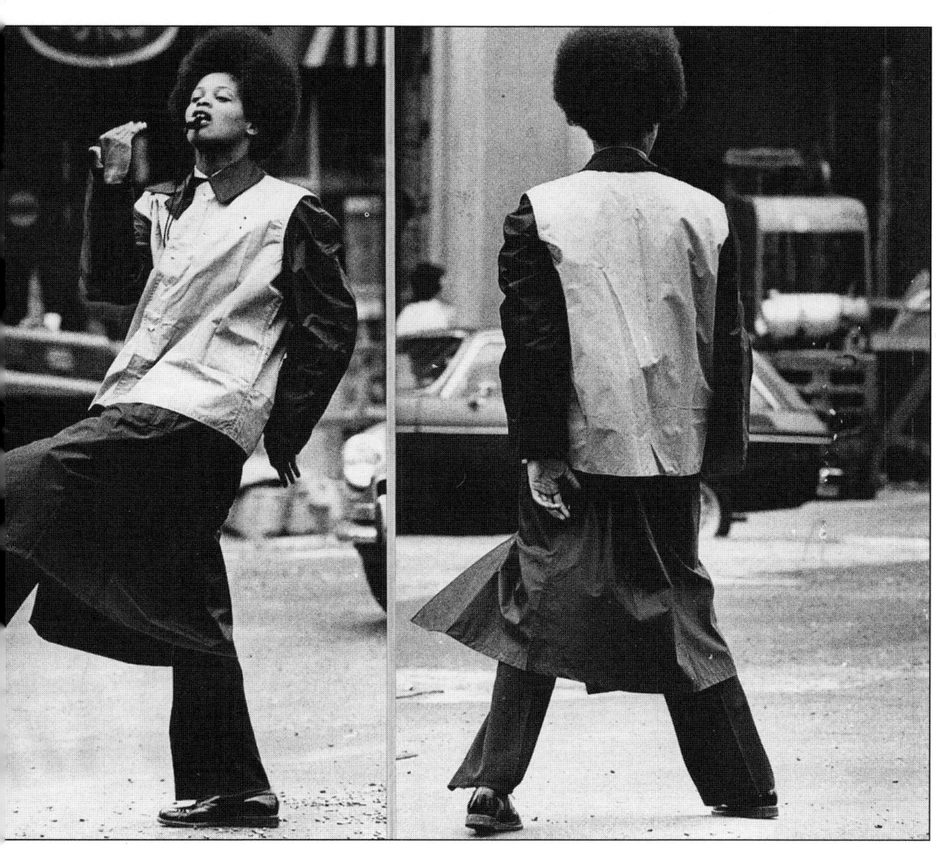

and Loudoun in Virginia and Howard and Charles in Maryland.

Federal employment had declined to 2,799,020 by the end of 1998, according to the Office of Personnel Management, the lowest level since 1966. Yet businesses that fed the government were flourishing—and Washington's suburbs sprouted first-rank high-technology companies like America Online along the Dulles Airport corridor in Virginia and prominent biotech firms along Interstate 270 in Maryland. A one-industry "company town" had at last become a commercial center as well, giving the area a fundamentally different identity.

Yet Washington's sharp separation between rich and poor remained as wide as ever. Fairfax and Montgomery counties were routinely among the most affluent jurisdictions in the world. Prince George's County had the highest per-household income among African American residents of any jurisdiction in the world. Washington-area residents owned more foreign cars—and more expensive makes—than in any metropolitan area in the world. But the poor continued to get poorer. While unemployment in the 1990s never exceeded 5.3 percent in the Washington area as a whole, it averaged 27 percent at the end of 1998 for those in the haggard sections of far Southeast Washington. For men under 25 in those neighborhoods, unemployment averaged 40.5 percent.

Where will the evolution of Washington lead? Some things seem clear, others cloudy.

What, for example, will happen to population trends? Most

likely, for one thing, the city will have even greater ethnic diversity. Washington has historically been a destination for political refugees from around the world. Latinos have quietly become more than 10 percent of the city's population. Asians now account for just under 3 percent. If all politics is local, and if the lion's share of Washington politics is racial, the dynamics promise to be more complicated than ever. But the city also may lose more residents, becoming a capital of greater extremes, of the very rich and the very poor. Metro construction that has brought another wave of gentrification to in-town neighborhoods, pushing out renters and pulling in home-buyers, raises that prospect.

Will the downtown get economically stronger? A new two-square-block convention center near the MCI Center suggests that possibility. But the suburbs' striking growth of employment at high-tech and biotech firms, at a thriving media company like Discovery Communications and at suppliers to these and other companies shows no signs of flagging.

Politically, the city's future is as uncertain as it was in 1800. Despite flurries of activity on behalf of statehood and full congressional representation, serious political change has never come close to happening. Neither major political party has endorsed full home rule or full voting rights for city residents. With no prospect of political change, voter turnout in Washington is traditionally low. Only 26 percent of District residents went to the polls during the 1998 general election for mayor and City Council—among the

Some of the more than 50,000 who traveled free on Metro's first day in March 1976 throng the Rhode Island Avenue station during opening ceremonies.

Intrepid bicycle commuter Kathleen Harte threads her way down Wisconsin Avenue, N.W., towards M Street in 1983.

An opening-day train sweeps past the Capitol along the first piece of the Red Line, a ride of less than 10 minutes from Rhode Island Avenue to Farragut Square. The estimated cost of the 103-mile system when completed: $10 billion.

With dramatic suburban growth, a still-unfinished Metro and Washingtonians' reluctance to give up their cars, commuters of the 1980s came up with creative solutions. These workers are part of a "slug" line at a Springfield, Va., parking lot, where drivers create informal carpools to qualify for the HOV (high-occupancy vehicle) express lanes on I-395. The lanes were built for buses, but Virginia opened them to carpools of four in 1973.

lowest such percentages in the country. Could retrocession to Maryland be the best long-term answer for the District of Columbia? The idea began to attract attention during the 1990s, mostly from Capitol Hill conservatives but also from some business leaders, but it has had no significant momentum behind it.

What can be said with some confidence is that the public Washington, the city of grand buildings and monuments, will continue to draw the families and children from across the nation and around the world who descend on the center of global power each year. Indeed, tourism has grown every year since 1970, and the crowds do not come because of the suburbs.

Lunchtime crowds fill the sidewalks of the 1700 block of K Street, N.W. in 1978. Ten years after the riots, many Washington law firms, associations and other businesses dependent on the federal government were concentrated along the K Street corridor west of 14th. Department stores had folded or departed for bigger and grander suburban shopping malls, such as White Flint in Montgomery County (below right), which opened in 1977. The old downtown was left with increasingly common scenes of boarded up storefronts and offices, like these (below left) at 9th and F streets in 1979.

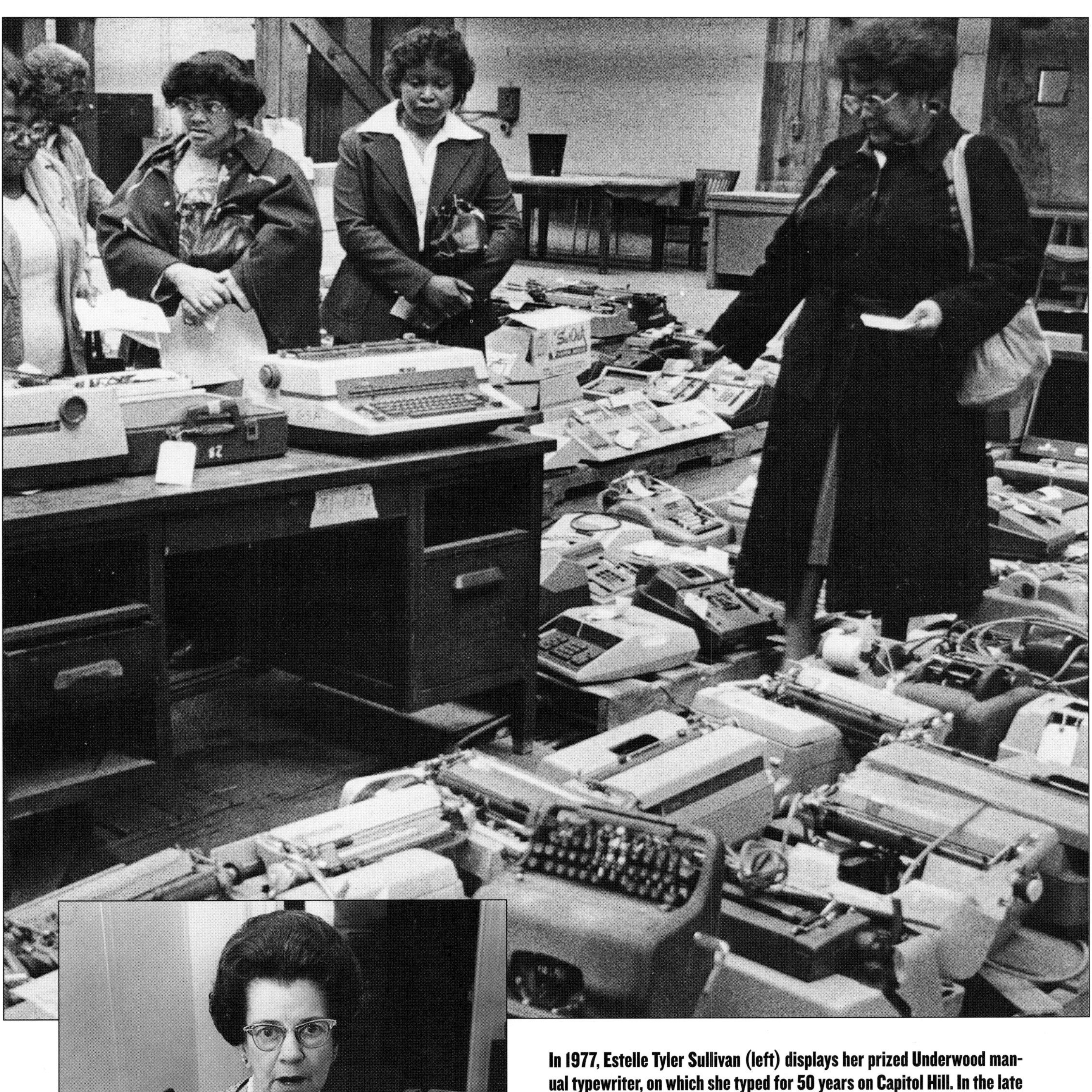

In 1977, Estelle Tyler Sullivan (left) displays her prized Underwood manual typewriter, on which she typed for 50 years on Capitol Hill. In the late 1970s, Washington offices still relied on typewriters, with most typists preferring electric models. By the early 1980s, the personal computer was rendering typewriters obsolete, although they were still valued, as these customers (above) at a 1982 GSA surplus sale attest.

Hundreds of young people register for summer jobs at the D.C. Employment Commission in March 1980. While Marion Barry's four terms as mayor left a legacy of racial division, failing schools, a bloated bureaucracy and a takeover by a congressionally appointed Control Board, Barry did consistently find funding for summer jobs for the city's youth. At right, youths cool off in the summer of 1980 by playing Frisbee amid sprinklers.

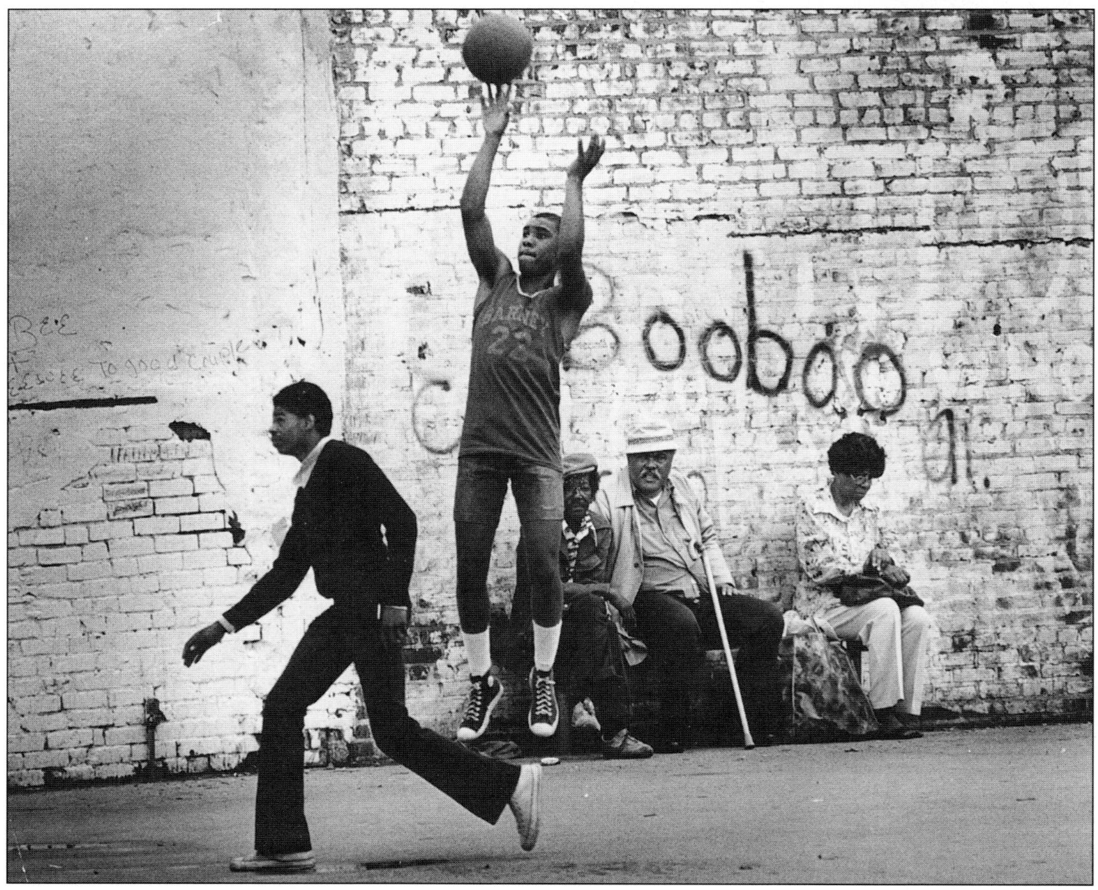

Two young hoopsters show their stuff for some bench-sitting elders.

Residents gather in front of newly renovated public housing in the James Creek project in Southwest. Built on the eve of World War II, James Creek escaped the wrecking ball during the urban renewal of Southwest. By the late 1970s, it was a series of rundown, barracks-like buildings. Housing officials, mindful of the mistakes of 20 years earlier, chose to rehabilitate houses for those living there instead of razing structures and removing people.

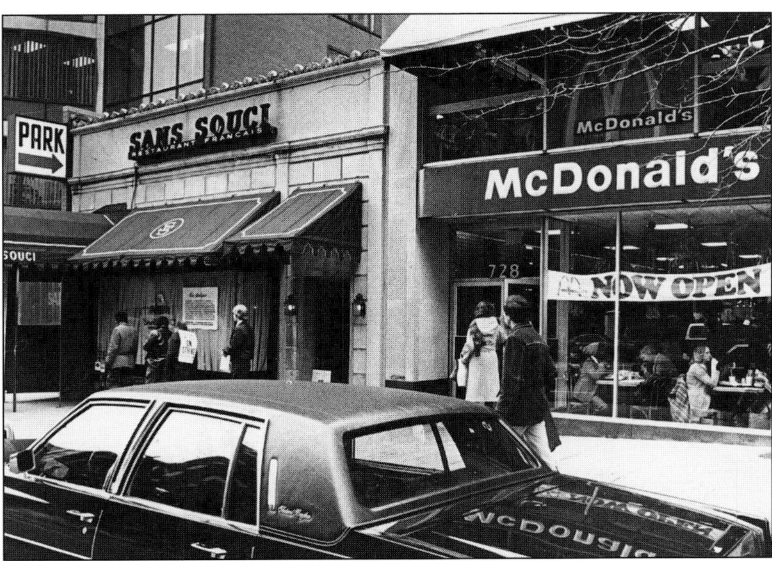

The Sans Souci, a block from the White House and home of the "Sans Souci lunch," a euphemism for the three-martini meal that once lubricated Washington power plays, gets a new neighbor in January 1979. Today, an even newer McDonalds is found on the same block of 17th Street, but the Sans Souci closed in 1981, a victim chiefly of competition and labor troubles.

Pressman Hugh Ball holds the last edition of the *Washington Star* on August 7, 1981. Born as the *Evening Star*, the influential daily was long the city's leading newspaper. Evening TV news and auto commuting hurt the *Star*, as they did afternoon papers everywhere. The *Star* outranked the *Post* in revenues and circulation until the late 1950s, when the *Post*, after its 1954 purchase of the *Times-Herald* gave it a morning monopoly, took the lead.

Tyson's Corner, Va., was a country crossroads when this photo (right) was taken circa 1935, and it remained essentially rural through the 1950s. Soon after Tyson's Corner Center, then the nation's largest single-level mall, opened in 1968, the area became a hub of employment — the first major one created by the Capital Beltway. In 1999, some 115,000 people worked in Tyson's Corner's shops and high-rise offices (below), and northern Virginians coped with some of the area's worst traffic congestion.

A new speed bump on Nutley Street in Vienna, Va., in 1987. Drivers complained that the bumps damaged their cars. By the 1980s, despite efforts to promote carpooling and public transportation, heavy auto traffic prompted the drivers to seek the least congested routes—often through neighborhoods where residents resorted to bumps to slow them down.

At left, Kelly Parker, Jody Long, Mari Satterly, Mary Bloss and Catherine Bloss of Magruder High School in Gaithersburg, Md., touch up their makeup in a retreat to the ladies' room at their 1984 prom. Below, Alvin Dan, Lisa Ng, Long Hoang, Thao Ton Tri Ngo and Shiun Oh enjoy their stretch limo en route to the 1987 prom for Silver Spring's Springbrook High School. By the 1980s, Washington and its suburbs had taken on a multicultural look, with dramatic growth in the Asian and Latino populations.

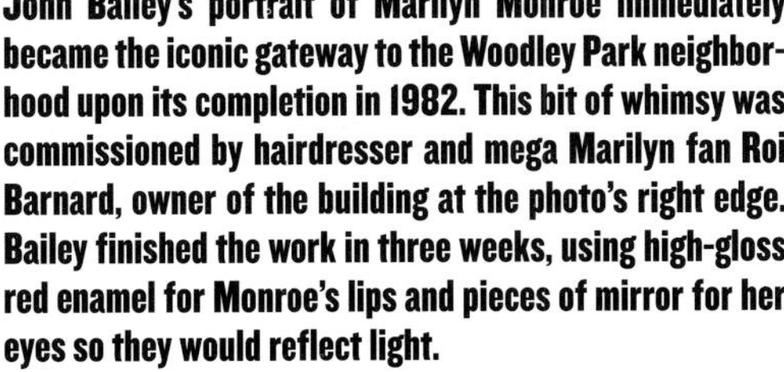

John Bailey's portrait of Marilyn Monroe immediately became the iconic gateway to the Woodley Park neighborhood upon its completion in 1982. This bit of whimsy was commissioned by hairdresser and mega Marilyn fan Roi Barnard, owner of the building at the photo's right edge. Bailey finished the work in three weeks, using high-gloss red enamel for Monroe's lips and pieces of mirror for her eyes so they would reflect light.

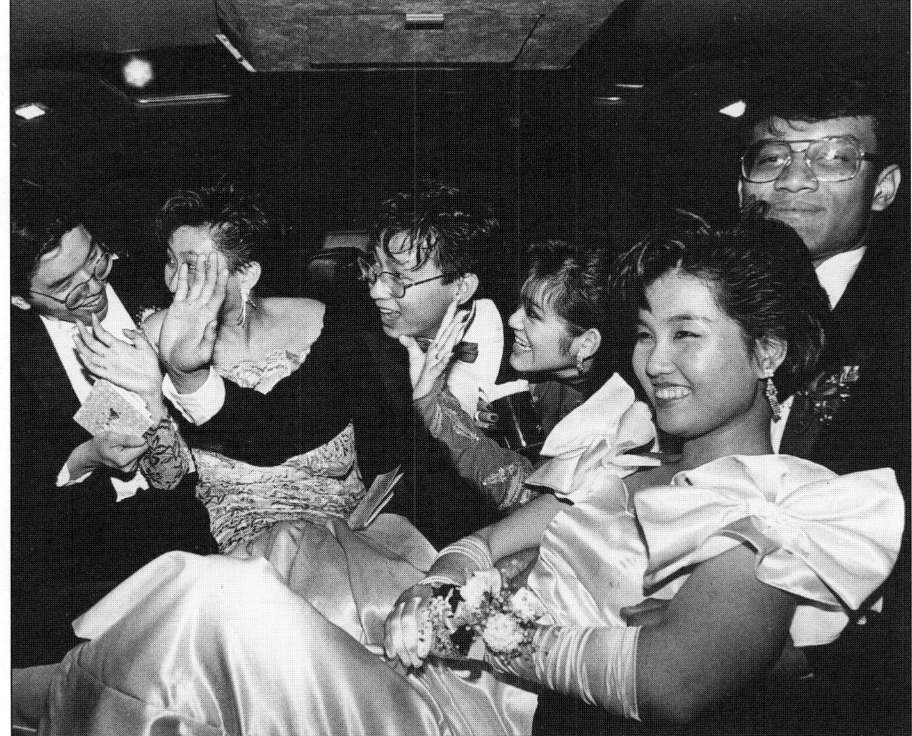

Anna Laubert, a waitress at a Sholl's Cafeteria on the corner of Vermont Avenue and K Street, N.W., kisses longtime customer Judy Garris as Nancy Kendall, left, watches. All three hold hands in a farewell on the restaurant's final day in November 1984, after it lost its lease. Sholl's remains a low-cost and old-choice at its one surviving location, on K Street.

The gold-topped spires of the Mormon Temple (left) greet westbound drivers coming over a Capital Beltway hill, between Georgia and Connecticut avenues. Some wag, reminded of the Land of Oz, painted the declaration on the bridge. Like other major religious institutions, the Church of Latter Day Saints sought a presence in Washington in part as a quasi-embassy to represent its interests to the government. In 1994, the Ahmadiyya Movement, an offshoot of traditional Islam, opens a 22,000-square-foot mosque (above) in Silver Spring, at Good Hope and Briggs Chaney roads.

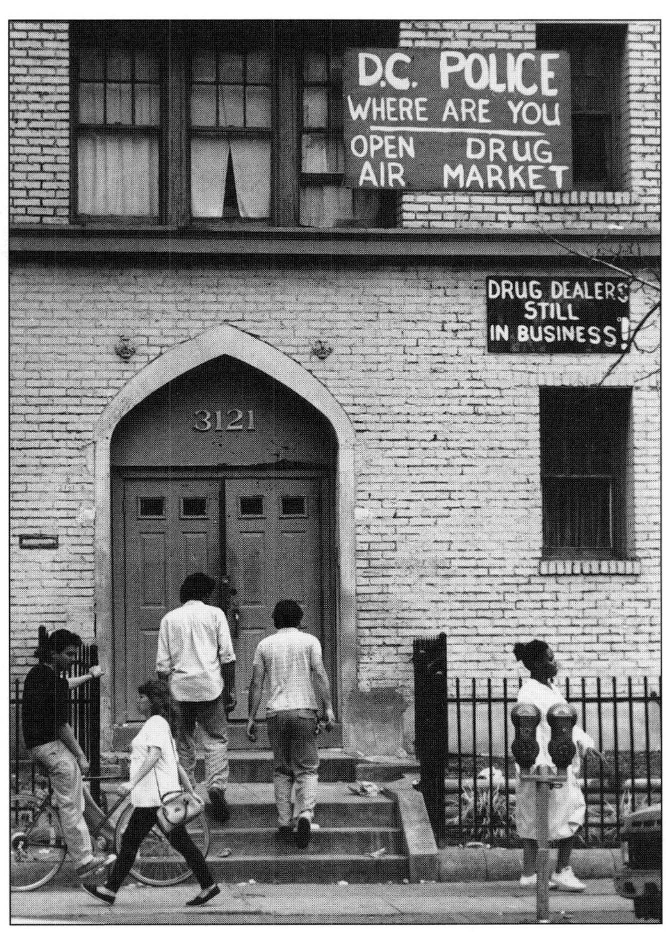

Above, plainclothes officers arrest suspects in 1981 after witnessing drug buying on 14th Street, N.W. At right, residents of an apartment building on Mount Pleasant Street, N.W., appeal for police in 1989 to rid their street of drug dealers. Below, members of the D.C. Narcotics Task Force arrest a suspect on Blaine Street, N.E. In the 1980s, without drug rehabilitation programs and effective educational and vocational training, the easy money of drug dealing continued to appeal to large numbers of poorer youths.

Ahmed Ali, left, continues rehearsing as his Duke Ellington School of the Arts classmates take a break in preparing for a public school orchestra concert at the Kennedy Center in 1991. Ellington opened in Georgetown's former Western High School in 1974 to offer high-level training in the arts.

Elke Ohnoutka, Sonia Martinez, Andrea Kolessar and Kelly Waggoner, four of six young women from Columbia, Md., sharing an Ocean City, Md., hotel room, prepare to go out during beach week, a traditional wild farewell to high school for affluent area teenagers.

Bargain hunters surge through the 14th Street, N.W., entrance of Garfinckel's department store during its 1990 going-out-of-business sale. Founded in 1905, the chain was bought in 1991 by Allied Stores Corp., the first in a series of owners who changed the store's upscale image. Unable to reach younger new consumers, the successors only alienated loyal customers. The arrival of national powerhouses such as Bloomingdale's, Neiman Marcus, Nordstrom and even Payless Shoes eventually overwhelmed Garfinckel's and almost all other homegrown chains. Gone are Kann's, Lansburgh's, Woodward & Lothrop, Dart Drug, Hahn Shoes and Rich's Shoes.

Washington Redskins owner Jack Kent Cooke gestures to Prince George's County Executive Wayne Curry as Cooke announces plans to build a new stadium in Landover, Md., in 1995. In the early 1990s Cooke had decided to seek a bigger and more profitable stadium for the three-time Super Bowl champions. Cooke died in 1997 as the stadium was under construction. Two years later, his estate sold the team to Bethesda businessman Daniel Snyder and several associates.

Latino day workers, most recent immigrants with few vocational skills, crowd around a contractor in need of help in 1991 at the corner of Silver Spring's Piney Branch Road and University Boulevard. Under President George Bush, Washington granted temporary legal status to undocumented Salvadorans and Guatemalans, letting them receive work permits. Immigrants now dominate the area's laboring and domestic service jobs.

Mayor Marion Barry enters the federal courthouse in 1990 (above) for arraignment on misdemeanor cocaine-possession charges. Barry's arrest at the Vista Hotel by hidden FBI agents worsened the city's racial divide. As his trial proceeded, supporters expressed hope via tee shirts (facing page, top) that he would be exonerated. Five years later, after serving a six-month sentence in a federal prison, Barry was elected to a fourth term despite opposition from the media, the white community and some members of the black middle class. He retook the reins on January 3, 1995 (below) from the incumbent, Sharon Pratt Kelly. Former Mayor Walter E. Washington, left, and Barry's wife Cora, right, look on. He declined to run again in 1998.

Mayor Anthony Williams in 1999 raises a soccer ball in celebration of D.C. United, the city's three-time Major League Soccer champions. Williams, an experienced government bureaucrat, was elected the year before by a city ready to move on from Marion Barry's politics of patronage and passion. The District's congressionally appointed Control Board, which had stripped Barry of authority over public works, administrative services, fire and emergency medical services, police, financial and personnel management, among other city functions, slowly began returning power to the mayor's office.

By 1987, Washington was no longer a black city surrounded by white suburbs. Instead, the majority of African Americans in the metropolitan area lived in the suburbs, with Prince George's County having the highest per-family income of any predominantly black area in the nation. Carol McGhee Taylor (above), a real estate agent who lives and works in the Mitchellville, Md., area, poses on the grand staircase of a house for sale in 1999 near the intersection of Enterprise and Lottsford roads. Nakia Turner, Carolyn Malachi and Chanita Arett (above right) watch the dancers at a cotillion in Largo, Md., that year.

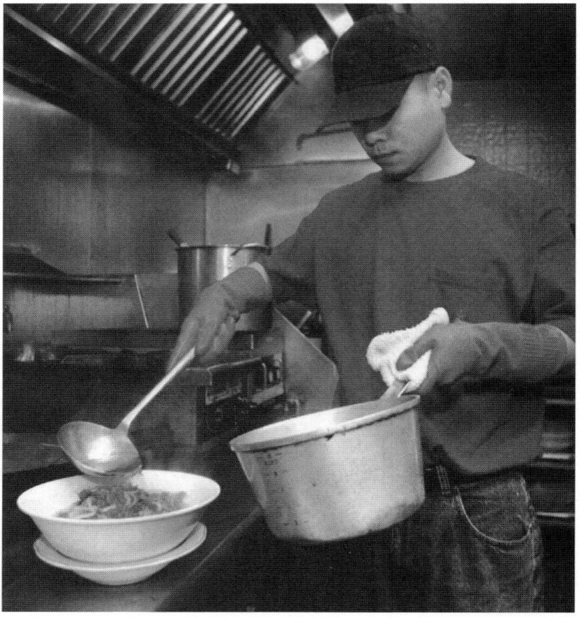

Nhan Phan (right) ladles Vietnamese beef soup at the Vietnam Grill in Manassas, Va. After 1950, thousands of new immigrants came to Washington, enriching the area with new cuisines and cultures. The fall of Saigon in 1975 triggered an influx of Vietnamese, especially those who had worked with U.S. forces or the South Vietnam government. The story was the same for citizens of other nations in political turmoil, including Cambodia, Laos, El Salvador, Iran, Ethiopia and Eritrea. As the saying goes, "Whenever a regime falls abroad, a new restaurant opens in Bethesda."

On the MCI Center's opening day in December 1997, fans watch the Washington Wizards play the Seattle Super Sonics. When Wizards owner Abe Pollin opened the arena in 1997, some credited him with beginning the reversal of nearly 50 years of suburban flight. The center on 7th Street, N.W., home also of the Washington Capitals hockey team, helped spark a revival of the surrounding neighborhood.

STATEHOOD

Washington is the only American city run by Congress and suffering from taxation without representation, an anomaly that has long been the subject of protests. Native Washingtonian Theodore Noyes, editor-in-chief of his family's newspaper, the *Evening Star*, constantly promoted home rule in the first half of the 20th century. His chief political cartoonist, Clifford Berryman, regularly produced drawings promoting home rule, such as this one from 1924. In 1947, members of the American Veterans Committee (below), a biracial group of activists who played key roles in challenging legally sanctioned segregation, urge citizens to approve a suffrage initiative. In 1973, supporters of home rule (left) rally at the District Building.

In the 1960s, frustrated local activists tried a new approach: statehood for Washington, whose population exceeds that of three existing states. The idea of statehood was first suggested in connection with New York City in 1969, when Norman Mailer and Jimmy Breslin ran for mayor there. D.C. journalist and politico Sam Smith translated the notion into a platform for Washington in 1970. Josephine Butler (below left), a union organizer, educator and community activist until her death in 1997, worked with Statehood Party founders Julius Hobson, Sr., Smith and others for statehood. During the 1980s and 1990s, citizens and the City Council endorsed the idea. By the end of the 1990s, both the statehood initiative and an alternative—a constitutional amendment granting the District voting rights in Congress, with two senators and two representatives—had failed.

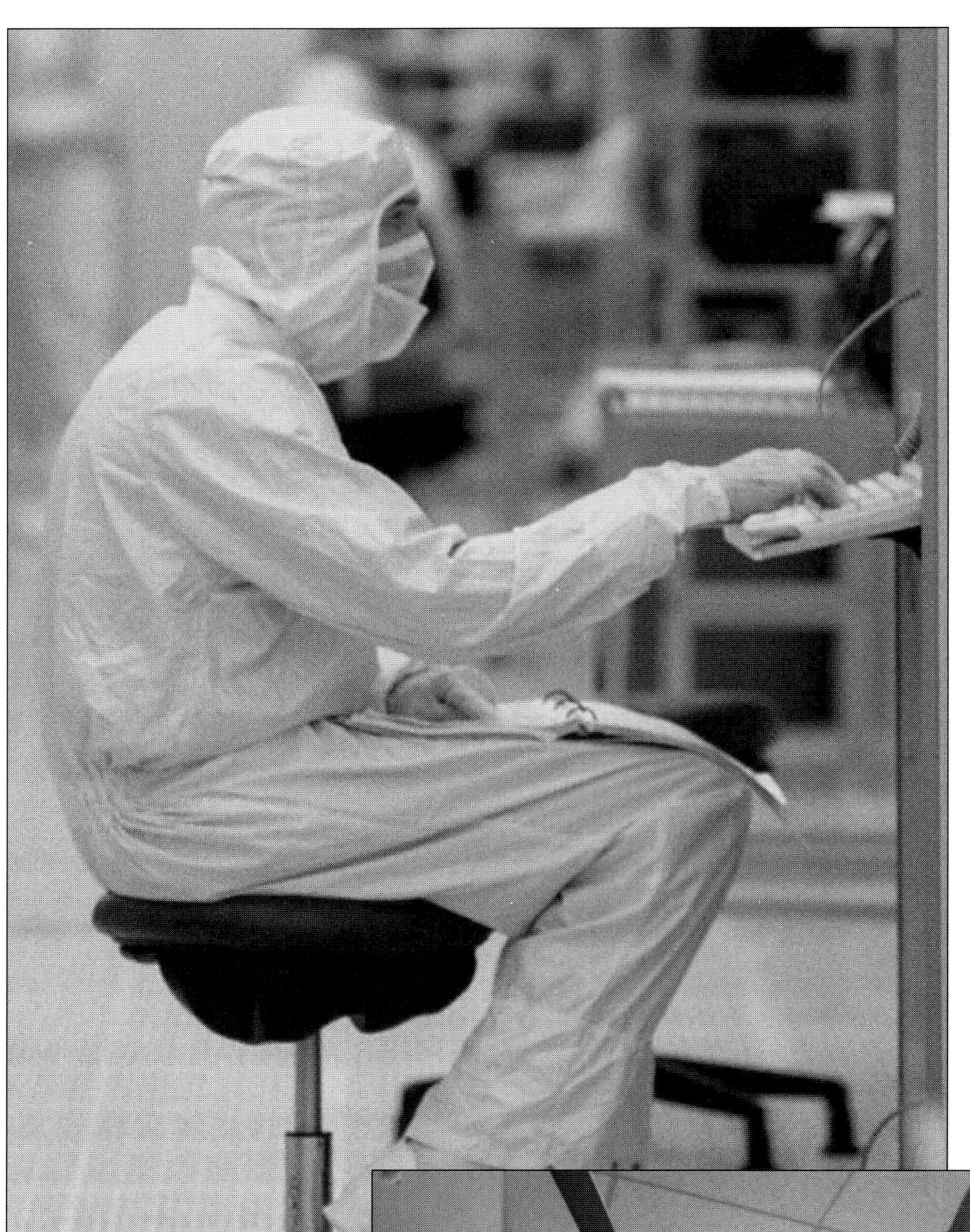

By the late 1990s, the national capital area had achieved one of George Washington's dreams: to create a center of commerce and industry as well as of government. In the suburbs, high-tech, biotech and other firms sprouted, and by 1999 technology workers outnumbered those who toiled for the government. At left, a dust-free technician operates a computer at Dominion Semiconductor in Manassas, Va., a $1.7 billion facility where IBM computer chips are made. Below, students Heath Mullins, foreground, and Chris Orange, seeking marketable computer skills, work on the insides of a computer at the Computer Learning Center, also in Manassas.

SELECTED BIBLIOGRAPHY

Listed here are the most important sources consulted for *Washington Album.* In addition, hundreds of *Washington Post* and *Evening Star* articles were reviewed.

Alfers, Kenneth G. *Law and Order in the Capital City: A History of the Washington Police, 1800-1886.* Washington: GW Washington Studies, George Washington University, 1976.

Bedini, Silvio A. "The Survey of the Federal Territory." *Washington History* 3-1 (spring/summer 1991): 76-95.

Borchert, James. *Alley Life in Washington: Family, Community, Religion, and Folklife in the City, 1850-1970.* Urbana: University of Chicago Press, 1980.

Boswell, Thomas, et al. *Redskins: A History of Washington's Team.* Washington: Washington Post Books, 1997.

Bowling, Kenneth R. *The Creation of Washington, D.C.: The Idea and Location of the American Capital.* Fairfax, VA: George Mason University Press, 1991.

Brinkley, Alan. *American History: A Survey.* New York: McGraw-Hill, 1995.

Brinkley, David. *Washington Goes to War.* New York: Alfred A. Knopf, 1988.

Buchholz, Margaret Thomas. "Josephine: The Washington Diary of a War Worker, 1918-1919." *Washington History* 10-2 (fall/winter 1998-99): 4-23.

Bustard, Bruce I. *Washington: Behind the Monuments.* Washington: National Archives and Records Administration, 1990.

Butler, J. George. *Simpler Times: Stories of Early Twentieth Century Life.* Arlington, VA: Vandamere Press, 1997.

Caplan, Marvin. "Eat Anywhere!" *Washington History* 1-1 (spring 1989): 25-40.

Cary, Francine Curro. *Urban Odyssey: A Multicultural History of Washington, D.C.* Washington: Smithsonian Institution Press, 1996.

Clark-Lewis, Elizabeth, ed. *First Freed: Washington, D.C., in the Emancipation Era.* Washington: A.P. Foundation Press, 1998.

Davis, John. "Eastman Johnson's *Negro Life at the South* and Urban Slavery in Washington, D.C." *Art Bulletin* 80-1 (March 1998): 67-92.

Dickens, Charles. *American Notes.*1892; reprint ed., New York: Fawcett Publications, 1961.

Dickson, Paul. *Timelines: Day by Day and Trend by Trend from the Dawn of the Atomic Age to the Gulf War.* New York: Addison Wesley, 1990.

Diner, Steven J. et al. *Housing Washington's People: Public Policy in Retrospect,* Studies in D.C. History and Public Policy. Washington, D.C.: University of the District of Columbia, 1983.

Elfenbein, Jessica. *Civics, Commerce, and Community: The History of the Greater Washington Board of Trade, 1889-1989.* Washington: Center for Washington Area Studies, George Washington University, 1989.

Elliott, Laura and Rudy Maxa. "This Is the Way It Was." *Washingtonian* 21-1 (October 1985): 179-221

Ellis, John B. *The Sights and Secrets of the National Capital.* Chicago: Jones, Junkin, 1869.

Federal Writers Project. *Washington: City and Capital.* Washington: Government Printing Office, 1937.

Fitzpatrick, Sandra and Maria R. Goodwin. *The Guide to Black Washington,* revised edition. New York: Hippocrene Books, 1999.

Gilbert, Ben W. and the Staff of *The Washington Post. Ten Blocks from the White House: Anatomy of the Washington Riots of 1968.* New York: Frederick A. Praeger, 1968.

Gillette, Howard Jr. *Between Justice and Beauty: Race, Planning, and the Failure of Urban Policy in Washington, D.C.* Baltimore: Johns Hopkins University Press, 1995.

Gillette, Howard Jr., ed. *Southern City, National Ambition: The Growth of Early Washington, D.C., 1800-1860.* Washington: American Architectural Foundation and George Washington University Center for Washington Area Studies, 1995.

Goldfield, David R. "Antebellum Washington in Context: The Pursuit of Prosperity and Identity." In Howard Gillette, Jr., ed., *Southern City, National Ambition: The Growth of Early Washington, D.C., 1800-1860.* Washington: American Architectural Foundation and George Washington University Center for Washington Area Studies, 1995.

Gutheim, Frederick. *Worthy of the Nation: The History of Planning for the National Capital,* National Capital Planning Commission Historical Studies. Washington: Smithsonian Institution Press, 1977.

Green, Constance McLaughlin. *The Secret City: A History of Race Relations in the Nation's Capital.* Princeton: Princeton University Press, 1967.

________. *Washington, D.C.: A History of the Capital,* 1800-1950. Princeton: Princeton University Press, 1962, paperback ed. 1967.

Green, Paul S. and Shirley L., "Old Southwest Remembered: The Photographs of Joseph Owen Curtis." *Washington History* 1-2 (fall 1989): 42-57.

Harris, C.M. "Washington's Gamble, L'Enfant's Dream: Politics, Design, and the Founding of the Nation's Capital." *William and Mary Quarterly,* 3d series, 56-3 (July 1999): 527-62.

Harris, Charles Wesley. *Congress and the Governance of the Nation's Capital: The Conflict of Federal and Local Interests.* Washington, D.C.: Georgetown University Press, 1995.

Hines, Christian. *Early Recollections of Washington City.* Washington: 1866. reprint ed., Junior League of Washington, 1981.

Jackson, Kenneth T. "Federal Subsidy and the Suburban Dream: The First Quarter-Century of Government Intervention in the Housing Market." *Records of the Columbia Historical Society* 50 (1980): 421-451.

Jacob, Kathryn Allamong. *Capital Elites: High Society in Washington, D.C., After the Civil War.* Washington: Smithsonian Institution Press, 1995.

Jaffe, Harry S. "Mocha Town." *Washingtonian* 35-2 (November 1999): 65-164.

__________ and Tom Sherwood. *Dream City: Race, Power, and the Decline of Washington, D.C.* New York: Simon & Schuster, 1994.

Johnson, David K. " 'Homosexual Citizens': Washington's Gay Community Confronts the Civil Service." *Washington History* 6-2 (fall/winter 1994-95): 44-63.

Junior League of Washington. *The City of Washington: An Illustrated History.* ed. Thomas Froncek. New York: Wings Books, 1977.

Kimmel, Stanley. *Mr. Lincoln's Washington.* New York: Coward-McCann, 1957.

King, LeRoy O. Jr. *100 Years of Capital Traction: The Story of Streetcars in the Nation's Capital.* Dallas, TX: LeRoy O. King, Jr., 1972.

Kiplinger, Austin with Knight Kiplinger. *Washington Now.* New York: 1975.

Kiplinger, W.M. with Austin Kiplinger. *Washington Is Like That.* New York: Harper & Brothers, 1942.

Klaus, Susan. " 'Some of the Smartest Folks Here': The Van Nesses and Community Building in Early Washington." *Washington History* 3-2 (fall/winter 1991-92): 22-45.

Kluger, Richard. *Simple Justice: The History of Brown v. Board of Education and Black America's Struggle for Equality.* New York: Vintage Books, 1977.

Korr, Jeremy. "The Birth of the Capital Beltway in Maryland." *Montgomery Gazette,* Feb. 19, 1999.

Lait, Jack and Lee Mortimer. *Washington Confidential: The Lowdown on the Big Town.* New York: Crown, 1951.

Leech, Margaret. *Reveille in Washington: 1860-1865.* New York: Harper & Brothers, 1941.

Levey, Bob and Steve Wursta. *Washington: City on a Hill.* Memphis: Towery, 1997.

Levey, Jane Freundel. "The Levitt Legacy." *Regardie's* (May 1984): 78-86.

________. "The Scurlock Studio," *Washington History* 1-1 (1989): 41-58.

________. "Segregation in Education: A Basis for Jim Crow in Washington, D.C., 1804-1880. M.A. thesis, George Washington University, 1991.

________. "The Way We Were [Woodward & Lothrop]." *Washingtonian* 31-3 (December 1995): 78-81.

Look, David W. and Carole L. Perrault. "The Interior Building: Its Architecture and Its Art." Preservation Case Studies, U.S. Department of the Interior, National Park Service, Preservation Assistance Division, 1986.

Longstreth, Richard W. "The Mixed Blessings of Success: The Hecht Company and Department Store Branch Development after World War II." Center for Washington Area Studies Occasional Paper No. 14, George Washington University, January 1995.

McNeil, Genna Rae. *Groundwork: Charles Hamilton Houston and the Struggle for Civil Rights.* Philadelphia: University of Pennsylvania Press, 1983.

Melder, Keith et al. *City of Magnificent Intentions: A History of Washington, District of Columbia.* Washington: Intac, Inc., 1997.

Miller, Fredric M. and Howard Gillette, Jr. *Washington Seen: A Photographic History, 1875-1965.* Baltimore: Johns Hopkins University Press, 1995.

Mitchell, Mary. *Divided Town.* Barre, MA: Barre Publishers, 1968.

Offutt, William. *Bethesda: A Social History.* Bethesda, MD: The Innovation Game, 1995.

Ogilvie, Philip W., comp. "Chronology of Some Events in the History of the District of Columbia." Unpub. ms., 1992.

Pacifico, Michele F. "'Don't Buy Where You Can't Work': The New Negro Alliance of Washington. *Washington History* 6-1 (spring/summer 1994): 66-88.

Paynter, John H. *Horse and Buggy Days With Uncle Sam.* New York: Margent Press, 1943.

Perl, Peter. "Nation's Capital Held at Mercy of the Mob," *Washington Post Magazine,* July 16, 1989, 18-39.

Poore, Ben: Perley. *Reminiscences of Sixty Years in the National Metropolis.* Philadelphia: Hubbard Brothers, 1886.

Reiff, Daniel D. *Washington Architecture: 1791-1861.* Washington: U.S. Commission of Fine Arts, 1971.

Reps, John W. *Monumental Washington: The Planning and Development of the Capital Center.* Princeton: Princeton University Press, 1967.

Roberts, Chalmers M. *In the Shadow of Power: The Story of The Washington Post.* Cabin John, MD: Seven Locks Press, 1989.

Scott, Pamela. *Temple of Liberty: Building the Capitol for a New Nation.* New York: Oxford University Press, 1995.

__________ and Antoinette J. Lee. *Buildings of the District of Columbia.* New York: Oxford University Press, 1993.

Smith, Kathryn Schneider. *Port Town to Urban Neighborhood: The Georgetown Waterfront of Washington, D.C., 1880-1920.* Washington: Center for Washington Area Studies, George Washington University, 1989.

_________. *Washington at Home: An Illustrated History of Neighborhoods in the Nation's Capital.* Northridge, CA: Windsor Publications, 1988.

Smith, Sam. *Captive Capital: Colonial Life in Modern Washington.* Bloomington: Indiana University Press, 1974.

Sween, Jane C. *Montgomery County: Two Centuries of Change*. Woodland Hills, CA: Windsor Publications, 1984.

Thursz, Daniel. *Where Are They Now? A Study of the Impact of Relocation on Former Residents of Southwest Washington Who Were Served in an HWC Demonstration Project*. Washington: Health and Welfare Council of the National Capital Area, 1966.

Terrell, Mary Church. *A Colored Woman in a White World*. Washington: National Association of Colored Women's Clubs Inc., 1968.

Van Dyne, Larry. "The Making of Washington." *Washingtonian* 23-2 (Nov. 1987): 161-320.

Wansy, Henry, et al. *The District in the XVIIIth Century: History, Site-Strategy, Real Estate Market, Landscape, &c. as Described by the Earliest Travellers*. Washington: Judd & Detweiler, 1909.

Warden, David Baillie. *A Chorographical and Statistical Description of the District of Columbia*. Paris: Smith, 1816.

Washington, D.C., with Its Points of Interest Illustrated. New York: Mercantile Illustration Co., 1894.

Weinstein, David. "Women's Shows and the Selling of Television to Washington, D.C." *Washington History* 11-1 (spring/summer 1999): 4-23.

Wetterau, Bruce. *The New York Public Library Book of Chronologies*. New York: Prentice Hall, 1990.

Williams, Juan. *Eyes on the Prize: America's Civil Rights Years, 1954-1965*. New York: Viking, 1987.

Young, James Sterling. *The Washington Community: 1800-1828*. New York: Harcourt, Brace, 1966.

ILLUSTRATION CREDITS

Wherever possible, photographers' names are included.

Chapter 1

17: Top, © The George Washington University 2000, The George Washington University Permanent Collection, Courtesy of The Dimock Gallery; bottom right, Library of Congress.
18: Library of Congress.
18-19: Courtesy, Don A. Hawkins.
20: Top, Kiplinger Washington Collection; middle, Historical Society of Washington, D.C.; bottom, Library of Congress.
21: Top, Allentown Art Museum, Purchase: Public Subscription by Citizens of Allentown and the Lehigh Valley, 1987; bottom, Historical Society of Washington, D.C.
22: Top, Library of Congress; bottom, James A. Parcell for The Washington Post.
23: Top, National Archives; bottom, Library of Congress.
24-5: Top, Dumbarton House; bottom, Kiplinger Washington Collection.
25: Library of Congress.
26: Historical Society of Washington, D.C.
26-7: Courtesy, Henry E. Huntington Library.
27: Top, Historical Society of Washington, D.C.; middle, The Historical Society of Pennsylvania, accession #1892.1; bottom, Library of Congress.
28: Top, White House Collection, courtesy, White House Historical Association; bottom left, White House Collection, courtesy, White House Historical Association; bottom right, The Octagon, the museum of the American Architectural Foundation.
29: Top, Maryland Historical Society, Baltimore, Maryland; bottom, Andrew W. Mellon Collection, Photograph © Board of Trustees, National Gallery of Art, Washington.
30: All, Kiplinger Washington Collection.
31: Top, National Park Service; bottom, Library of Congress.
32-3: Library of Congress.
34: Top, The Metropolitan Museum of Art, Purchase, Joseph Pulitzer Bequest, 1942. Photograph © 1989 The Metropolitan Museum of Art; middle left, *Ben: Perley Poore's Reminiscences of Sixty Years in the National Metropolis*; middle right, Library of Congress; bottom, © Collection of the New-York Historical Society, accession number 1832.41.
35: Top, White House Collection, courtesy, White House Historical Association; bottom left, Historical Society of Washington, D.C.; bottom right, Collection of Tudor Place Foundation, Inc. (Joel Breger).
36-37: Library of Congress.
38: All, *Poore's Reminiscences.*
39: Top, Diplomatic Reception Rooms, United States Department of State; bottom, Kiplinger Washington Collection.
40: Top left, Library of Congress; top right, The Washington Post; bottom, © Collection of the New-York Historical Society, accession number S-225.
41: Top, Library of Congress; bottom, © Collection of the New-York Historical Society, negative number 1574.

Chapter 2

43: Top, Library of Congress; bottom, National Park Service.
44-5: All, Library of Congress
46-7: Historical Society of Washington, D.C.
47: Bottom, Library of Congress.
48: Top, National Park Service; bottom, Moorland-Spingarn Research Center, Howard University.
49: Library of Congress.
50: Bottom, Historical Society of Washington, D.C.
50-1: Library of Congress.
52-3: Library of Congress.
54: Top, National Archives; bottom, Historical Society of Washington, D.C.
55: *Celebration of the One Hundredth Anniversary of the Establishment of the Seat of Government in the District of Columbia.*
56: Top, Library of Congress; bottom left, Historical Society of Washington, D.C.; bottom right, Library of Congress.
57: Top, National Archives; bottom, Historical Society of Washington, D.C.
58: All, Library of Congress.
59: Top, Moorland-Spingarn Research Center, Howard University; bottom, Library of Congress
60: Top left, Historical Society of Washington, D.C.; top right, courtesy, HarpWeek; bottom, Library of Congress.
61: Top, courtesy, Kathryn Schneider Smith; bottom left, Washingtoniana Division, D.C. Public Library, © The Washington Post; bottom right, Library of Congress.
62: Top, Library of Congress; bottom left, *Poore's Reminiscences;* bottom right, *Poore's Reminiscences.*
63: Top, Library of Congress; bottom left, Historical Society of Washington, D.C.; bottom right, Library of Congress.
64: Top, Historical Society of Washington, D.C.; bottom left, Annalisa Kraft for The Washington Post; bottom right, The Washington Post.
65: Top, The Washington Post; bottom, Linda Wheeler for The Washington Post.

Chapter 3

67: Top, The Washington Post; bottom, Library of Congress.
68: National Archives.
69: Top, Historical Society of Washington, D.C.; bottom, Washingtoniana Division, D.C. Public Library.
70: Top, National Archives.
70-1: The Washington Post.
71: Top, Historical Society of Washington, D.C.
72: All, Historical Society of Washington, D.C.
73: Top, *Washington, D.C., with Its Points of Interest Illustrated*; bottom, Moorland-Spingarn Research Center, Howard University.
74: All, Library of Congress.
75: All, Library of Congress.

76-7: All, Library of Congress.
78: Bottom, The Washington Post.
78-9: Library of Congress.
79: Bottom, The Mariners Museum, Newport News, Va.
80: All, Library of Congress.
81: All, The Washington Post.
82: Top, Historical Society of Washington, D.C.; bottom left, Washingtoniana Division, D.C. Public Library; bottom right, Historical Society of Washington, D.C.
83: Top left, Historical Society of Washington, D.C.; top right, Historical Society of Washington, D.C.; bottom, Smithsonian Institution Archives, Alice Pike Barney Papers, Accession # 96-153.
84: Library of Congress.
85: Top left, Library of Congress; top right, Library of Congress; middle, Montgomery County Historical Society; bottom, Library of Congress.
86: All, Library of Congress.
87: Top, Library of Congress; bottom, The Washington Post.
88: Top left, The Washington Post; top right, Library of Congress; bottom, The Washington Post.
89: Top, The Washington Post; bottom, Moorland-Spingarn Research Center, Howard University.
90: All, Library of Congress.
91: All, Library of Congress.
92: All, Library of Congress.
93: Top left, The Washington Post; top right, Library of Congress; middle, Library of Congress; bottom, Library of Congress.
94-5: Library of Congress.
95: All, Library of Congress.
96: Top, Library of Congress; bottom, Scurlock Photo, Library of Congress.
97: All, Library of Congress.

Chapter 4

99: Top, Library of Congress; bottom, The Washington Post.
100: Bottom, courtesy, Ford Archives, Dearborn, Mich.
100-1: The Washington Post.
101: Bottom, Historical Society of Washington, D.C.
102: All, Washingtoniana Division, D.C. Public Library.
103: Top left, Star Collection, © The Washington Post, D.C. Public Library; top right, Library of Congress; bottom, Star Collection, © The Washington Post, D.C. Public Library.
104: All, The Washington Post.
105: All, The Washington Post.
106: Bottom, The Washington Post.
106-7: Library of Congress.
107: Bottom, The Washington Post.
108: All, Library of Congress.
109: Top left, The Washington Post; top right, The Washington Post; middle, The Washington Post; bottom left, Library of Congress; bottom right, The Washington Post.
110: Top, Robert McNeill photograph, Moorland-Spingarn Research Center, Howard University; bottom, Star Collection, © The Washington Post, D.C. Public Library.
111: All, The Washington Post.
112: Top, National Archives; middle, The Washington Post; bottom, Martin Luther King Library.
113: Top, The Washington Post; bottom left, Library of Congress; bottom right, Library of Congress.
114: All, The Washington Post.
115: Top, Gus Chinn for The Washington Post; bottom left, The Washington Post; bottom right, The Washington Post.
116: Top right, Associated Press; top left, Associated Press; middle, Library of Congress; bottom, Library of Congress.
117: Top, The Washington Post; bottom, Library of Congress.
118: Top, The Washington Post; bottom left, Library of Congress; bottom right, Library of Congress.
119: Top left, The Washington Post; top right, The Washington Post; bottom left, Library of Congress; bottom right, Library of Congress.
120: Top left, Library of Congress; top right, The Washington Post; bottom left, Library of Congress; bottom right, Martin Luther King Library.
121: Top, Associated Press; bottom, The Washington Post.
122: Top, The Washington Post; bottom left, Library of Congress; bottom right, The Washington Post.
123: Top, Library of Congress; bottom, The Washington Post.

Chapter 5

125: Tom Kelley for The Washington Post.
126-27: The Washington Post.
127: Top, Star Collection, © The Washington Post, D.C. Public Library; bottom left, The Washington Post; bottom right, Library of Congress.
128: The Washington Post.
129: All, Star Collection, © The Washington Post, D.C. Public Library.
130: Top, Star Collection, © The Washington Post, D.C. Public Library.
130-31: Star Collection, © The Washington Post, D.C. Public Library.
131: Top, Pittsburgh-Courier (Washington Edition), Moorland-Spingarn Research Center, Howard University.
132: Top, The Washington Post; bottom, Moorland-Spingarn Research Center, Howard University.
133: All, The Washington Post.
134: Top, Library of Congress; bottom, National Archives.
135: Top, Library of Congress; bottom, John Daly for The Washington Post.
136: Top, Jack Lartz for The Washington Post; bottom, Robert Burchette for The Washington Post.
137: Top, Arthur Ellis for The Washington Post; bottom, The Washington Post.
138: Top, Department of Defense; bottom, The Washington Post.
139: Top, Pittsburgh-Courier (Washington Edition), Moorland-Spingarn Research Center, Howard University; bottom, Arthur Ellis for The Washington Post.
140: Top, Norman Driscoll for The Washington Post; middle, Charles Del Vecchio for The Washington Post; bottom, Jim

McNamara for The Washington Post.
141: Top, The Washington Post; bottom left, Star Collection, © The Washington Post, D.C. Public Library; bottom right, Star Collection, © The Washington Post, D.C. Public Library.
142: Bottom, Pittsburgh-Courier (Washington Edition), Moorland-Spingarn Research Center, Howard University.
142-43: Pittsburgh-Courier (Washington Edition), Moorland-Spingarn Research Center, Howard University.
144: Top, Henry Rohland for The Washington Post; bottom left, Historical Society of Washington, D.C.; bottom right, Charles Del Vecchio for The Washington Post.
145: Top left, Jim McNamara for The Washington Post; top right, Scurlock photo, Pittsburgh-Courier (Washington Edition), Moorland-Spingarn Research Center, Howard University; bottom, United Press International.
146: Top left, Harry Goodwin for The Washington Post; top right, The Washington Post; bottom left, Star Collection, © The Washington Post, D.C. Public Library; bottom right, Robert McNeill photograph, Pittsburgh-Courier (Washington Edition), Moorland-Spingarn Research Center, Howard University.
147: Top, Star Collection, © The Washington Post, D.C. Public Library; middle, Harry Naltchayan for The Washington Post; bottom, Star Collection, © The Washington Post, D.C. Public Library.
148: Top, Star Collection, © The Washington Post, D.C. Public Library; middle, Washingtoniana Division, D.C. Public Library; bottom left, Harry Naltchayan for The Washington Post; bottom right, Arthur Ellis for The Washington Post.
149: Top, National Archives; bottom, Arthur Ellis for The Washington Post.
150: Vic Casamento for The Washington Post.
151: Top, The Washington Post; middle, Library of Congress; bottom, courtesy, Joseph Owen Curtis.
152: Top left, Vic Casamento for The Washington Post; top right, Vic Casamento for The Washington Post; bottom, Wally McNamee for The Washington Post.
153: Left, courtesy, Kay Tobin Lahusen; bottom right, The Washington Post.
154: Top, Douglas Chevalier for The Washington Post; bottom, Robert Burchette for The Washington Post.
155: Top, Frank Hoy for The Washington Post; middle, Harry Naltchayan for The Washington Post; bottom, Vic Casamento for The Washington Post.

Chapter 6

157: Courtesy, John W. Hechinger, Sr.
158: Top, Frank Johnston for The Washington Post; bottom, The Washington Post.
158-59: Robert Burchette for The Washington Post.
159: Bottom, Harry Naltchayan for The Washington Post.
160: Top, Linda Wheeler for The Washington Post; bottom, United Press International/Bettman Newsphotos.
161: Top left, Ken Feil for The Washington Post; top right, Gerald Martineau for The Washington Post; bottom, Frank Johnston for The Washington Post.
162: Top, John McDonnell for The Washington Post; bottom, Frank Johnston for The Washington Post.
163: Top, The Washington Post; bottom, Harry Naltchayan for The Washington Post.
164: Top, James A. Parcell for The Washington Post.
164-65: Frank Johnston for The Washington Post.
165: Top, Larry Morris for The Washington Post.
166: Top, James A. Parcell for The Washington Post; bottom, Gary A. Cameron for The Washington Post.
167: Top, Charles Del Vecchio for The Washington Post; bottom, James A. Parcell for The Washington Post.
168: Top, Larry Morris for The Washington Post; bottom left, Douglas Chevalier for The Washington Post; bottom right, Harry Naltchayan for The Washington Post.
169: Top, Vanessa Barnes Hillian for The Washington Post; bottom, Linda Wheeler for The Washington Post.
170: Top left, Larry Morris for The Washington Post; top right, Larry Morris for The Washington Post; bottom, James A. Parcell for The Washington Post.
171: Top, James A. Parcell for The Washington Post; bottom left, Harry Naltchayan for The Washington Post; bottom right, James A. Parcell for The Washington Post.
172: Top, courtesy, Fairfax County Public Library, Photographic Archive; middle, Craig Herndon for The Washington Post; bottom, James A. Parcell for The Washington Post.
173: Top, Lucian Perkins for The Washington Post; bottom left, Milbert Orlando Brown for The Washington Post; bottom right, Elizabeth Richter for The Washington Post.
174: Top, Dudley M. Brooks for The Washington Post; bottom left, United Press International; bottom right, Juana Arias for The Washington Post.
175: Top left, James A. Parcell for The Washington Post; top right, Carol Guzy for The Washington Post; bottom, Craig Herndon for The Washington Post.
176: Top, Lucian Perkins for The Washington Post; bottom, Juana Arias for The Washington Post.
177: Top, Bill Snead for The Washington Post; bottom left, The Washington Post; bottom right, Bill Snead for The Washington Post.
178: Top, Joel Richardson for The Washington Post; bottom, Frank Johnston for The Washington Post.
179: Top, Carol Guzy for The Washington Post; bottom, Rick Bowmer for The Washington Post.
180: Top left, Dudley M. Brooks for The Washington Post; top right, Mark Gail for The Washington Post; middle, Margaret Thomas for The Washington Post; bottom, Joel Richardson for The Washington Post.
181: Top left, Margaret Thomas for The Washington Post; top right, *Our National Capital and Its Un-Americanized Americans*; bottom left, Lucian Perkins for The Washington Post; bottom right, The Washington Post.
182: Top, Frank Johnston for The Washington Post; bottom, Larry Kobelka for The Washington Post.

ABOUT THE AUTHORS

BOB LEVEY's column, "Bob Levey's Washington," which explores all aspects of life in the capital, has appeared in *The Washington Post* since 1981. During his 32-year career at *The Post*, Levey has covered presidential politics, Congress, local news and sports. In 1985, 1988 and 1997, *Washingtonian* magazine named him one of the top five columnists in the capital, and in 1999 the magazine selected him as a "Washingtonian of the Year."

Levey also has maintained careers in television, radio and the Internet. He hosts a talk show on cable TV NewsChannel 8 and serves as a commentator for WTOP-AM and FM. In addition, Levey hosts "Levey Live," an hour-long "chat show" appearing Tuesdays and Fridays on *The Washington Post's* Web site, washingtonpost.com.

Levey holds a bachelor's degree from The University of Chicago.

JANE FREUNDEL LEVEY is the editor of *Washington History: Magazine of The Historical Society of Washington, D.C.*, a consulting historian specializing in D.C. history and a founder of Summit Historians, a group that produces corporate histories and exhibits.

She holds a master's degree in American Studies from George Washington University and a bachelor's from Wellesley College. She speaks and publishes frequently on Washington history topics.

The Leveys have two teenaged children, Emily and Alexander.